NOTTINGHAM FORES
VIV ANDE

NOTTINGHAM F.
FOREST
JOHN O'HARE

SUN SOCCERCARD No 659
J. McGOVERN (Nottingham F.)

NOTTINGHAM F.
CW01064277
PETER SHILTON

NOTTINGHAM F.
FOREST

NOTTINGHAM FOREST
PETER WITHE

NOTTINGHAM F.
FOREST
FRANK CLARK

NOTTINGHAM F.
FOREST
KENNY BURNS

JAY DEES
NEWSAGENTS
LTD
The Cornish Match Company Ltd
Average Contents 48 Finnish Sticks
David Needham

NOTTINGHAM FOREST
LARRY LLOYD
D

NOTTINGHAM FOREST
COLIN BARRETT
D

SUN SOCCERCARD No 543
C. WOODS (Nottingham Forest)

NOTTINGHAM F.
PETER SHILTON
BRIAN
CLOUGH
MANAGER
FOREST
NOTTINGHAM FOREST

JOHN McGOV
NOTTINGHAM F.
IAN BOWYER

NOTTINGHAM F.
FOREST
MARTIN O'NEILL

First published in Great Britain by

www.pineapplebooks.co.uk

Pineapple Books Limited
246 Nottingham Road
Burton Joyce
Nottingham
NG14 5BD

ISBN 0-9543576-1-2

Printed by : Neartone, Unit 16 Catton Road, Arnold, Nottingham, NG5 7JD

Design by : i4c, Sparkhouse Studios, Ropewalk Street, Lincoln, LN6 7DQ

All photographs used by permission and supplied by
The Nottingham Evening Post Group
JMS Photography
Keith Gibson / Alpha Graphics
Bob Thomas / Popperfoto
Mirrorpix
Empics
[For individual photograph credits see back of book]

Football cards / stickers used by permission of Topps and Panini

Nottingham Forest Programmes used by permission of Nottingham Forest Football Club

Memorabilia supplied from the collections of John McGovern and Rob Jovanovic

British Library Cataloguing-in-Publication Data.
A catalogue record for this book is available from the British Library.

FOREST GIANTS

THE STORY OF

NOTTINGHAM FOREST F.C.

1975 – 80

By
John McGovern
&
Rob Jovanovic

Foreword by
Brian Clough OBE

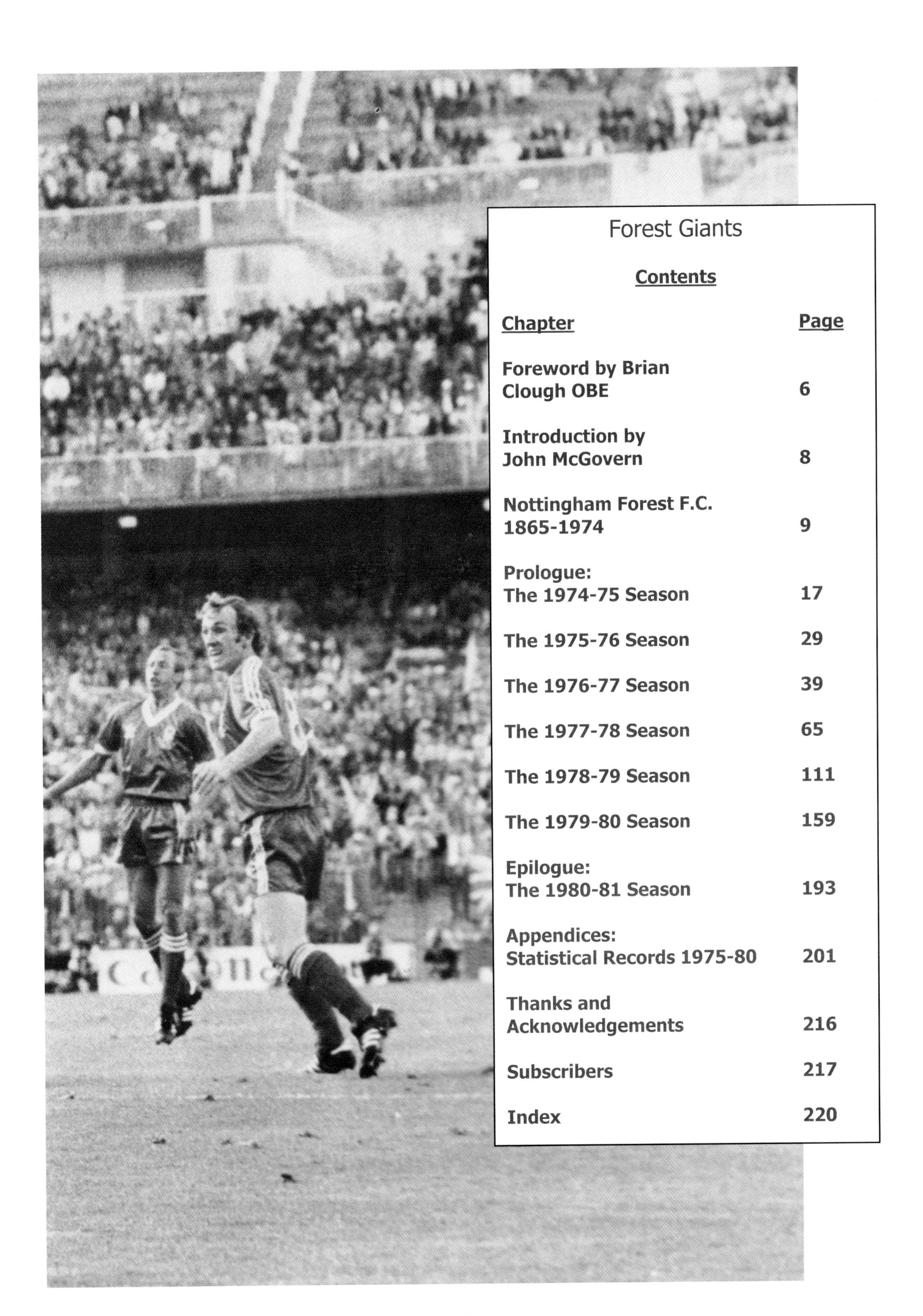

Forest Giants

Contents

Brian Clough

Manager of the Year 1978

Foreword

At the time Forest wanted me I was out of work, so that was important. I was approached by a very genuine man called Stuart Dryden and by a gentleman called Derek Pavis. I arranged to have dinner with them and it progressed from there. I got the job rubber stamped and I was back in work, simple as that. I contacted Peter Taylor, having spent the first few months at Forest on my own. We'd had a successful relationship both on and off the field, as players when I was at Middlesbrough and in management obviously with Derby. He jumped at it.

John McGovern was one of my first signings for Forest. He was languishing at Leeds, him and John O'Hare. I knew their pedigree. When the usual euphoria started to wear off at Forest, after a couple of wins, everything settled down and we found our true level in the bottom six or wherever it was. Two years later I got them into the First Division.

The season when we got promoted out of the Second Division is forgotten now in the things we achieved and yet it was the most important thing in some respects. Without that base we couldn't go anywhere else. We couldn't go and win the First Division Championship. We couldn't go and win in Europe if that wasn't there. We captured everybody's imagination.

We got to the League Cup Final and won it, which was unheard of for Nottingham Forest. The usual quips came out: 'We don't have a coach driver to take our coach to Wembley because we go so often the coach knows its own way there.'

There's a number of things that managers say and do now that we were doing twenty-five years ago. We introduced the ball to feet system of playing in this country more than anybody else did. We kept possession. We played it. We didn't kick bloody long balls. We never criticized referees, we'd commit the same fouls as anybody else, we got the same injustice as anybody else, but we never argued, it was a waste of time.

My pinnacle was going forty-two league games undefeated, because I was always a league man but it went so unheralded. If anybody else had done what we'd done in such a short spell of time we wouldn't have only gone down in history as we are in history now we'd have gone down as the best thing ever. We'd have outdone Penicillin!

Brian Clough OBE
August 2003

Introduction

Brian Clough formed the perfect managerial partnership with Peter Taylor. Two men obsessed with constructing, then moulding together, the perfect football team. This unique, uncompromising duo were destined to startle the success-starved Nottingham Forest supporters while mesmerizing football followers countrywide. Their meticulously assembled side quickly produced consistently thrilling displays through a lustrum of record breaking non-stop triumphs. Being a player during that period of Nottingham Forest's history was equivalent to experiencing a priceless master class in football education.

The initial, but unheralded, step of winning promotion in 1977 was a humble prelude on the path to glory. A late season loss by Bolton Wanderers allowed the 'Reds' to creep into the First Division, taking the third promotion place by a single point. The club's progress then changed from a stumble to an all out sprint as the team construction gathered momentum. League Championship and League Cup victories in the 1977–78 season were celebrated ecstatically in Nottingham, yet attracted less than glowing tributes from a section of the national press. 'One hit wonders' or 'team of misfits' were undeserved, derogatory remarks attributed to many supposedly erudite sports writers. Winning the European Cup at the first attempt while retaining the League Cup the following season left many major critics eating copious amounts of humble pie. A second European Cup success in 1980 brought Nottingham Forest's trophy haul to five major pieces of silverware in three seasons.

Glasgow Celtic, Manchester United, Liverpool and Aston Villa are also amongst the British elite to have won the European Cup, yet they never experienced such a fairy tale rise to power as meteoric or dramatic as Nottingham Forest's.

Where passionate memories are merely remembered as nostalgia, results are there to be believed, cast in the annals of the game. When Nottingham Forest produced an unbeaten run of forty-two league matches from 1977 to 1979 they duly earned that almost invincible look of perfection, fought for and created by Brian Clough and Peter Taylor. This book is dedicated to the blood, sweat and tears shared by the men who can justifiably be called 'Forest Giants'.

John McGovern
August 2003

NOTTINGHAM FOREST F.C. 1865 - 1974 B.C. (Before Clough)

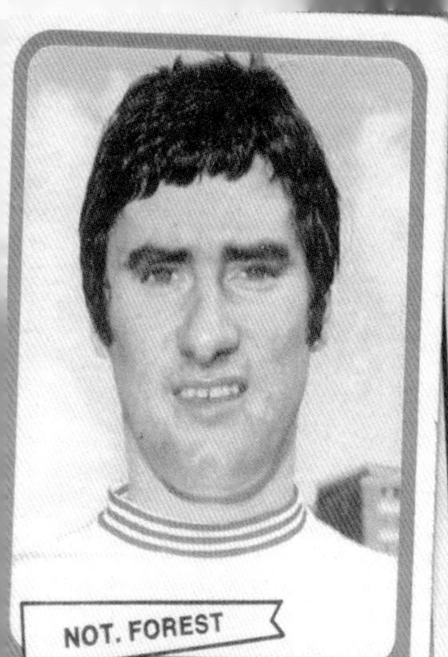

Back in the Nottingham of 1865, the major cultural event of the year was the opening of the Theatre Royal; the formation of a football club by a group of recreational shinney (a forerunner of hockey) players went widely unnoticed. After an initial meeting at the Clinton Arms on Sherwood Street they took the name of their playing area, 'the Forest' (just off Mansfield Road and the present day Goose Fair site) and became the Nottingham Forest Football Club. An early meeting called for the purchase of a set of red caps and the club's colours were set for the next 130+ years. The first recorded game was on 22 March 1886 and ended in a 0-0 draw against the world's oldest club – Notts County, which had formed slightly earlier in 1862. For a couple of years Forest played both hockey and football but then after a vote the hockey was given up.

Through the early years the club played only friendly games, usually less than a dozen a season, but by 1877 were drawing crowds of up to two thousand. The opposition was growing more diverse too. Instead of the perpetual local derbies, the opponents began to come to Nottingham from further afield. First it was the likes of Sheffield Norfolk and Birmingham and by the late 1870s Glasgow Rangers and Ayr Thistle were regular opponents. Early players included William Gunn (who co-founded the Gunn & Moore sports shop) and Dr Tinsley Lindley. Lindley was involved in one of the more bizarre injuries in football history when he missed a game after being bitten by a rat, but other players also missed matches after suffering from lead poisoning after a dodgy pre-match fish meal.

Forest's first competitive game took place in 1878 as the club entered the FA Cup for the first time (the competition was in its seventh season); they drew Notts County in the first round. A 3-1 win set Forest on their first cup run and they progressed past four hurdles before losing 2-1 to Old Etonians in the fifth round. Forest continued to enjoy early Cup success with a semi-final run the next season, beating Sheffield in the quarter-final after the latter refused to play extra time. The game had ended in a 2-2 draw but with no Sheffield players on the pitch Forest kicked off anyway and Sam Widdowson ran down the pitch and planted the ball into the absent team's goal. Forest later lost 1-0 to Oxford University in the semi-final. In the 1884-85 season Forest again reached the semi-final and faced Scottish opposition in the shape of Queen's Park. Unfortunately a 1-1 at Derby was followed by a 3-0 replay defeat in Edinburgh. Around this time Forest also became the first provincial team to play in London. (They had also played in the first game to take place in Birmingham.)

The game of football was still very much in its formative stages, teams often lining up with twelve (or more) players a side; goalkeepers were allowed to approach the taker of penalty kicks and could pick up the ball anywhere on the pitch (the first set of rules had not been set down in writing until 1877).

Another bit of Forest trivia history was made when London team Woolwich Arsenal were struggling to find a kit to use and Forest presented them with a set of red shirts, a colour that the club wears to the present day. In Forest's centenary year of 1965 Arsenal returned the gesture when they presented a special set of shirts to Forest to wear in their centenary match against Valencia at the City Ground.

The year after Forest's gift to Arsenal the Football League was founded for the 1888-89 season by twelve clubs, eleven of which are still members: Accrington are the only one of the initial dozen to have dropped out, while Stoke, Derby, Notts County, Burnley, Everton, West Bromwich Albion, Bolton, Blackburn, Wolverhampton Wanderers, Aston Villa and debutant champions Preston are still going strong. The league expanded by leaps and bounds and Forest soon joined it. In 1891-92 Forest swept to the upstart Football Alliance Championship edging out Newton Heath (the future Manchester United) by two points. This achievement led to the club being admitted directly into the Football League's First Division for the 1892-93 season as the league grew to two divisions of sixteen and twelve teams respectively. Gradually the league expanded further until the two divisions had sixteen teams each, then eighteen, twenty and finally twenty-two. The league later underwent a massive increase to three divisions of twenty-two with another twenty clubs being admitted the following year, forming a Third Division North and a Third Division South.

Six years after Forest were admitted to the league, they captured their first major trophy by winning the FA Cup with a 3-1 victory over Derby County at Crystal Palace. The previous twenty years had seen an explosion of interest in football both locally and nationally: a crowd of over sixty-two thousand witnessed the Final that year, and home games at the Gregory Ground (the club's fifth home pitch in two decades) just off Derby Road in Lenton often attracted over ten thousand people.

F.A Cup Run 1898

1st Round [29/1/98]
Grimsby Town (H) 4-0

2nd Round [12/2/98]
Gainsborough (H) 4-0

3rd Round [26/2/98]
W. B. Albion (A) 3-2

Semi-Final [19/3/98]
Southampton 1-1
(Bramall Lane, Sheffield)

S-F Replay [24/3/98]
Southampton 2-0
(Crystal Palace)

Cup Final [16/4/98]
Derby County 3-1
(Crystal Palace)

Forest had gained a reputation as a club of innovation and firsts – a theme that continued right through the glory days of the late 1970s and beyond, as we shall see. Sam Widdowson was behind much of the moving and shaking. A powerful 'superman' of the age, he had a long career at Forest while playing county cricket for Nottinghamshire in his spare time. He also spent many hours thinking about the game and how it could be improved. Widdowson introduced the referee's whistle (Forest v Sheffield Norfolk in 1878) and was the first player to wear shin guards, which he placed on the outside of his socks in 1874. He also took one James Brodie's idea of introducing goal nets and a crossbar, which he introduced for a game in Nottingham in 1891. He was clearly a man of vision, but it was two more of his ideas that made the longest lasting impressions on the game into the twentieth century. The first of these was his insistence on trying to find ways of playing the game at night. He was involved in the first attempt at a floodlit game in October 1878, when a strip of twelve gaslights was strung along the side of the pitch in a game against Aston Villa. In 1889 he was behind the first match ever to be played under electric lighting when he arranged for the use of fourteen electric 'Wells' lamps to light up a game versus Notts Rangers in front of a five thousand strong crowd. He was so far ahead of the rest that floodlights weren't regularly used in league football until 1958!

Widdowson's other great legacy was a tactical one, his introduction of the 2-3-5 formation in the 1880s. Most teams at the time played a variation of the 1-2-7 formation, with one full-back, two half-backs and seven forwards. Widdowson changed the Forest line-up to include two full-backs, three half-backs and only five forwards. Though initially criticized, the formation soon spread. Preston famously used it to win the first League Championship, and most teams used it (or variations of it) until the early 1960s.

The turn of the century saw Nottingham as a centre of football excellence, as both Forest and Notts County proved to be formidable forces in the English game. County had won the FA Cup in 1894 and Forest's triumph four years later gave the city the rare distinction of having two clubs win the trophy. The two local rivals were also doing well in the league with County and Forest coming third and fourth respectively in the First Division in the 1900-01 season, but things soon took a turn for the worse. By 1906 Forest had been relegated (on goal difference from Middlesbrough) but they bounced straight back as champions of the Second Division in 1906-7 largely thanks to the twenty-one goals of prolific Welsh marksman Grenville Morris (*pictured left*) and another 14 from the local boy Enoch 'Knocker' West. Morris was the Red's first star striker of the twentieth century, was Forest's top scorer eight times between 1902 and 1912, and is still the club's all-time leading scorer.

Second Division, Final Table 1906-07	Pld	Pts	GD
FOREST	**38**	**60**	**+38**
Chelsea	38	57	+46
Leicester Fosse	38	48	+23
West Bromwich Albion	38	47	+38

(*top 4 of 20*)

In the summer of 1905 Forest embarked on an ambitious tour of Argentina and Uruguay. After a long voyage, Forest won all seven games by a combined score of 52-2.

In the first half of the twentieth century things were up and down, but more often down than up. Relegation to the Second Division was brightened only by winning the Victory Shield over Everton during suspension of the league due to the First World War. When normal activities resumed in peacetime the club yo-yoed between the top two divisions before settling as a mid-table Second Division outfit through the 1930s. By the time war broke out again in 1939 the club had finished above midway in the division just once in the preceding decade.

Second Division, Final Table 1921-22	Pld	Pts	GD
FOREST	**42**	**56**	**+21**
Stoke City	42	52	+16
Barnsley	42	52	+15
West Ham	42	48	+13

(*top 4 of 22*)

When the league reopened for business in 1946-47 Forest continued their run as an average mid-table Second Division side. The most notable just-post-war event was probably when the City Ground was flooded in 1947. Swans were seen swimming over the pitch which was covered almost to the top of the crossbars. Billy Walker had been appointed manager just as war broke out and his initial post-war results didn't give the Forest faithful too much optimism for the future. In 1949 Forest were relegated to the Third Division for the only time in their history, but the seeds of better times to come were sown with the signing of Wally Ardron (*pictured below left*) from his hometown team, Rotherham United. The all-action forward often made himself goal scoring chances by the simple use of his physical strength. Ardron notched up twenty-five goals in forty-one league games as the Reds finished fourth in his debut season and followed it up with thirty-six goals in forty-five league games as Forest won promotion as champions in 1950-51. The team as a whole bagged a massive 110 goals in the league campaign. These impressive feats are still club records over fifty years later. The following year Forest missed out on promotion to the First Division by just two points (Ardron hitting another twenty-nine league goals in just thirty-nine league games).

Division Three (South) Final Table 1950-51	Pld	Pts	GD
FOREST	**46**	**70**	**+70**
Norwich	46	64	+37
Reading	46	57	+35
Plymouth	46	57	+30
Millwall	46	56	+23

(*top 5 of 24*)

The mid-1950s saw Walker consolidating Forest's Second Division placing while rebuilding the squad for another promotion push. Ardron retired in 1955 but two years later Forest gained promotion back to the top flight after an absence of twenty-three years. The first game back was marked by Tom Finney leading out the visiting Preston side and then shaking the hand of every Forest player before kick-off. A more than respectable tenth place was secured and fans came flooding to the City Ground (at which the club was celebrating sixty years) and a then-record 47,804 passed through the turnstiles for the visit of Manchester United. One of the main reasons for the growing interest was the attractive, attacking football that Walker had introduced.

The start of the 1958-59 season was no different from the previous one; the aim was to stabilize a solid mid-table position and anything else would be icing on the cake. While they were a skilful attacking side, they were always likely to concede goals too. This was amply illustrated just two games into the season after defeats at Wolverhampton Wanderers (5-1) and at home to Manchester United (3-0). Things picked up during the autumn, but the inconsistency proved to be a season long ailment. In the third round of the FA Cup Forest drew a potential banana skin in the shape of a trip to non-league Tooting & Mitchum. In the second half Forest found themselves 2-0 down. An own goal and a penalty were required to force a replay which the Reds cruised comfortably through. Grimsby were swept aside in the fourth round and then two replays were required before Birmingham were finally dispatched on the end of a 5-0 drubbing. Forest suddenly found themselves in the quarter-finals of the FA Cup for the second time in three years and were drawn to face the holders, Bolton Wanderers, at the City Ground. Over forty-four thousand crammed in to witness a Tommy Wilson brace that edged Nat Lofthouse and the holders 2-1. The semi-final brought up Aston Villa and a single Johnny Quigley goal was enough for a 1-0 win at Hillsborough in front of almost sixty-six thousand. Forest would be embarking on their first ever trip to Wembley.

The 1958-59 FA Cup winning squad. Back row, left to right: Graham (trainer), McDonald, Whare, Thompson, McKinlay, Burkett, Whitefoot. Front row, seated left to right: Dwight, Quigley, Wilson, Walker (manager), Gray, Imlach.

But there was a gap of almost two months between the semi-final and the Final, and in that time Forest seemed to have Wembley on their minds as their league form dipped. After qualifying for the Final they won just three of their last thirteen league games to finish the season in thirteenth place.

3rd Round [10/1/59]
Tooting & Mitcham (A) 2-2
3rd Round Replay [24/1/59]
Tooting & Mitcham (H) 3-0
4th Round [28/1/59]
Grimsby Town (H) 4-1
5th Round [14/2/59]
Birmingham City (A) 1-1
5th Round Replay [18/2/59]
Birmingham City (H) 1-1
5th Round 2nd Replay [23/2/59]
Birmingham City 5-0
(at Filbert Street, Leicester)
6th Round [28/2/59]
Bolton Wanderers (H) 2-1
Semi-Final [14/3/59]
Aston Villa 1-0
(Hillsborough, Sheffield)
Cup Final [2/5/59]
Luton Town 2-1
(Wembley)

On 2 May 1959, captain Jack Burkitt led Forest out to face Luton Town, who had just avoided relegation from the First Division. The Forest eleven was the same one that had started every single round, and the Reds were soon in command. Roy Dwight fired Forest ahead after just eight minutes and Tommy Wilson added a second with a header five minutes later. Forest were cruising until the thirty-third minute when Dwight broke his leg. This was in the days before substitutes were allowed and so the Reds played almost the last hour with ten men. Luton did manage to pull a goal back in the sixty-second minute, but the Reds held on for a famous victory. Dwight watched Burkitt lift the cup on television from his hospital bed. An estimated two hundred thousand fans welcomed the team back to Nottingham as they were given a reception at the Council House. It was the first such occasion, as the building had not been built the last time they had won the FA Cup, and it would be almost twenty years before the team had another such achievement to celebrate. It had been the pinnacle of Billy Walker's tenure as manager and the following summer he retired to a position on the club's committee which he held until his death in 1964.

Above left: Roy Dwight heads Forest into the lead.
Above right: Captain Jack Burkitt receives the FA Cup from the Queen.
Below left: Jack Burkitt and manager Billy Walker arrive back at the Midland Station.
Below right: The victory parade begins.

Andy Beattie became Forest's second post-war manager in 1960, but had a difficult time. The club languished in the lower reaches of the First Division, though they did manage to attain a ninth place finish in his final year, 1962-63. He was succeeded by an Irishman, Johnny Carey. Carey had played for Manchester United before having a successful managerial career with Blackburn, Everton and Orient. He immediately went about putting his stamp on Forest and their style of play. He had inherited a group of promising young players that included Bobby 'Sammy' Chapman and Ian Storey-Moore (*pictured bottom right*) and Bob McKinlay (*pictured middle, right*) who still holds the record for the most games played for Forest. He also brought in a number of players to blend in with his attacking philosophy: Alan Hinton, John Barnwell, Colin Addison and Joe Baker all coming Trentside.

It all came together beautifully in the 1966-67 season. After an indifferent league start, Forest lost just once in the twenty-two league games between 6 November and 18 April. That single loss was crucial though as the 1-0 defeat at Old Trafford ultimately meant that Manchester United pipped Forest to the League Championship. United went on to the win the European Cup the following year while Forest were left to wonder about what might have been. To rub salt into the wound, the Reds also lost an FA Cup semi-final to Tottenham at Hillsborough, its the closest the club has ever been to a League and FA Cup double. The following year they tasted some European action in the Inter City Fairs Cup, going out to Zurich on away goals after beating Eintract Frankfurt 5-0 on aggregate in the first round.

First Division, Final Table 1966-67

	Pld	Pts	GD
Manchester United	42	60	+39
FOREST	**42**	**56**	**+23**
Tottenham Hotspur	42	56	+23
Leeds United	42	55	+20
Liverpool	42	51	+17
Everton	42	48	+19

(*top 6 of 22*)

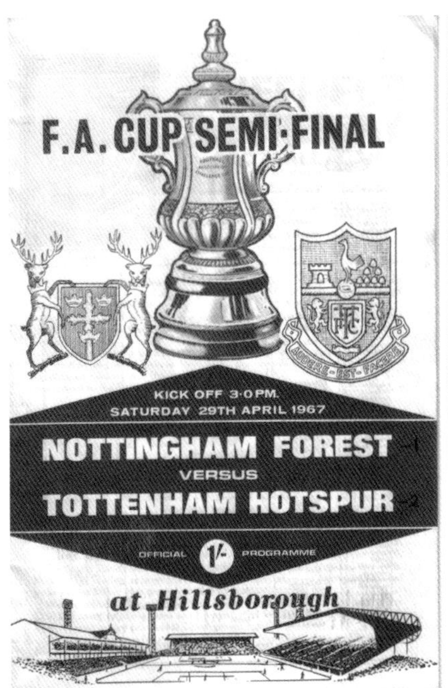

Pictured above, the 1966-67 team. Back row (left to right): Carey, Hindley, McKinlay, Grummitt, Winfield, Newton, Cavanagh. Front row (left to right): Lyons, Baker, Barnwell, Hennessey, Wignall, Storey-Moore.

Fading into obscurity.....			
1969-70	Division 1	15th	38 pts
1970-71	Division 1	16th	36 pts
1971-72	Division 1	21st	25 pts
1972-73	Division 2	14th	40 pts
1973-74	Division 2	7th	45 pts

Carey left the club in December 1968 after the board went behind his back, and against his wishes, to sign volatile Scotsman Jim Baxter, and the club began a downward spiral. Baxter left after producing just three goals in forty-eight games. Matt Gillies took over, but could not halt the slide into the Second Division that eventually came in 1972. Ex-Derby captain Dave MacKay took over for less than a year and then Allan Brown was given the task of resurrecting the fading fortunes of Forest. In his first season, 1973-74, the Reds managed a seventh place finish in the Second Division and had a creditable FA Cup run.

The run started with an exciting 4-3 home win over Bristol Rovers, the first City Ground game to be played on a Sunday. In the fourth round Forest were given another home tie, this time against high flying First Division outfit Manchester City. This game turned out to be the most memorable of the early 1970s for Forest fans. The flamboyant Duncan McKenzie (*pictured left with Barry Lyons*) had the game of a lifetime, scoring one and setting up three others as Forest ran wild and won 4-1 before a delirious 41,472 crowd. The Reds only went out of the FA Cup in the sixth round to Newcastle under very controversial circumstances. The Geordie fans invaded the pitch when Forest were leading 3-1 and forced a replay that Newcastle won 1-0 at the second attempt. Now it was hoped that 1974-75 might bring an outside chance of promotion.

Left: The Forest youth team, c. summer 1973. Back row, far left are the two future England internationals Tony Woodcock and Viv Anderson.

Right: John Robertson in action shortly before the Reds relegation from the top flight in 1972.

Some Forest Records

Biggest Win:	14-0 v Clapton (1891)
Most Goals In A Game:	Sandy Higgins (5)
Most Goals In a Season:	Wally Ardron (36)
Most Goals:	Grenville Morris (217)
Most Games Played:	Bob McKinlay (682)
Highest Home Attendance:	49,946 (28/10/67)

FOREST

Since being relegated to the Second Division, the Forest squad had undergone a major overhaul. Successive managers had made their own changes and then moved on leaving a team that resembled a patchwork quilt that no single manager had wanted. Gone were the likes of Peter Cormack, Ian Storey-Moore and Barry Lyons while new faces included left-back Paddy Greenwood from Hull, Irish international Miah Dennehy, Scottish international Neil Martin (who had crossed the Midlands from Coventry) and a bevy of young apprentices struggling to hold down a regular first team spot. Crowds at the City Ground had slumped to just over the ten thousand mark, fighting on the terraces was a regular occurrence and Forest fans had the reputation as one of the most violent sets of supporters in the Second Division. Things weren't exactly looking rosy.

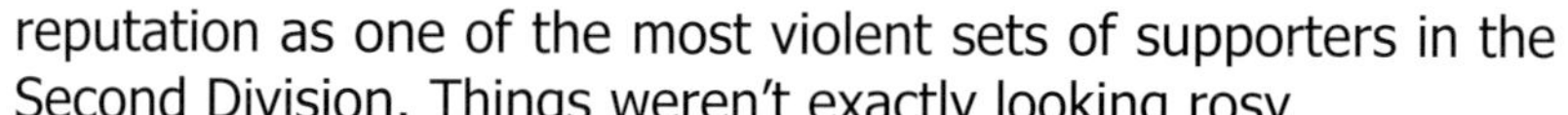

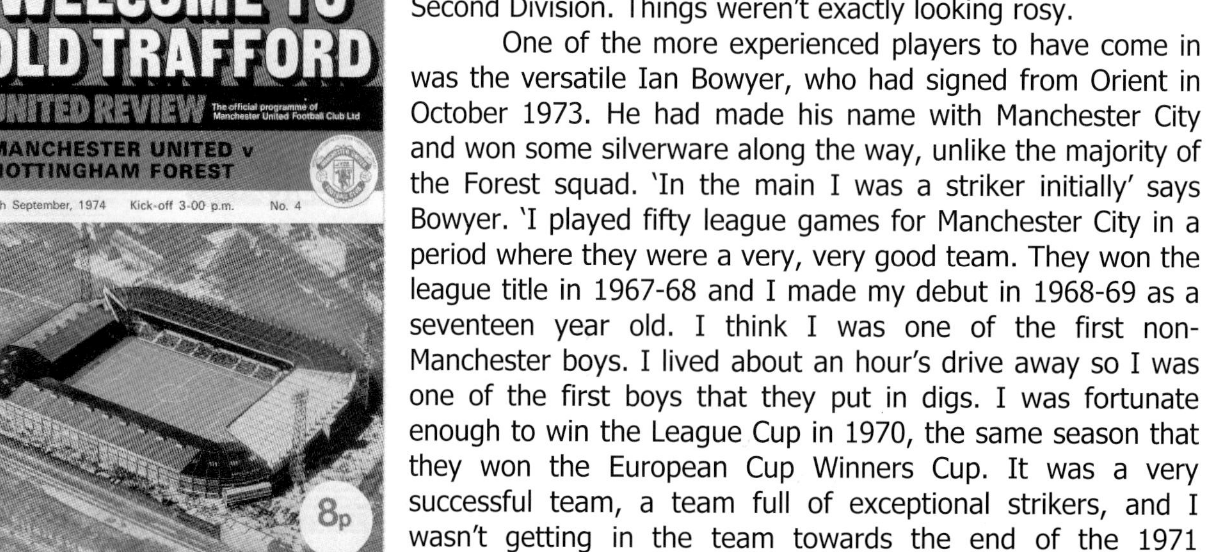

One of the more experienced players to have come in was the versatile Ian Bowyer, who had signed from Orient in October 1973. He had made his name with Manchester City and won some silverware along the way, unlike the majority of the Forest squad. 'In the main I was a striker initially' says Bowyer. 'I played fifty league games for Manchester City in a period where they were a very, very good team. They won the league title in 1967-68 and I made my debut in 1968-69 as a seventeen year old. I think I was one of the first non-Manchester boys. I lived about an hour's drive away so I was one of the first boys that they put in digs. I was fortunate enough to win the League Cup in 1970, the same season that they won the European Cup Winners Cup. It was a very successful team, a team full of exceptional strikers, and I wasn't getting in the team towards the end of the 1971 season, I'd kind of hit a brick wall there. There was a lot of speculation; City were signing Rodney Marsh and I decided that I needed to play. So with that in mind, I went to Orient in the Second Division and had two seasons there. My first season I really enjoyed it but the second season, I think the London thing got to me and I came from basically a country background, a village. Then in 1973 David Mackay brought me to Forest. I was predominantly a left-sided midfield player, and I played there but I also played up front at Forest.' Bowyer had signed for Mackay but before he settled in Mackay had left the club. This wasn't the first time it had happened to Bowyer: 'When I moved from Manchester City to Orient the manager that signed me was Jimmy Bloomfield. He signed me one week and he effectively moved out the next week to Leicester in the First Division. So he got a promotion out of it. And then it happened again when I came to Forest; Dave Mackay left here after I think I had played two games for him, so I didn't know either of those two very well.' In the wake of Mackay's departure Allan Brown was appointed as the new Forest manager.

Bowyer's first game for Forest, against Blackpool, had been an interesting one. 'First of all I stayed in a room with Duncan McKenzie, which was an experience in itself,' he laughs. 'He could talk three hundred words per second, most of it about Duncan. So he was an incredible room-mate. In the game itself we were losing 2-0, Jim Barron [the goalkeeper] got carried off and John Galley ended up in goal. In those days we only had one substitute and we'd already used it, but we managed to get from 2-0 down back to 2-2.'

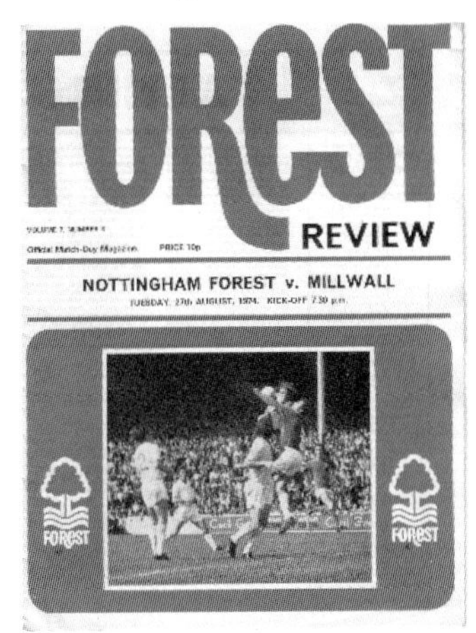

The major talking point for Forest fans that season, and the most memorable event in Allan Brown's time at Forest, was a controversial FA Cup quarter final at St James' Park against Newcastle United. The Reds took a commanding lead late into the game but a pitch invasion by the home fans caused the players to evacuate the pitch and on their return the Geordies managed to come back and take the lead. Eventually the tie was declared void, but Newcastle won after two replays. Ian Bowyer remembers it well: 'The game was incredible on reflection now. I think to a degree they let Newcastle off lightly. Bearing in mind we were winning 3-1, probably with about twenty minutes to go, they had just had their centre half Pat Howard sent off and then there was a pitch invasion. I'm not sure what kind of effect the pitch invasion had on our players but I do know that it broke the rhythm of the game so when things resumed after fifteen or twenty minutes the game wasn't quite the same again. The way it was going we were playing against ten men and the score of the game was going to go 4-1, 5-1. That flow of the game was broken, we never got it back, and effectively we managed to lose the game 4-3.'

'When the fans came on I think one or two of our lads got a slap around the head. Dave Serella got a bit of a bash around the head. The referee took us off and there was a lot of scratching of heads and "What do we do now?" The FA decided the game was null and void. So we had to go to Goodison Park and we drew the game 0-0. We had a goal disallowed and it was a goal that I actually scored from a free kick. We had actually worked on this routine in training for weeks and the first time we got the opportunity to score from it, the referee disallowed it. It was almost as if there was a bit of play-acting – that we had made a mess of the free-kick. I didn't see anything wrong with it; obviously our manager at the time didn't see anything wrong with it. Anyway we had played Newcastle twice, both away from the City Ground and the FA decided that we had to play again for a third time, again it was at Goodison Park. So we had played Newcastle three times and we hadn't had a home game. It's probably one of the only times it has happened in the history of the FA Cup, and in the third game we lost 1-0."

Though Forest had an indifferent start to the 1974-75 season, Ian Bowyer had a blistering one. By 7 September the Reds had won only one of their first five league games but Bowyer was on a scoring run. He scored again in a 2-2 draw at Old Trafford and then again against Newcastle in a League Cup tie. The visit to Old Trafford emphasized the quality of the Second Division line-up that season. Along with Manchester United there was Aston Villa, Newcastle, Sheffield Wednesday, West Bromwich Albion and Forest, all vying for the three promotion places. It's worth noting that it was just six years before that Manchester United and Forest had finished first and second in the First Division. As the summer turned to autumn Forest settled into a position of midtable obscurity, just behind the promotion challengers and just above the relegation battle. In October the Forest committee gave manager Brown a club record £120,000 to buy Barry Butlin, a forward well known for his aerial ability. He had previously played for Derby, had a loan spell across the river at Notts County and had started the current season at Luton. On his debut he scored at the City Ground but the Reds went down 3-1 to Norwich. Despite this debut goal, Butlin's arrival failed to provide the spark that Brown had hoped for and he continued to shuffle his pack. Young goalkeeper John Middleton took over the green jersey in November when Dennis Peacock was replaced, Northern Irish winger Martin O'Neill (*pictured left with two brothers and two sisters on a visit to Nottingham in the early 1970s*) was in and out of the first team; and Scotsman John Robertson was banished to the reserves after falling out of favour.

By Christmas it was clear that Forest would be going nowhere that season. The lead up to the 28 December clash at home against Notts County had seen just one win in five matches, and Barry Butlin had scored only one goal in his last twelve games. When Notts County won the local derby 2-0 they couldn't have known what an effect it would have on the fortunes of their city rivals. The match was the final straw for the committee and Allan Brown was relieved of his duties. He left Forest thirteenth in the Second Division, seven points off promotion and five points above relegation.

	Pld	Pts
Manchester United	25	37
Sunderland	24	33
Norwich City	24	31
West Bromwich Albion	25	29
Bristol City	24	27
Oxford United	25	27
Aston Villa	24	26
Blackpool	25	26
Notts County	25	26
Hull City	25	25
Fulham	25	24
Bolton Wanderers	24	24
FOREST	**25**	**24**
Bristol Rovers	25	22
Orient	24	22
York City	25	21
Southampton	23	21
Cardiff City	24	20
Oldham Athletic	23	19
Portsmouth	25	19
Sheffield Wednesday	25	18
Millwall	24	17

(Second Division table on 4/1/75)

Finding a replacement didn't take long at all: Brown hadn't even cleared out his office before the *Nottingham Evening Post* was naming his successor – the outspoken ex-Derby manager Brian Clough.

FOREST ARE ALL SET FOR TALKS WITH CLOUGH

By JOHN LAWSON

ALLAN BROWN was today dismissed from the Nottingham Forest managership just over 13 months after taking on the job of steering the club back into the First Division.

The move ends his appointment as manager at noon today. ... for a number of reasons they did not prove it.

The chances of Forest landing such a high profile manager at the start of the campaign had seemed remote at best. Brian Clough had gained his reputation as one of the game's brightest young managers by taking a small provincial club like Derby County from the lower reaches of the Second Division to the League Championship in just five seasons. He had also just missed out on a European Cup Final with

Derby in 1973. After things soured between Clough and Derby chairman Sam Longson he walked away from the club and took a job at Brighton in the Third Division. Of course a manager of his calibre wasn't going to stay long in the lower divisions, and soon Leeds United came calling, after the departure of their legend of a manager, Don Revie. Clough famously lasted just forty four days at Leeds and by Christmas 1974 he had been out of work for three months. When Forest approached him it didn't take long for a deal to be struck. 'Stuart Dryden was a very influential member of the so called committee that they had at Forest at that time,' says Clough: 'it progressed from there. I then went to see [committee member and future chairman] Brian Appleby QC and I was back in work, simple as that. I was easy to contact because I was only down the road and if they didn't know about pedigree at that particular time then I didn't know who did.'

Bill Anderson, Brown's assistant was named acting manager for Forest's next game, an FA Cup match at home to First Division Tottenham Hotspur. It was an end to end cup tie. Tottenham took the lead through Martin Chivers, Dave Jones equalized in the sixty-eighth minute and Barry Butlin had a chance to win it late on but couldn't beat Pat Jennings in the visitor's goal. Clough was officially named manager the following day and his first game in charge was the replay in London on Wednesday 8 January 1975.

'It was obviously a big thing, having Brian Clough come in as manager,' recalls Viv Anderson, then in his first season as a first-teamer. 'When we played Tottenham at home I came off with cramp with about ten minutes to go, and then he took the majority of the squad to London for the replay but left me behind, so I thought the writing was on the wall for me! My first impressions weren't the best.' However, missing the replay wasn't to prove detrimental to his long term aspirations however and he went on to become the first black player for England. Neil Martin, on the other hand was given the chance to play in the replay, and went down in history as scoring the winner in Brian Clough's first game as Nottingham Forest manager. Clough spent the evening in the directors box and was typically bullish after the game, exclaiming that 'Nottingham Forest have one thing going for them right now – me!' The team stayed in London following the game and trained at Bisham Abbey in preparation for another London encounter, at Fulham the following Saturday. Another 1-0 win courtesy of a Barry Butlin goal sent the Reds home in high spirits, but the mood didn't last.

'Well the usual euphoria started because we started off with a couple of wins,' says Clough. 'We won in the FA Cup and then we won a league match, but everything settled down eventually and we found our true level. It was a comparable situation to when I was at Derby as well, where I'd had the same problems. I took over there from a guy called Tim Ward who was very highly thought of in Derby and there was opposition when I came, being a young man at thirty-one, and I was taking over from an established manager. He was entrenched in Round Tables and all sorts of organizations and I was trying to instil this new feeling in Derby and of course it closed doors on me on a lot of occasions. Nottingham were regarded as an amateur club and they were amateurs. The people who ran the club were nothing short of incredible amateurs. The first chairman I served under was a gentleman called Jack Willmer. Well I've never seen anybody less chairman of a football club in all my life! I don't know what he'd be now in present day chairmanship ratings. In fact he wouldn't even get a mention in the book, in any book. They'd have to leave a blank space for some of the chairmen Nottingham Forest had.'

Like he had done in his short stay at Leeds, Clough immediately set about bringing in his own people, people he knew would get the job done. The initial task was to ensure Second Division survival. His first signing wasn't a high profile player, it was a tried and trusted member of his back room staff – trainer Jimmy Gordon. Gordon had been a player for both Newcastle and Middlesbrough, which was where he'd started his coaching career and met a couple of young players named Brian Clough and Peter Taylor. After moving to coach at Blackburn he first joined up with Clough and Taylor at Derby and had followed Clough to Leeds. He'd spent the previous couple of months out of football, working as a storeman at Rolls–Royce in Derby. 'I contacted Jimmy a second time,' recalls Clough. 'I'd first contacted him whilst I was with Derby. Jimmy wasn't a very adventurous guy but he'd spent a lifetime in football. I can remember saying to him for example, "How is the accommodation and everything?" He said "Well I'm still in the clubhouse," you know and that was absolutely laughable. There was this so-called top coach living in the clubhouse and he thought it was great. He was brought up in an old-fashioned way where it was taken that you were lucky to get a job in football when you finished playing. Jimmy had played well into his thirties in top class football and he was a well thought of coach.' An initial approach to Peter Taylor wasn't as successful, though, and the partnership made famous with Derby would have to wait a little while longer before being rekindled in Nottingham.

Next on the Clough shopping list was to bring some stability to the centre of the Forest midfield. To achieve this he went back to Leeds and plucked out a couple of players that he'd initially taken to Elland Road with him from Derby – John McGovern and striker John O'Hare (*pictured signing for Forest on left*). The pair, McGovern especially, had fallen out of favour at Leeds after Clough's departure and were signed by Forest in February 1975 for a combined fee of £60,000, a fraction of the £150,000 it had cost Leeds to take them from Derby in the first place.

John McGovern had known Brian Clough for virtually all of his footballing life, but he had been a late starter as far as the round ball game was concerned. He had been born in Montrose, Scotland, in 1949 and moved south to Hartlepool aged seven. His early sporting endeavours included captaining both the rugby and cricket teams at his grammar school, while his long-term ambition was to become a tennis player. There was a problem with this plan though: 'None of the kids in Hartlepool wanted to play rugby, cricket or tennis, so I started playing football,' explains McGovern. 'There was no football at school but I used to spend my summer holidays at Bo'ness, just outside of Edinburgh, and they all used to play football there. When I was fifteen I joined a local team but it was an under-eighteen league and they said I was a bit young and a bit frail. So the first time I pulled on a football shirt for any kind of organized game was when I was fifteen. I found out pretty soon afterwards that I was pretty good at this and I got some enthusiasm to continue it. I was given a trial against a Hartlepool's United Youth Eleven. They were just starting up and had never had a youth team before – this was in 1965 –

and I was trying to get into the youth team. The Rolling Stones and Beatles were around and I fancied myself as a bit of a Mick Jagger. I played the harmonica a little bit as well as playing football and had shoulder length hair which Brian Clough didn't really appreciate.'

McGovern obviously made an impression in the trial game and he was soon in the Hartlepool United team playing against a Leeds United XI as a fifteen year old. He made his league debut against Bradford City on the last day of the season, aged sixteen, and never looked back. 'The following year I played a few games,' he recalls. 'This was while still going to school, and I did disappointingly in my O levels because football had become an obsession. My father, Robert, had died when I was eleven and my mother, Josephine, was wondering what I was going to do. Brian Clough persuaded her to let me sign on as an apprentice. Then when I turned seventeen I was on £17 a week, plus an extra £5 appearance money, so I was earning a fortune!'

At the end of the 1966-67 season Clough departed Hartlepool for Derby and Gus McLean took over. McLean led Hartlepool to promotion in his first season but took a dislike to McGovern from the off. 'The first thing he said to me was, "You were Brian Clough's blue-eyed boy, well I'm going to change all that!" Soon afterwards I got the chance to go down to Derby. McLean didn't appreciate what I did which was pass the ball and have a football brain.' McGovern's early appearances had all been as a right winger and this is where he initially played at Derby. 'Peter Taylor said, "You aren't getting a kick out wide,"' says McGovern, 'and I said "I can't get the ball" to which he replied "If we had someone like you in the middle to pass the ball out to you, you might get it!" So from then on I played in the of midfield and took to it as a natural progression.'

At Derby, McGovern won promotion to the First Division and a League Championship medal, which led to his first taste of European Cup football. Derby got as far as the semi-finals where they met Juventus. 'In the semi-final we were absolutely cheated by the referee in Italy. He never officiated a major game in Europe again after that. I could not believe what was going on. It was so obvious it nearly had me in tears as I could not believe that it could happen in football at that level.'

Eighteen months later McGovern was on the move, to Leeds, following Clough to their third team together. "He [Clough] got away after forty-four days but I was there for seven months!' quips McGovern. 'I knew after one day it was the wrong move. I didn't realize there was such resentment among the players. His brusque manner upset them and after Clough left I never had a chance. One day I was called in and told that Leeds had agreed a fee of £50,000 for me with Carlisle where Alan Ashman was the manager and they'd also agreed a fee with Norwich of £75,000 where John Bond was the manager. They told me I could go to either one, they didn't even mind losing out on £25,000 so long as I'd go. So I spoke with Carlisle but didn't fancy moving up there then I spoke with John Bond and agreed wages and everything with him on the Saturday and then read in the paper on Monday that he'd signed Mick Maguire from Coventry.' Norwich's loss became Nottingham Forest's gain as Clough stepped in to bring McGovern and John O'Hare to the City Ground.

John O'Hare, another Scotsman, is quick to tell you that his home-town team from Renton in Dumbartonshire was the unofficial world champion of 1888 and also one of the first winners of the Scottish Cup. Unlike McGovern, he started playing very early and was in all his school teams from primary age and up. He would play in five-a-sides and in as many tournaments around southern Scotland as possible. By his early teens O'Hare's side had won the Glasgow league and he came to the attention of Sunderland's chief scout Charlie Ferguson. 'My dad wanted to get me out of where I lived,' says O'Hare. 'To get me out of the local environment. It was a lovely little village but a bit roguish really. There was a lot of violence; you didn't need a cinema, you just watched the fights at the weekend from the window! So he really wanted me to get out of that.' Get out of it he did, and he landed on his feet at Sunderland in 1962. 'It was a fantastic club to go to,' he recalls, 'because you didn't have to do all the menial tasks like cleaning terraces, polishing boots, painting, you just went to be a footballer – not like any other club I knew, where you had these jobs to do for years and years. We got paid £4 a week, of which £2 went home and £2 was to spend. Our board was paid for so we actually we got a full £4 a week, which went a fair way back then.' O'Hare worked his way into the first team at Sunderland and made over fifty appearances before moving to Derby and having the same success as John McGovern, but playing up front as a target-man.

'I had a fantastic time at Derby and got into the Scotland team in 1970,' says O'Hare. 'First I was in the Under-23s where I scored three goals. Then I made my full debut against Northern Ireland at Windsor Park. We won 1-0 and I scored so that was fantastic. I played for Scotland for about three seasons as centre forward and played thirteen games, scored five goals. I turned down a couple of trips in the summertime. Brian Clough didn't want us to go away, he wanted us to take a break. Tommy Docherty took over as national team manager from Bobby Brown and he wanted us to go to Brazil to play in a mini tournament. I'd like to have gone but I wasn't going at that point because I was enjoying my summer holiday. The same thing when they were going to Moscow and Denmark. Looking back I think Russia was a place I'd like to have gone to but never managed to get there, that was the only chance I had ever got to go Moscow. I used to enjoy the travelling and I'd like to have seen Moscow but didn't.'

'Leeds offered me big money,' he remembers, 'more than Derby would pay me. At Derby it was about £110 per week and Leeds offered me £150 per week, which was quite a big difference. So that was that, I went.' O'Hare recalls that Clough's down to earth training and managerial methods were in stark contrast to the in-depth ones used by Revie. 'Most of the stuff with Brian Clough was sort of enjoyable, not like hard work. It used to be warm up then have a game. He didn't do any real free-kick work or anything. You didn't know what you'd get from one day to the next, there was no routine as such. You went on Monday and you'd do this, you'd go Tuesday and do that. You just didn't know. It was that thing about being alive and alert and his training was really good, probably not the textbook coaching thing, but enjoyable, really enjoyable training. It was totally alien for the Leeds players. With Revie they had all this technical jargon and these dossiers on opposing players on each team that they played, things like the goalkeeper kicked to his left, all these sort of things like. With Clough it was, "It's about how we play, that's the important thing."' Jimmy Armfield took over from Clough and agreed the deal that sent the pair of Scots south for a discounted fee. 'It was a massive drop in wages,' recalls O'Hare. 'I had to sell my house that I was actually living in at the time, which when I look back on it wasn't the most sensible thing to do, but there you go.'

The pair instantly found themselves in a relegation fight. Despite the initial promise of a couple of away wins, the reality was that Forest had a set of players suited for below the halfway mark in the Second Division. The eight games after the win at Fulham had brought just three draws and five defeats, which was worse than Allan Brown's run before Christmas. McGovern made his debut in a 0-0 home draw with Cardiff City, and O'Hare started at Oxford the following week in another draw. Clough had made a couple of subtle changes within the staff that he'd taken over as well as bringing the new faces in. First he persuaded Martin O'Neill to withdraw a transfer request that he'd put in to Brown, and reinstated John Robertson in the centre of midfield with McGovern. Ian Bowyer patrolled one wing and George Lyall the other while O'Hare and Butlin linked up as a new look strike force. This new look team managed to hit the net fairly regularly but conceded even more often. Two goals at Aston Villa weren't even enough to get a point and the same happened later at Bristol Rovers. At one stage they slipped to just three points above the relegation places.

'It was just a case of trying to get some results,' recalls McGovern. 'It took a while to settle in and it was a while until we actually won.' It was more than a while: Forest went sixteen games between wins, finally getting two points at bottom club Sheffield Wednesday on 1 April. 'I was really suffering with a groin strain,' McGovern continues, 'and you can imagine what a handicap that is when you're the slowest player on the team anyway! Clough said, "We've got ten games left and you're playing in all of them."'

'I said "I can't run." He said, "It doesn't matter you never could. Think about some of the others, they can't play!" So I lasted through to the Norwich game, which was the second-to-last game of the season.' The league season ended with a 2-1 win over West Bromwich Albion and the two points gave Forest a slightly healthier look to their league position, but only slightly. The last match of the year was a 1-0 loss to Notts County in the County Cup Final at Meadow Lane.

Of course it didn't really matter if Forest avoided relegation by two points or twenty, as long as they did. Clough was in it for the long haul and spent the summer further stamping his authority more firmly on all areas of the club. 'There was a massive change when Brian Clough arrived,' says John Robertson, 'and nobody could fail to notice what an impact he made. He gave me a fair crack of it, but as far as atmosphere was concerned everybody knew that they would have to buck up, they'd have to be on their toes.'

It was also the time for some of Forest's promising youngsters to be given a chance. John McGovern recalls that 'I was really impressed with John Middleton – he had some fantastic performances that year to keep us up – and I'd never seen anyone run as fast as Viv Anderson. Then in training there was this kid called Tony Woodcock and I asked "Who's that lad? He can play!"' The next season would see these players get their chance as the Clough revolution by the Trent started to gather momentum.

Second Division, Final Table 1974-75

	Pld	Pts
Manchester United	42	61
Aston Villa	42	58
Norwich City	42	53
Sunderland	42	51
Bristol City	42	50
West Bromwich Albion	42	45
Blackpool	42	45
Hull City	42	44
Fulham	42	42
Bolton Wanderers	42	42
Oxford United	42	42
Orient	42	42
Southampton	42	41
Notts County	42	40
York City	42	38
FOREST	**42**	**38**
Portsmouth	42	37
Oldham Athletic	42	35
Bristol Rovers	42	35
Millwall	42	32
Cardiff City	42	32
Sheffield Wednesday	42	21

August 1974				
3	Port Vale	A	3-1	PSF
6	Walsall	A	1-1	PSF
10	Leicester	H	1-3	PSF
17	Bristol City	H	0-0	
19	Millwall	A	0-3	
24	Portsmouth	A	0-2	
27	Millwall	H	2-1	
31	Oxford United	H	1-2	
September				
7	Manchester United	A	2-2	
10	Newcastle United	H	1-1	LC2
14	Hull City	H	4-0	
17	Portsmouth	H	1-2	
21	Sheffield Wednesday	A	3-2	
25	Newcastle United	A	0-3	LC2R
28	Sunderland	H	1-1	
October				
2	Aston Villa	A	0-3	
5	Southampton	A	1-0	
12	Norwich City	H	1-3	
19	West Bromwich Albion	A	1-0	
26	Bristol Rovers	H	1-0	
29	Coventry City	H	1-1	F*
November				
2	Bolton Wanderers	A	0-2	
9	Oldham Athletic	H	1-0	
16	Cardiff City	A	1-2	
23	York City	H	2-1	
30	Orient	A	1-1	
December				
7	Fulham	H	1-1	
14	Bristol City	A	0-1	
21	Blackpool	H	0-0	
26	Hull City	A	3-1	
28	Notts County	H	0-2	
January 1975				
4	Tottenham Hotspur	H	1-1	FAC3
8	Tottenham Hotspur	A	1-0	FAC3R
11	Fulham	A	1-0	
18	Orient	H	2-2	
28	Fulham	A	0-0	FAC4
February				
1	Oldham Athletic	A	0-2	
3	Fulham	H	1-1	FAC4R
5	Fulham	A	1-1	FAC4R2
8	Bolton Wanderers	H	2-3	
10	Fulham	H	2-3	FAC4R3
14	York City	A	1-1	
22	Cardiff City	H	0-0	

28	Oxford United	A	1-1	
	March			
8	Aston Villa	H	2-3	
15	Sunderland	A	0-0	
22	Manchester United	H	0-1	
25	Notts County	A	2-2	
29	Blackpool	A	0-0	
	April			
1	Sheffield Wednesday	H	1-0	
5	Bristol Rovers	A	2-4	
12	Southampton	H	0-0	
14	Worksop Town	A	2-1	F
19	Norwich City	A	0-3	
21	Grantham Town	A	1-0	F*2
26	West Bromwich Albion	H	2-1	
28	Biggleswade	A	6-1	F
	May			
8	Notts County	H	0-1	CCF

Overall Record

	Pld	W	D	L	F	A	PTS	GD
Home	28	7	11	10	28	34	25	-6
Away	30	10	10	10	38	41	30	-3
League	42	12	14	16	43	55	38	-12
League Cup	2	0	1	1	1	4	0	-3
FA Cup	6	1	4	1	6	6	6	0
County Cup	1	0	0	1	0	1	0	-1
Friendlies	7	4	2	1	16	9	10	+7
Total	**58**	**17**	**21**	**20**	**66**	**75**	**55**	**-9**

Record Under Brian Clough

	Pld	W	D	L	F	A	PTS	GD
Home	11	2	4	5	12	15	8	-3
Away	16	5	8	3	20	18	18	+2
League	17	3	8	6	16	23	14	-7
League Cup	-	-	-	-	--	--	--	0
FA Cup	6	1	4	1	6	6	6	0
County Cup	1	0	0	1	0	1	0	-1
Friendlies	3	3	0	0	10	3	6	+7
Total	**27**	**7**	**12**	**8**	**32**	**33**	**26**	**-1**

* = Peter Hindley Testimonial

*2 = Bloomer/ Norris / Benskin Testimonial

Note –
Allan Brown's last match as manager was versus Notts County on December 28th 1974. Bill Anderson stood in as acting manager for game versus Tottenham Hotspur on January 4th 1975 and Brian Clough took over as manager from the game at Tottenham Hotspur on January 8th 1975.

Back row (left to right): Richardson, O'Kane, Serella, Peacock, Bowyer, Chapman, Cottam.
Middle row (left to right): Galley, O'Neill, Dennehy, Robertson, Lyall, Martin, Jackson.
Front row (left to right): Anderson, McIntosh, Woodcock, Dulson.

1974-75 Player Statistics

	League	FA Cup	LCup	CCup	F	Totals
Liam O'Kane	41	5	2	1	3	52
George Lyall	36(1)-7	6	2	1	5-4	50(1)-11
Paul Richardson	37(1)-4	4	1(1)	0	5	46(2)-4
Sammy Chapman	31	6-1	1	1	5	44-1
Dave Jones	36-1	3-1	2	0	2	43-2
Ian Bowyer	30(2)-6	6	2-1	0	3-1	41(2)-8
Barry Butlin	29(1)-7	5	0	1	4-1	39(1)-8
John Middleton	28	6	0	0	2	36
Neil Martin	26(1)-10	5(1)-2	1	0	3	35(2)-12
Miah Dennehy	26(1)-3	2(1)	2	0	5-1	35(2)-4
Martin O'Neill	16-1	5	2	1	4-2	28-3
John Robertson	17(3)	4-1	(1)	0	2	23(4)-1
John Cottam	14(1)-1	3(1)	1	1	4(1)	23(3)-1
Viv Anderson	14(2)	1	1	1	3	20(1)
Dennis Peacock	14	0	2	0	4(1)	20(1)
Paddy Greenwood	15	4	0	0	1	20
Tommy Jackson	14(2)-1	1	1	0	1	17(2)-1
Dave Serella	8(2)	0	1	0	3	12(2)
John O'Hare	10-2	0	0	0	1-1	11-3
John McGovern	8	0	0	0	0	8
Tony Woodcock	5(4)	0	0	1	2(3)-1	8(7)-1
Jim McCann	1	0	0	1	3-4	5-4
Jimmy McIntosh	3(1)	0	0	1	(1)	4(2)
John Galley	3(1)	0	1	0	0	4(1)

Also: G. Dulson (F 2), G. Saunders (F (1)), P. Wells (CC 1), B. Bowery (F 1) and I. Miller (F 1).
Note – full team v Biggleswade (28/4/75) is unknown.

LCup = League Cup, CCup = County Cup, F = Friendlies

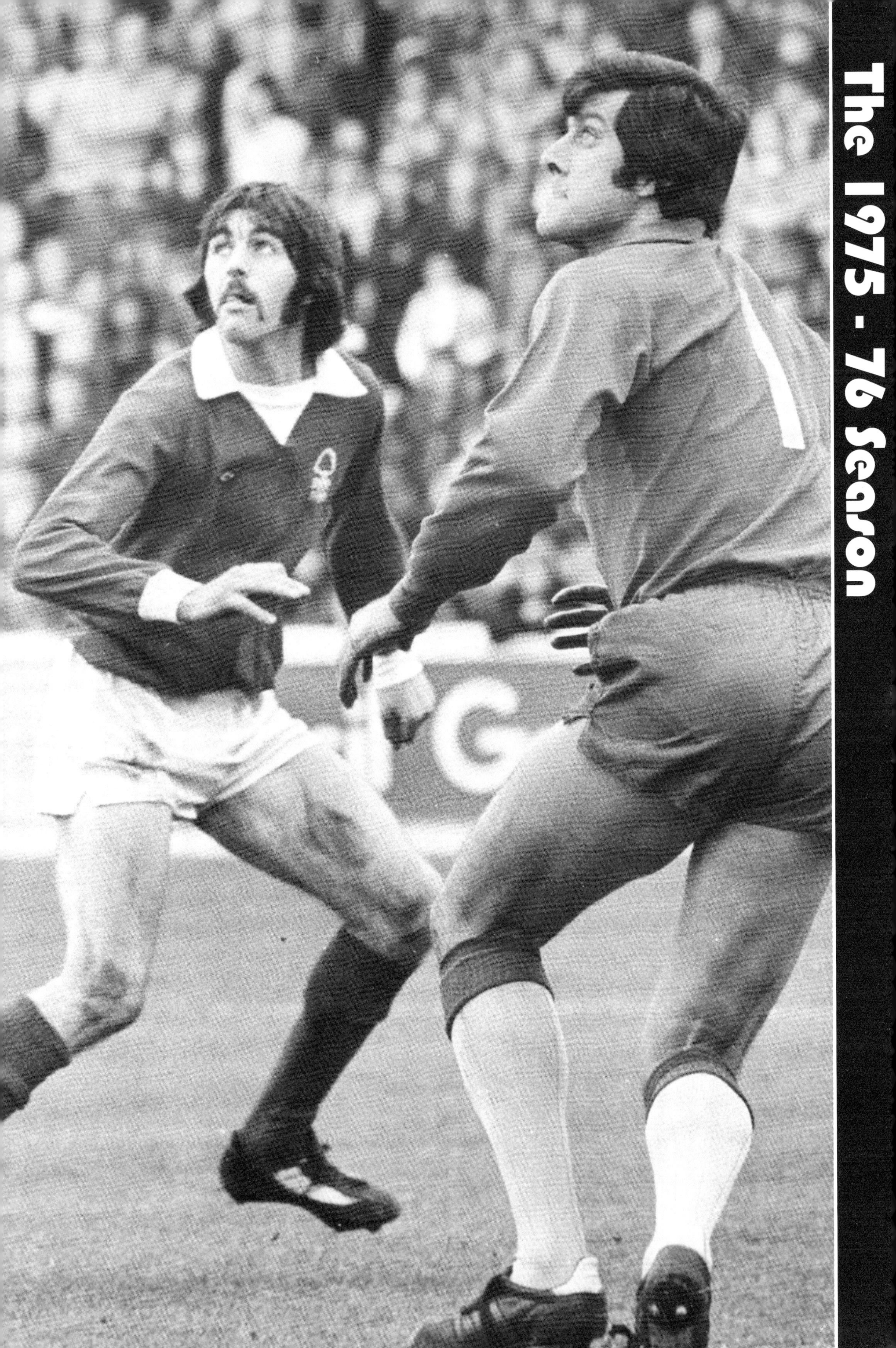
The 1975 - 76 Season

One of Brian Clough's many stellar attributes was the ability to stoke the fires of interest in his team. During the summer of 1975 season ticket sales at the City Ground reached their highest level for many years. However, the manager was still left with limited funds for the transfer market, but made himself busy enough during the close-season. A trio of players were allowed to leave on free transfers: Tommy Jackson, out of favour striker Neil Martin and reserve team centre-half Steve Baines were all shown the door. Clough also obtained a small fee for selling Irishman Miah Dennehy to Walsall, but he still didn't have any ready cash despite lowering the wage bill. He did make one signing, though, and a surprising one at that. Frank Clark was Clough's target, a thirty-two year old veteran full back thought to be coming to the end of his career at Newcastle United. Like many signings Clough made, there was more than a little method in this supposed madness. Clark would become a valuable addition to the shoring up of the Forest defence with his calming demeanour, and also brought a wealth of experience.

Clark (*pictured below*) had been born in County Durham and had planned to go to university. 'I was going to do chemistry' he explains. 'I don't know what I was going to do at the end of it, but I took maths physics and chemistry at A level and my intention was to go to university. I've been that way all my life. These people who say "I always knew what I was going to do, I have this plan and that plan," I admire them, because I've never made plans, I've really just gone along. Whilst I was doing my A levels I was playing for Crook Town, an amateur team, and I actually played in an amateur cup final whilst I was still at school in 1962 and I also played for the full England amateur side. Eventually I got two Bs and a D in my exams and that really wasn't good enough to get me into university as science courses at that time were quite popular. I didn't want to be a teacher, so I worked in the RVI [hospital] in Newcastle in the Biochemistry Department for a year and played part-time at Newcastle. I broke my leg and was out for about ten months because in those days if you had a broken leg – and I broke both bones – it was quite significant. So I was off work for about four months and the professor wasn't happy about that and I had to choose really, between football and biochemistry. I decide to go into football full-time.

'My parents were happy with my decision because they realized that's what I really wanted to do but the ironic thing is that my father died before I ever played league football. He'd have been absolutely thrilled the way it's turned out, but he died when I was only twenty, so he never actually saw me play in the league itself for Newcastle.' Clark soon broke into the first team and became a regular through the second half of the 1960s. In 1969 he was part of the Geordie team that unexpectedly won the Inter-City Fairs Cup. 'We stunned everybody, including ourselves, by actually winning it!' laughs Clark. 'We just thought it was a great adventure, kept winning, kept getting through – it was a magnificent experience.'

At the end of the 1974-75 season Clark had found himself ensconced as club captain, had played part of the season at centre-half and expected to end his career at St James' Park. So what transpired after the last game of the season came as a complete shock. 'I played over thirty games that season,' he recalls, 'and I'd just moved into a new house in Whitley Bay. We had had a difficult season and finished tenth. On the last day of the season we were playing Birmingham at home; I was playing in the team. We lost 2-1 and I was sitting in the dressing room – I was always last to leave. Joe Harvey came in and said, "I'm sorry to tell you, you're finished, you've got a free transfer." I was absolutely stunned. We'd been in this house about two months but that was how it was done. I was at the end of a contract, but in those days that wasn't unusual, we only ever got twelve month contracts. Usually at the end of the season the manager said, "I'll give you another twelve months and an extra fiver." You'd say, "Thanks, boss!" and get out before he changed his mind. The most you ever got was a two-year contract. I had this silly idea that I was going to stay there for the rest of my life – it was stupid and naïve in a way – so it was real bolt from the blue.'

So without any warning, Clark was out of a job, in his thirties and with a new mortgage to pay. Initial approaches came from a couple of local Fourth Division sides, Hartlepool and Darlington. As Clark began to take it all in he realized that this situation might actually be turned to his advantage and that he'd slipped into a rut at Newcastle and needed a new challenge. 'I was a typical Geordie,' he says, 'very parochial. I used to get nervous as soon as I crossed the Tyne Bridge coming south! But it forced us, as a family, to confront the thing, so we moved to Nottingham. I didn't really know Nottingham that well although I played quite a lot at Forest when they were a First Division side and of course we played against them in the infamous FA Cup tie eighteen months earlier. I knew Brian, having played in the north east, and I'd played in his testimonial at Sunderland. Our first conversation I had with him, I said I had spent most of the last season at Newcastle playing centre-back and I thought, This will do for me, this will extend my career here – I could play until I was forty. I used to think it was quite easy at centre-half; I never used to head it, I used to let the other fella head it! So I said this to Brian and he said, "You can forget about that. I've got about eight centre-halves!" The Newcastle directors had used publicly the excuse for getting rid of me that I was an injury problem, but I proceeded never to miss a game for two seasons.'

Clark puts part of his longevity at Forest down to the rigorous pre-season training regime that Jimmy Gordon and Brian Clough put the players through. For the 1975-76 season there was also a demanding seven match pre-season schedule in place. 'Brian had got this reputation of not liking anybody to train too hard, and once the season had started that might be true, but the pre-season was bloody hard, which was good, I thrived on that. Unless you were an international, you always had about twelve weeks off which is a long time and some players used to come back grossly overweight. I didn't: by that time I used to keep myself in shape. What I would do when the season ended was I would always have a couple of weeks doing nothing, then I would do a little bit, plenty of running, not quick running, then I would go on holiday for a couple of weeks and do nothing at all. After that I used to try and time it so I would have at least two or three weeks before the actual pre-season started, but some of them would do nothing. In those days you worked so hard in the first three days: you couldn't walk for the next three days you were stiff all over which was daft really. Whereas now you come back and they break you in a little more gently. Once the season started we used to get a lot of days off. I had adopted this philosophy, I had read it somewhere – because don't forget in those days there wasn't a great deal of scientific research put into training football, you did what the managers had been doing themselves for twenty years – I had read somewhere that when you get older and want to prolong your career you should be training harder instead of training less, which is what people used to do. So I got into this habit, especially if we had played on the Saturday, sometimes he would give us the Monday off as well as the Sunday. I didn't like to go two days of not having done anything after a game, so I would go out and run around the road in Lowdham where we lived. One time someone saw me and told him [Clough] and he gave me the biggest bollocking! He said, "When I give you a day off, you have a day off!" Two years later I'd played nearly a hundred consecutive games and he said, "Who's right now?" Well, you couldn't argue with that!'

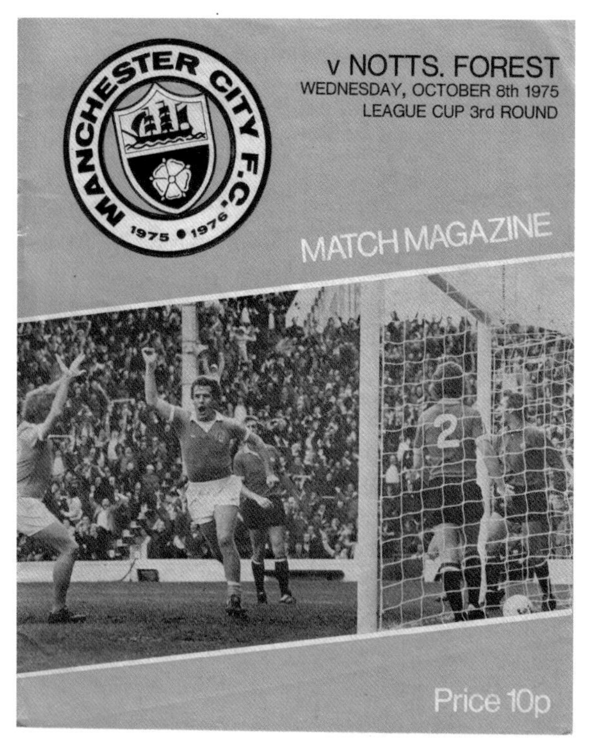

After the tough initial training sessions at Wollaton Park, the next stage was a West German visit. The squad flew out in late July for a series of five games in a week. The first four were against lower division opponents and Forest won fairly easily before a 1-0 reverse to First Division Stuttgart. The fifteen man squad that travelled to Europe included a trio of youngsters in the shape of Tony Woodcock, Ian Miller and Jimmy McCann. The three places had become vacant after Ian Bowyer, John Robertson and Martin O'Neill were all dropped because of a series of pay disputes as they were negotiating new contracts.

After the official party returned from the Continent there was a three day break before they were due to fly to Northern Ireland for two more games in the week before the opening league fixtures. If the contract sagas were going to be sorted before the new season started for real they would have to be sorted now. 'I actually wrote off to the Professional Footballers Association,' reveals Ian Bowyer, 'and I was granted a free transfer. The club appealed that decision, so we had a hearing set for London; I was being represented by Derek Dougan. So Brian turns up – I don't think he wanted to go to the meeting. It was at Lancaster Gate, it's the middle of London, and he comes over in his shorts with a squash racket in his hand. Between Derek Dougan and Brian Clough we sorted it out and I was happy with what I was offered and so our appearance at this tribunal lasted thirty seconds! It was typical and in many ways I think I gained respect from Brian because I didn't give in, but he never let me forget it. He used to say, "You took me to London" and I used to say "No gaffer, you appealed. *You* took *me* to London."'

The resigning of Bowyer, Robertson and O'Neill was possibly the biggest trio of signings that Nottingham Forest have ever made and it paid immediate dividends. All three were included in the Irish trip and over the two games, which Forest won 3-0 and 3-2, Bowyer scored two hat-tricks. Not only that, but John Robertson (*pictured on right*) was given a place on the left wing which took him back to his earliest days at Forest. In the second game his crosses led to two of Bowyer's goals. Though no one realized it at the time, it was a glimpse of the future.

The opening league match of the season was at home to Plymouth. Brian Clough had been in charge for eight months now and already the team was showing signs of being in the manager's image. Viv Anderson was promoted to right-back and Clark was at left-back, with Robertson left-wing and O'Neill on the right. An impressive start was produced and when Notts County visited on 30 August, the Reds were four games unbeaten (including a brace of wins over Rotherham in the League Cup first round which they'd had to enter because of the previous season's lowly league finish). The game went County's way as they nicked a late winner in what was the debut game for a young winger called Terry Curran. Curran had just been signed from Doncaster Rovers for £60,000 (with goalkeeper Dennis Peacock and reserve team-winger Ian Miller going in the opposite direction) and was given an attacking role from the right-hand side.

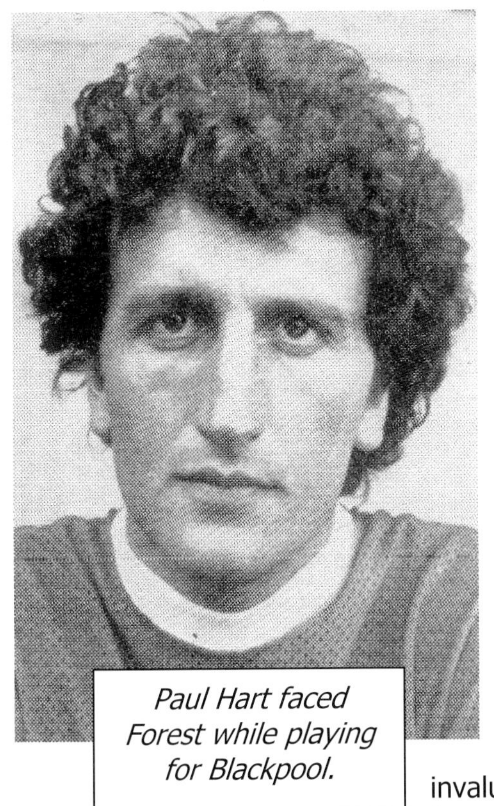

Paul Hart faced Forest while playing for Blackpool.

September and October proved to be tough hunting grounds for the Reds. A single league win in each month left them at the wrong end of the table and a defeat at First Division Manchester City knocked them out of the League Cup. This period did however sow more seeds that would reap benefits in later years. After George Lyall missed a spot kick at Portsmouth John Robertson was installed as the penalty taker. His first chance to prove himself came a few weeks later, at home to Hull City. Unfortunately, when Forest were awarded a penalty in the first half Robertson shot it straight at the keeper, though he did manage to score with the rebound. In the second half the Reds were again awarded a penalty – Robertson stepped up and missed it. Forest lost the game 2-1 and Robertson had to endure a hail of abuse from the home fans. How things would change. 'I went off them [penalties] then, well I think I got taken off them' says Robertson, 'but I wasn't too keen anyway.' Terry Curran took over and had more luck with them until he was injured the following season. This injury led to Robertson giving penalties another go and at the second attempt he found that he actually had a natural gift for them which would prove invaluable in Forest's future.

More changes were obviously needed to gain some consistency in the league. Seventeen-year-old Bryn Gunn got a couple of games (but wouldn't figure regularly in the first team for a few years yet); David Jones was sold to Norwich and then John Middleton was struck down with a broken leg in a training accident. This latter event was particularly galling as he had been showing signs of developing into a top quality goalkeeper. The previous summer had seen him picked for the England youth team and he'd played all five games as they won the Mini World Cup in Switzerland and then been called into a training camp with the full England squad by Don Revie. Middleton's misfortune opened the door for Peter Wells to make his league debut. Just before Christmas the City Ground's revolving door clicked into action again and George Lyall was on his way to Hull for £20,000.

Colin Barrett

Things had picked up in November, and convincing wins over Carlisle United (4-0), Southampton (3-0) and Blackburn (4-1) left the league position looking healthier and giving the club some reason to be optimistic heading into 1976. Inconsistency plagued Forest again though as they lost in the third round of the FA Cup to Third Division Peterborough United after a replay. Rubbing salt into the wound was the loss of the cash boost that would have been picked up by the fourth round trip to Old Trafford that awaited. A disappointing January culminated with a 3-1 loss at home to Chelsea and a 1-1 draw at Luton.

Next up was a run-of-the-mill league game at home to Blackpool. Forest put in one of their better performances of the season and won 3-0. This win seemed to give the team a spark and they went on a great run that would continue not just for the rest of the season but for the next few years.

While results were picking up Brian Clough was still tinkering with the squad. Jimmy McIntosh was sold to Hull and Tony Woodcock was loaned out to Graham Taylor's Lincoln City in the Fourth Division. When Liam O'Kane sustained what would turn out to be a career ending injury Clough got his chequebook out again. His target this time was Manchester City defender Colin Barrett. Stockport-born Barrett had been a sought-after teenager but all attempts by league clubs to sign him had been rejected by Barrett's father and he went to work at Hawker Siddeley Aviation while still playing local amateur football. After almost three years in a 'proper' job, Manchester City came in for him and he signed for them in 1970 under the warning of 'On your head be it!' from his father. Barrett had played over fifty games for City before dropping into the reserves. 'I was in and out of the side at City,' says Barrett. 'I had asked for a transfer because I couldn't see any future and then Brian Clough came in and said he wanted me to go on loan, which I declined. I preferred to have a permanent move if I could, so I wasn't really interested.' City manager Tony Book relayed Barrett's decision to Forest, but Clough wasn't about to give up the chase. 'He got me on the phone,' recalls Barrett, 'and he said "I want to speak to you. You might not like me and I might not like you, but you're playing in the reserves and I've got a place in the first team here." So I agreed to meet him outside the Leek Town football ground and he got me to come on loan. He'd said a month's loan because it was towards the end of the season, but then he said he wanted to extend it to three months after the first month was up. As I wanted a permanent move I thought, Oh, here we go, because I'd heard what normally happens is they just have you for a few months and say, "We don't want you any more" but at the end of the season he said, "No problem, we'll get a contract sorted out."'

Barrett played every game after arriving at Forest, initially at right-back (replacing the injured Liam O'Kane) and sometimes at centre-half, and this coincided with the club's good run. As well as dropping down from a relatively big First Division club to a Second Division one, Barrett found major differences in his everyday activities at Forest. 'Training was pretty unusual,' he says. 'I was used to being told what to do, what not to do, but with Clough it was different. The first time I met him on the Saturday before the first game he turned round and said "Do you want a drink?" I said, "No I'm OK, I've got a match this afternoon." He said, "If it makes you play better have a drink." It was a case of getting used to fact that he gives lads days off and I said, "I will go in and train at City." This was while I was still on loan. "No," he said: "If I give you a day off you have a day off!"'

Following on from the convincing Blackpool win the goal scoring floodgates opened for the Reds. Terry Curran became the star of the show with some breathtaking performances – a goal against Blackpool and another in a 2-0 win at Bristol City set them on their way. A 2-2 draw at Charlton was followed up by an exciting 4-3 win over Oldham with Curran hitting the net again. Between the February and the end of the season Forest had a run of nine wins and just two losses in their last fifteen games, with John O'Hare (*pictured bottom left on opposite page*) scoring four goals in a seven game span and rose to an eighth place finish.

'Expectations had been very low,' says Frank Clark. 'They had finished pretty close to the bottom the season before and there was no money available. The playing squad was fairly average and we just muddled through that season. I think everybody was more than happy with how the season ended because I think Brian, I know people think he is a miracle worker and what he subsequently did could almost be akin to a miracle, but even he knew he wasn't going to do it so quickly, so the first year was fairly unspectacular but satisfying nevertheless. I was able to just relax and almost enjoy it. I find this concept, where people say you've got to enjoy the game, difficult to grasp because it's too important. You enjoy all the lifestyle through the week, the training, the build-up, the afterglow if you've won, you enjoy all that, but the actual ninety minutes, it's too important. But I did enjoy my time because of that.'

By the end of the season the team was almost unrecognizable from the slumped side that Allan Brown had left behind. Six of the first team (Wells, Barrett, Clark, McGovern, O'Hare and Curran) had been introduced to the side by Clough and another two (Robertson and O'Neill) had been rescued from the reserves and given a confidence boost. This solid nucleus was being shaped for a concerted promotion push and the late season burst of good form catapulted them into eighth place – just seven points from the last promotion spot. A better autumn, which had seen them collect just eight points from a possible twenty-two at one stage, could well have put them back in the First Division. As things turned out they wouldn't have to wait much longer anyway.

Second Division Final Table 1975-76

	Pld	Pts
Sunderland	42	56
Bristol City	42	53
West Bromwich Albion	42	53
Bolton Wanderers	42	52
Notts County	42	49
Southampton	42	49
Luton Town	42	48
FOREST	**42**	**46**
Charlton Athletic	42	42
Blackpool	42	42
Chelsea	42	40
Fulham	42	40
Orient	42	40
Hull City	42	39
Blackburn Rovers	42	38
Plymouth Argyle	42	38
Oldham Athletic	42	38
Bristol Rovers	42	38
Carlisle United	42	37
Oxford United	42	33
York City	42	28
Portsmouth	42	25

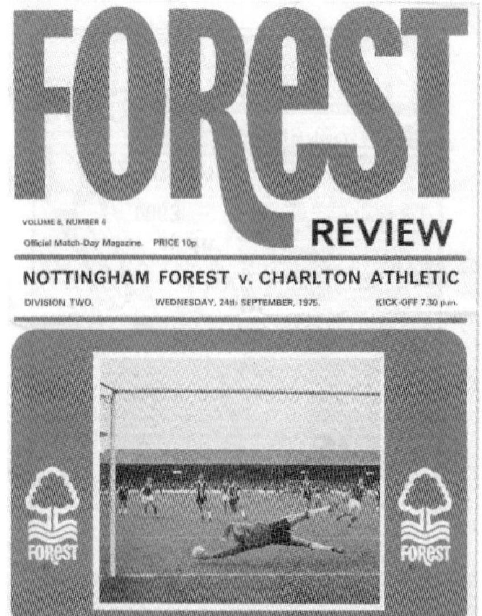

July 1975				
29	TSV Geingen, West Germany	A	2-0	PSF
31	SV Kaufbeuren, W. Germany	A	1-1	PSF

August				
1	BC Aichach, West Germany	A	1-0	PSF
3	TSV Gamersheim	A	9-0	PSF
5	Stuttgart Kickers, W.Germany	A	0-1	PSF
9	Ballymena, N. Ireland	A	3-0	PSF
11	Coleraine, Northern Ireland	A	3-2	PSF
16	Plymouth Argyle	H	2-0	
19	Rotherham United	A	2-1	LC1, 1
23	Portsmouth	A	1-1	
27	Rotherham United	H	5-1	LC1, 2
30	Notts County	H	0-1	

September				
6	Chelsea	A	0-0	
10	Plymouth Argyle	H	1-0	LC2
13	Hull City	H	1-2	
20	Oxford United	A	1-0	
24	Charlton Athletic	H	1-2	
27	Bolton Wanderers	H	1-2	

October				
4	Bristol Rovers	A	2-4	
8	Manchester City	A	1-2	LC3
11	Fulham	A	0-0	
18	Southampton	H	3-1	
21	Luton Town	H	0-0	
25	Oldham Athletic	A	0-0	

November				
1	Carlisle United	H	4-0	
4	Blackpool	A	1-1	
8	Sunderland	A	0-3	
15	Bristol City	H	1-0	
17	Hartlepool United	A	0-0	F
22	Southampton	A	3-0	
29	York City	H	1-0	

December				
6	Orient	A	1-1	
9	Qatar National IX	A	1-1	F
13	Portsmouth	H	0-1	
20	Plymouth	H	0-1	
26	West Bromwich Albion	H	0-2	
27	Blackburn Rovers	A	4-1	

January 1976				
1	Peterborough United	H	0-0	FAC3
7	Peterborough United	A	0-1	FAC3R
10	Hull City	A	0-1	

17	Chelsea	H	1-3	
23	Mansfield Town	H	2-1	CCSF
31	Luton Town	A	1-1	

February

2	Corby Town	A	2-1	F
7	Blackpool	H	3-0	
21	Bristol City	A	2-0	
24	Charlton Athletic	A	2-2	
28	Oldham Athletic	H	4-3	

March

6	Carlisle United	A	1-1	
13	Fulham	H	1-0	
17	Sunderland	H	2-1	
20	York City	A	2-3	
27	Orient	H	1-0	

April

3	Bolton Wanderers	H	1-0	
10	Oxford United	A	2-4	
13	Notts County	H	0-0	
17	West Bromwich Albion	A	2-1	
20	Blackburn Rovers	A	0-3	
24	Bristol Rovers	A	1-0	
26	Don Revie All- Stars	H	2-1	F*
28	Louth	A	6-0	F
30	CD Severance, Spain	A	10-0	F

* = Sammy Chapman Testimonial

Overall Record

	Pld	W	D	L	F	A	PTS	GD
Home	26	15	3	8	37	22	33	+15
Away	35	14	13	8	64	31	41	+33
League	42	17	12	13	55	40	46	+15
League Cup	4	3	0	1	10	4	6	+6
FA Cup	2	0	1	1	0	1	0	-1
County Cup	1	1	0	0	2	1	2	+1
Friendlies	12	8	3	1	34	7	19	+27
Total	**61**	**29**	**16**	**16**	**101**	**53**	**73**	**+48**

Back row (left to right): Gordon, Richardson, Bowyer, O'Kane, Peacock, Middleton, Anderson, O'Neill, Robertson, McIntosh, Clough.
Front row (left to right): McGovern, Jones, O'Hare, Butlin, Chapman, Lyall, Clark, Cottam.

1975-76 Player Statistics

	League	FA Cup	LCup	CCup	F	Totals
Frank Clark	42	2	4	1	9	58
John McGovern	41	2	4-1	1	11	57-1
John O'Hare	39(1)-9	2	4	0	10-4	55(1)-13
Sammy Chapman	37-1	2	4-1	1	10	54
Ian Bowyer	40-13	2	4-3	1-1	6-7	53-24
John Robertson	37(2)-5	1(1)	4	1	7	50(3)-5
Barry Butlin	32-7	2	0	0	8-3	42-10
Paul Richardson	23(1)-1	1	4-2	1-1	8	37(1)-5
Terry Curran	33-6	0	0	1	3-2	37-8
Martin O'Neill	29(1)-5	0	2	1	4	36(1)-5
John Middleton	19	0	4	0	9	32
Viv Anderson	21	0	3	0	6-1	30-1
Peter Wells	23	2	0	1	2(1)	28(1)
Liam O'Kane	8	2	1	(1)	8	19(1)
Bryn Gunn	11	0	3	0	4	18
George Lyall	5(2)-2	0	2-2	0	7(1)-3	14(3)-7
John Cottam	8-1	0	1	0	3(1)	12(1)-1
Colin Barrett	10	0	0	0	2-1	12-1
Jimmy McIntosh	1(1)	2	0	0	7-1	10(1)-1
Jim McCann	1(4)-1	0	0	0	3(3)-2	4(7)-3
Bert Bowery	1-2	2	0	1	(1)	4(1)-2
Gary Mills	0	0	0	0	2(2)	2(2)
Tony Woodcock	0	0	0	0	2(1)-2	2(1)-2
Duncan MacKenzie	0	0	0	0	1-2	1-2
Joe Baker	0	0	0	0	1	1
Glyn Saunders	0	0	0	1	0	1
David Sunley	1	0	0	0	0	1
D Dall	0	0	0	0	(1)	(1)
J Powell	0	0	0	1	(1)	(1)

LCup = League Cup, CCup = County Cup, F = Friendlies

The summer of 1976 is remembered as one of the UK's hottest on record, and in Nottingham it was no different. *Phew! What a scorcher!* was the newspaper headline of choice, while hosepipe bans came into force, and ice cream sales rocketed.

Nottingham had been changing through the 1970s, having already undergone a series of major structural upheavals in the 1960s. The mid-70s saw the final demolitions on the old Meadows estate, and in the city centre the Victoria and Broadmarsh shopping centres opened for business in 1972 and 1975 respectively. Boots, Players and Raleigh were all going strong, despite the series of industrial disputes that disrupted the middle of the decade. In fact, by the end of the 1970s Raleigh would reach a record output level of around ten thousand cycles per week, having opened a new Ilkeston factory in 1974. Urban legend has it that when Forest won the productivity of all the local firms went up. If that was really the case then production figures must have gone through the roof over the next few years.

Although inflation was rising (in March 1977 it was announced that prices had risen 70% in just three years!) Nottingham's populace was still keen to go out and spend money on entertainment. Clubs like Isabella's were packed at the weekends, with the new sound of disco holding sway on the dance floors. At the other end of the musical spectrum punk rockers were increasingly being spotted in and around the Old Market Square and the Virgin record store on King Street was at the centre of a well-publicized court case over their right to advertise the Sex Pistols' album, *Never Mind The Bollocks*, in their shop window.

The summer of 1976 was also a golden one in sports fan's memories: James Hunt won the Formula 1 Grand Prix championship and Bjorn Borg won the first of his five Wimbledon Men's Singles titles. In football, the international landscape of the mid-1970s was almost completely dominated by West Germany, Holland and Belgium. The West Germans had beaten Holland in the 1974 World Cup Final and then lost to Czechoslovakia on penalties in the 1976 European Championship final hosted by Yugoslavia. The European Cup was won by Bayern Munich for the third straight time in 1976, with a 1-0 win over St Etienne at Hampden Park. Dutch masters Ajax had completed the same hat-trick between 1971 and 1973, using their free flowing 'total-football' approach. The 1976 European Cup Winner's Cup was captured by Belgian side Anderlecht, who also won it in 1978 but lost the 1977 final to Hamburg.

The 1976 UEFA Cup was taken home by Liverpool in Bob Paisley's second season in charge. This win over the Belgians from Brugge was just a prelude to the Merseysider's conquering of Europe with a mixture of strength at the back, guile in midfield and clinical finishing up front. They won the European Cup in 1977 after winning the First Division in 1976 when they edged the free-flowing football of Stan Bowles' Queen's Park Rangers by just a point. They would have laughed at the idea of a Second Division club rising up and knocking them from both of these lofty perches. The odds for such a bet were surely never investigated, but the odds for Forest getting into the top flight are a matter of record. In mid-August Forest were joint third favourites (with Bolton) for promotion with odds of 8/1 being offered, Wolves were the bookies' choice at 4/1. Other sources had higher expectations, and the

Sunday People placed Forest as their choice not just for promotion but to win the Second Division championship.

But why were Forest being touted for success in such circles? The answer is simple: Peter Taylor had come to Forest in June and re-formed the most famous managerial double act in football.

Taylor (*pictured right*) had been born in Nottingham in 1928 and played a couple of games for Forest during the Second World War. His professional career as a goalkeeper started at Coventry in 1950 after playing there part-time while completing his apprenticeship as a bricklayer. He moved north to Middlesbrough in 1955, where he met Brian Clough, who was just breaking into the first team set-up, and trainer Jimmy Gordon. Taylor retired as a player in 1965 and moved into management with Burton Albion in the Southern League. After Clough was offered the chance to manage Hartlepool he insisted that Taylor join him and the elder partner took a pay cut to move north once again. The partnership pushed Hartlepool up the Fourth Division, before taking Derby County to unheard of heights. The split came after the pair had moved to Brighton & Hove Albion in 1973. Taylor had been the motivating force behind taking on the Third Division side and Clough's heart was never really in it. When the chance came to rejoin the 'big time' at Leeds Clough took it. But Taylor declined and stayed behind at Brighton. At the end of the 1975-76 season Brighton missed out on promotion to the Second Division by just three points and Taylor resigned.

While Taylor was on holiday in Majorca Clough tracked him down and asked him to 'come home' to Nottingham, as he recalled: 'He [Taylor] failed to get promotion that particular season and he was on his own, having spent a lot of money on a lot of players. So being Nottingham born and bred he was the first one that came to my mind. We'd had a successful relationship both on and off the field, both as players when I was a player at Middlesbrough and in management. Peter retained a very, very strong friendship with me and it was a natural thing to ask "Do you fancy going back to your city of birth?" And of course he jumped at it. We had one meeting in Majorca, it was a half-an-hour job sitting in the sunshine in Majorca. He went on with his holidays and I came back to work and it all started from that."

Clough's work that summer had included trying to add some firepower to the Forest line-up by bringing Duncan Mackenzie back to the City Ground, but that fell through. Taylor would bring his own ideas of possible strikers when he started work in earnest during the pre-season trip to Germany in late July.

His arrival sent a shockwave through the playing staff and energized both players and management. His first task was analysing the current squad on a player-by-player basis and casting his acclaimed critical eye over whom to keep and whom to replace. The partnership had always worked that way and always would. Taylor would bring names to Clough for consideration and more often than not he was spot on. But his role wasn't just to review thee team, putting the players on edge, wondering where the axe was going to fall; Taylor also brought a wicked sense of humour that was often used to defuse tense situations and relax the team at key moments.

'I think that was the key,' says Frank Clark. 'Getting the two of them back together. You laughed more when Peter was around and I think it galvanized Brian more. A lot of people didn't like [Taylor] but there's nothing wrong with that, God rest his soul. It was because he used to get under people's skin – that was his style. All players had a weakness; they either drank, gambled or chased women, and his theory was he would always try and find out the weakness of each player so he could use it in a positive sense to get a better performance. This used to go right over my head, I thought it was good and I was very relaxed about it. I don't think he particularly rated me that highly as a player and sometimes he picked the team – I always knew when because I'd probably be left out if he picked the team.'

'I always thought that Clough was the "main man" no question,' says Colin Barrett. 'I didn't have a lot of time for Taylor, but Clough – you needed him there. When he wasn't there you knew there was a problem and you knew full well that if Taylor had said something to Brian Clough then you were in trouble.'

One of the players that Taylor had an immediate effect on was John Robertson (*pictured below*). The likeable Scot had played for Scotland Schoolboys and caught the eye of then Forest assistant manager Bill Anderson. Anderson had visited Robertson's parents and persuaded them to let their son come south to Forest and sign as an apprentice. He broke into the first team in 1970 while Forest were still in the First Division and had played twelve games the following season in central midfield. After relegation he appeared in twenty-eight league games and then just five in the 1973-74 season. By the time Clough arrived in January 1975 he was languishing in the reserves and on the transfer list. His move out to the left wing let him hold down a regular first team place but the general feeling was that he had not managed to play anywhere near his potential. The arrival of Peter Taylor at the club was a make or break period for Robertson: if he didn't buck-up his ideas he would be gone. The first time Taylor came across Robertson was on an Augsburg training pitch in Germany. 'We were on a German tour,' recalls Robertson. 'I think basically his first words to me were "And you, you can pop off back to the hotel. I'll see you later." And that was his first words to me. I didn't understand what I'd done. But he said he'd see me later so I went back. He said he'd watched me warming up and just walking about and not doing too much and then playing a bit of the game and obviously I didn't play too well, but he said he could see that I had a load of ability and that I was wasting my time at the minute and questioned my attitude and everything like that. We had a good chat but basically from then on it was uphill all the way.'

Peter Taylor's recollection of the same event was a little harsher, as he wrote in his 1980 book, *With Clough, By Taylor* – 'My first words to him were "You're a disgrace and ought to be sent home!"' Taylor was less than impressed with Robertson's warm-up routine, which consisted of 'not moving out of a five yard radius throughout the entire quarter of an hour'. Clough had told Taylor that Robertson 'thinks nobody cares about him and he dresses like a tramp'. Taylor laid down the law – shape up or ship out. He was on Robertson like the proverbial rash and the winger's attitude started to show signs of improving immediately.

The five games in West Germany were primarily aimed at getting match-sharp, as Colin Barrett remembers: 'We played against local sides for fitness training. A couple of weeks before that at Wollaton Park we'd done the really physical side of it. Then in Germany we went for some actual games. What most clubs did at that time for pre-season was play a couple of games against local sides so we never played against anybody top drawer, it was mainly Second Division sides and local amateur sides to basically get you to match fitness.'

After dropping the opening game 3-2 Forest won four straight and scored thirteen further goals from seven different players. The games were often played on pitches covered by three inches of grass making the five games in eight days even harder, but as the players all agreed, it was much better than another week up and down the hills in Wollaton Park.

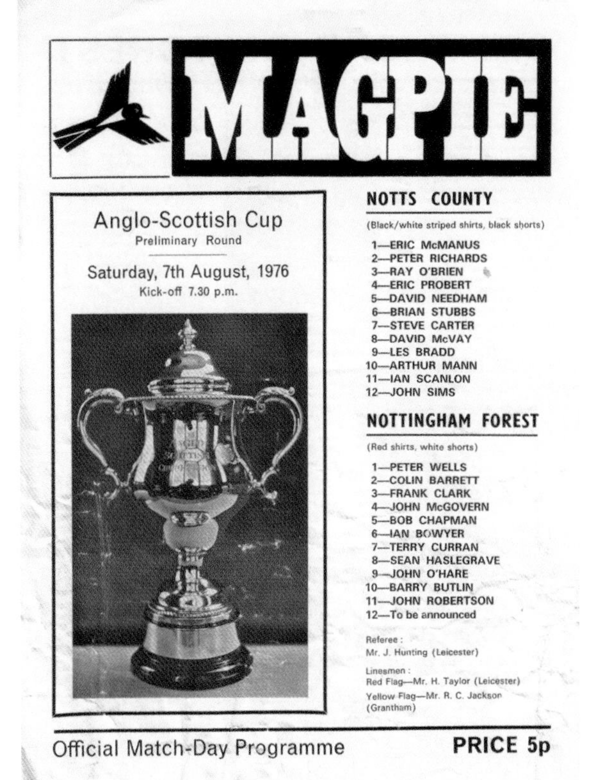

These games saw the debut of midfielder Sean Haselgrave, who had come in from Stoke City, and the promotion of full-back Glyn Saunders from the reserves to replace the still-injured Viv Anderson, who had picked up a late season knee injury with the reserves the previous May. John McGovern continued to fill in as centre-back alongside Sammy Chapman, a role he'd been slotted into the previous season. McGovern wrote a few notes about the tour in the club's match day programme and noted prophetically that it was a fitting spectacle to 'pass the World Cup stadium in Munich, just to remind us what it's all about – football!' If only he'd had a crystal ball to look three years into the future!

After the week in Germany the players returned home for a much earlier than usual start to the season. The first three games were a curious mix of pre-season friendlies and competitive games under the guise of the quirky Anglo-Scottish Cup. Forest had competed once before in this tournament which was previously under the sponsorship of Texaco. This 1971 entry, when Forest were still a First Division club, had ended early with the Reds going out in the first round to Airdrieonians on penalties. Initially the competition had included clubs from England, Scotland, Northern Ireland and Eire, with the English teams dominating. Wolverhampton Wanderers (1971), Derby County under the management of Brian Clough and Peter Taylor (1972), Ipswich Town (1973) and Newcastle (1974 and 1975) had all triumphed while Middlesbrough took the first non-Texaco trophy by beating Fulham in 1976.

The Reds were invited to join the revamped competition in 1976-77 and Brian Clough remembers a conversation that took place shortly before the season started: 'The Anglo Scottish Cup was very important to Brian Appleby QC [who had taken over as chairman]. Peter Taylor and I just happened to be talking to him in the car park, just outside the main entrance, and he said, "All we want to do here is win something." Peter Taylor, being the gentleman, turned around and said, "Something, you mean anything?" Brian Appleby said, "Yes, anything." "Oh,"'Peter Taylor said, "'well that's no problem, anything. I thought you were talking about the

First Division!" So Peter pinned him down there straight away and then Peter said to me afterwards, "What are we in?" So I told him about the Anglo-Scottish Cup and he said, "Well you'd better go and win it!"

The tournament was arranged with the English clubs starting in four groups of four with each team playing the others just once and the group winners going on to the knockout rounds with the four qualifying Scottish teams. Forest were placed into Group B with Division One sides Bristol City and West Bromwich Albion and local rivals Notts County. Group A housed Bolton, Blackpool, Burnley and Blackburn; Group C held Orient, Norwich, Chelsea and Fulham; and Group D included holders Newcastle, Middlesbrough, Hull City and Sunderland. Two points were awarded for a win, one for a draw, and a bonus point was available to any club scoring three or more goals in a single game – an experiment intended to promote attacking football and bring in some bigger crowds to these early August matches. It was expected that crowds would be smaller than average, with the majority of workers taking holidays in July and August, and even back in 1976 there was a feeling that the extremely hot summer break had been too short with too many TV matches being shown over the summer. The Home Internationals, European Championships and American Bicentennial Tournament had all been screened.

The three preliminary games took place over seven days and failed to catch the public's imagination. The largest attendance at the three Forest games was the eleven thousand that witnessed the 0-0 draw at Meadow Lane for the latest instalment in the Forest – Notts County rivalry. First Division outfit West Bromwich Albion brought a strong line-up to the City Ground that included Willie Johnston, John Wile and Tony Brown, but were dispatched on the end of a 3-2 scoreline which also gave Forest a bonus point for the three goals netted. The Reds got another bonus point in the next game, a 4-2 win over Bristol City, as they swept into the quarter-finals.

Anglo-Scottish Cup Group B Final Table

	Pld	W	D	L	F	A	BP	Pts
FOREST	**3**	**2**	**1**	**0**	**7**	**4**	**2**	**7**
Bristol City	3	2	0	1	5	4	0	4
West Bromwich Albion	3	1	0	2	5	5	1	3
Notts County	3	0	1	2	3	7	0	1

(BP = bonus points for goals scored)

Below – In an early season encounter Wolves' Steve Daley scores an own-goal, but Forest still lost 3-1.

'Martin O'Neill came to the fore, he scored about fifteen goals one season. I said, "Martin, do you know where you're getting them from?" He said, "Yes, I work hard, I tackle and I put them in the net. You keep saying it's the hardest thing in the game." I said, "Yes, it still is the hardest thing in the game, but they're all coming from the left wing [Robertson]," and Martin hadn't twigged that.' – Brian Clough

Despite the confidence boosting start, the opening games of the league campaign were rather tentative by comparison. Fulham, who had finished bottom of their Anglo-Scottish group, held the Reds to a 2-2 draw with Terry Curran notching one goal and setting up John O'Hare for the other in front of over two thousand away fans. Curran netted again in a 1-1 draw at home to Charlton and then a disappointing 3-1 home defeat to newly relegated Wolverhampton left Forest mid-table. The Wolves game was Glyn Saunders' last game at right-back as Colin Barrett took over the role.

The first break from league action came with a trip to Walsall in the second round of the League Cup, where the West Midlanders fielded a trio of ex-Foresters in the shape of Miah Dennehy, Dave Serella and Alan Buckley. Buckley gave the home side an early lead but Forest gradually took control and two goals from the emerging Martin O'Neill paved the way to a 4-2 win.

O'Neill had initially signed for Forest back in 1971 and like John Robertson he'd drifted out of the regular first-team squad. He'd played just forty-five League games over the previous two years but under Clough and Taylor he was a regular playing in thirty-eight League games in 1976-77. O'Neill famously gained a reputation as an opinionated, well educated, player who was quick to question the motivation behind management decisions. He'd been plucked from studying for a Law degree at Belfast's Queen's University and left his eight brothers and sisters to join Forest as a nineteen year old. He'd had some success in Northern Ireland playing for Distillery and winning the Irish Cup in 1971. That win catapulted the team into the European Cup Winner's Cup and the draw landed them with the mighty Barcelona. The home leg unsurprisingly brought a 3-1 loss for the Irishmen but a wonder goal from O'Neill is still talked about in the area. A month later he crossed the Irish Sea to Forest in October 1971.

The first time O'Neill was dropped for a game at Forest by then manager Matt Gillies, he asked for a transfer. 'I cringe with embarrassment when I think about that now,' admits O'Neill. He was one of the few players to openly stand up to Brian Clough and after one such 'discussion' he claimed that he could easily go back to Northern Ireland and continue his education. Clough called his bluff by providing a plane ticket for O'Neill the next day, which needless to say went unused, and nothing further was heard about the matter.

ATV's Midland TV cameras visited Nottingham on 11 September for a Midlands derby with Hereford United. United had been promoted the previous season under the tutelage of young manager John Sillett and came to the City Ground unbeaten. Sillett had put together an exciting team led by Terry Paine, ex-Red John Galley, young apprentice Kevin Sheedy and prolific marksman Dixie McNeil. McNeil had hit a hat-trick against Burnley the previous week and he would prove to be a thorn in the side of the Forest defence on this occasion too. Early on he got a step ahead of Sammy Chapman and planted a header past Peter Wells. He continued his assault on the Forest goal with a driving run before crossing for Peter Spiring to volley an unstoppable shot into the far corner for a shock 2-0 lead.

As in the early season, it was left to Terry Curran to try and get Forest back into the match. Curran started a run in his own half, tight to the touchline; his method was simple – push it by the defender and run like hell. On this occasion he pushed it by two Hereford markers, gave them a several-yard head-start and outpaced them to the ball even though he had to take a wide berth off the field of play and then back on to it to beat them. Once back in control he picked out John O'Hare inside the area. In a rare moment of mis-control O'Hare allowed the ball to skip up high in the air, but connected with an overhead kick which fell to the unmarked Barry Butlin, who buried the ball from ten yards to get Forest back into contention. It was a microcosm of Forest's season – some raw talent, a mis-cue and a rescuing of a situation that seemed to have got away.

This series of events was more or less repeated before half-time. This time Frank Clark's mis-hit cross fell to Martin O'Neill, who worked hard to find Ian Bowyer at the edge of the area and his shot took a deflection before finding the net (*pictured on previous page*).

In the second half John Robertson found the corner with a cross shot (*pictured below*) despite having three defenders on him; and then a stellar effort from Ian Bowyer seemed to put the game beyond Hereford's reach. He won a crunching tackle on the halfway line, took it past a couple of defenders and then unleashed a stunning eighteen-yard drive for a 4-2 lead. It wasn't the end of things, though, because Dixie McNeil, who else, pounced again to give the Reds a few anxious moments at the end. The popular saying is that a good team manages to win when they're not playing at the peak of their powers, and though Forest certainly had room for improvement but they were finding ways to win, usually by scoring bagfuls of goals.

The middle of the month saw a return to cup action, with two ties in a week. The Anglo-Scottish Cup was at the knock-out phase and Kilmarnock visited the city ground for a quarter-final first leg. The game took on a strange air when both Clough and Taylor were found to be missing from the dug-out on a scouting mission as they ran the rule over a mystery striker. The Reds didn't suffer too much from their absence though and won 2-1 which was better than the next cup tie, a League Cup match at home to Coventry. Three first half goals from the First Division side ended the tie and the Reds crashed out, spelling the end of Peter Wells' time as Forest's keeper – John Middleton took over for the rest of the season and Wells was sold to Southampton in December. In between the two cup ties, the subject of the management's scouting trip became apparent as Peter Withe joined from Birmingham City for a fee of £44,000. His debut came in the home game against Carlisle United and he grabbed a goal as the Reds continued their free-scoring ways at home with a 5-1 win.

The Withe signing was a typical piece of Peter Taylor manoeuvring. He had initially tried to sign the big centre-forward for Brighton, and when he missed out there he just bided his time for another chance to get his man. He knew that Withe thrived on getting good service from the wings and with Robertson and Curran supplying the ammunition from either flank he expected Withe to explode on to the Second Division scene – which he did.

The signing of Withe also had a knock-on effect on Ian Bowyer's role in the side. 'Peter Withe was one of Pete Taylor's recommendations,' says Bowyer. 'Ninety percent of the players thought Taylor was a great laugh but he could be very hard and very serious when it came to the games and he could be quite ruthless – you could be very very quickly out of the door. He would discuss tactics with Brian and I'm sure they had different ideas on some things. He was good for Brian and had a good sense of humour but without ever being accepted as one of the boys. Though Peter could make you laugh at anything, he kept you – and you kept him – at arm's length. He was top class at his job. Before Peter Withe joined us there was myself, Barry Butlin and John O'Hare and because Brian wanted all three players in the team he said, "You're better equipped to play midfield" and as a result of that I became a midfield player. We'd got off to an OK start but we knew that there was no way that mediocrity would be accepted. When we got Peter Withe we had some players that had played at a higher level but maybe hadn't achieved what they wanted and we had a team that was hungry, with the younger ones like Tony Woodcock and Viv Anderson coming through – and we had the best manager, so knew we had a chance.'

The return game with Kilmarnock came at the end of a lengthy and tiring journey to Scotland, made by coach due to the high cost of flying north, a situation that seems unbelievable in the twenty-first century. Viv Anderson came back into the side at right-back and made the position his own for the next few years. His long legs helped get him the nickname 'Spider' and he used them to good effect when quickly joining the attack and overlapping Terry Curran down the wing to get crosses in. Anderson was a local Nottingham lad and had played in junior teams with both Peter Wells and Glyn Saunders before being signed as a schoolboy by Manchester United. After dropping out of football and getting a job he later signed with Forest as a seventeen year old. The game at Rugby Park saw Terry Curran play in a central striker's role and he responded by scoring both of Forest's goals. The Reds actually trailed 2-0 but managed to get one back before the ninety minutes were up and as the aggregate score and away goals were equal the tie went into extra time. 'At Kilmarnock I got a rollicking,' remembers John McGovern. 'One of their strikers ran past me for one of the goals, I was playing sweeper. Clough said "If you can't play there I'll have to put you back in midfield!" At half-time he'd give you a quick analysis of how you were playing in the match. He never mentioned the opposition, we concentrated on what we were doing and how we did it. I had a great time playing at the back, it's simpler playing at the back because you're facing the ball all the time. When you're looking at the game it's easier but I would have liked an extra yard of pace!' Terry Curran saved McGovern's blushes though as he scored in extra time for a 2-2 draw on the night and a 4-3 aggregate win. The long journey home was a happy one and Frank Clark recalls that stories of his guitar playing on away trips was blown out of proportion. 'That was a myth really,' he says, 'My own recollection, but the other lads might tell you differently, was that it only ever happened once on the bus. We had a couple of good sing songs in different places, but on the team coach – no.

A disappointing 1-0 loss at Billy Bremner's Hull City came after the Scottish trip. The game was significant for being the Forest debut of imposing centre-half Larry Lloyd, who had signed on a short term loan deal from Coventry City. The Bristol-born Lloyd had won a League Championship under Bill Shankly at Liverpool but had latterly fallen into reserve team football at Coventry. Lloyd takes up the story: 'What basically happened is that while I was training one day Gordon Milne, who was the manager of Coventry, said that Peter Taylor and Brian Clough had been on and would I go to Forest on a month's loan? Well, I immediately looked at the league table and Forest were about halfway in the old Second Division and Coventry were no great shakes in the First Division but at least it was top flight football. So I was very, very reluctant to go. Then Gordon Milne made it plain to me I wasn't wanted at Coventry, so I thought, OK, well at least I know I'd be regaining a bit of fitness. So I went there for the month of October 1976 on loan. I did pretty well and they wanted to sign me after my first game against Hull. I said, No, let's see the month out. I saw the month out and then went back to Coventry because I really wanted to build it up again at Coventry. I'd just had a back operation and I wanted to sort of prove myself at Coventry. But Gordon Milne made it clear again that he didn't want me there and he said, "Cloughie's been on a few times now so go back and talk to him." Cloughie and Taylor made it clear that despite being mid-table they weren't that far behind and that they needed me at the back. They wanted to build around me, and first and foremost they needed a big lad at the back to do the job that I was capable of doing.'

With Lloyd at the back, the Forest forwards continued to do their job as the side carried out a 6-1 demolition of Sheffield United at the City Ground. Ian Bowyer smashed in number one on eleven minutes and Barry Butlin added a second before Hamilton pulled back a penalty for the visitors. The game then turned into the Terry Curran Show. First he chased down a loose ball and twice challenged the United keeper Jim Brown, and when the ball ran loose Ian Bowyer smashed it into the roof of the net. In the second half Curran went on a mazy run past four United defenders before playing a neat one-two with Viv Anderson and side-footing number four. The fifth goal came from another Curran move which ended when he fed Peter Withe to score from close range. The icing on the Forest cake came from a period of sustained Forest pressure. Three times the Reds went close and three times United tried to get the ball out of their danger area, but on each occasion Forest's hard-working midfielders closed them down before they could reach the halfway line. The pressure finally told as Viv Anderson sprinted into the area to gleefully slam in his first competitive goal for the club (*pictured above*). The win was the Reds' biggest for nineteen years and pushed Forest up to fifth in the table before a difficult trip to Blackpool.

Second Division Table – Top 6

	Pld	Pts	GD
Chelsea	9	13	+2
Wolverhampton W.	9	11	+10
Oldham Athletic	9	11	0
Blackpool	9	10	+5
FOREST	**9**	**10**	**+7**
Charlton Athletic	9	10	+1

(*after games of October 9th 1976*)

Like many instances during this season, just as Forest seemed about to put in a serious challenge they threw in an unpredictable performance to drop back just off the leaders pace. This time it was ex-Reds boss Allan Brown's Blackpool side that held on for a 1-0 win. Two home wins then followed, over Ayr in the Anglo-Scottish Cup semi-final, first leg (2-1) and Burnley in the league (5-2). This second win came at a high cost though as Terry Curran was carried off with a serious knee injury. (*Curran is pictured scoring in this game on opposite page, top right*) Brian Clough commented that 'Our promotion hopes just limped out of the door.'

The 5-2 win meant that in the last four home league games Forest had scored four, five, six and five goals respectively. Unfortunately they couldn't take this scoring form on the road with them, and they went down to a third successive 1-0 away loss at Oldham.

November 3 saw Forest's first chance to reach a cup final since the FA Cup semi-final loss to Tottenham in 1967. (The last final they'd reached had been way back in 1959.) The second leg of the Anglo-Scottish Cup semi-final saw the Reds 2-1 up from the first leg (a game which had seen the appearance of the youngest ever Forest player: Steve Burke was just sixteen years and twenty-two days old), but the close game at Kilmarnock in the previous round meant they were taking nothing for granted. The game took place in a torrential downpour and showcased a new strike partnership that would carry Forest for the next two years. Young striker Tony Woodcock had just returned from a month on loan at Doncaster and was paired with Peter Withe for the game. Both players scored in the 2-0 win and launched the side forward on a fourteen game unbeaten streak.

Woodcock made this break into the first team fairly late and the loan at Doncaster had been his second such move. Earlier he'd had a spell at Lincoln, where Graham Taylor had tried to sign him permanently but when Peter Taylor arrived he vetoed the sale of any players until he'd had the chance to check them out for himself. Woodcock had also been a relatively late starter as far being a footballer was concerned. 'I was pretty late and I didn't start having any interest until I was about twelve years of age,' he says. 'My brother-in-law bought me a pair of football socks just out of the blue and that was what started it off. Soon I was playing football every day and started getting in small teams, then local area teams and stuff like that, and it just carried on from there, step by step. There were one or two clubs that started looking at me and Alan Hill came to look at one of my best friends, Martin Smith the goalkeeper. It might have just been lucky that he saw me playing then invited me down for trials.' Woodcock's parents decided that he should sign for Forest and continue living at home and he later signed as an apprentice. By the time Clough and Taylor were in charge Woodcock was out in the wilderness and couldn't break out of the reserve team. 'I wasn't really performing in the reserves,' he admits, 'and I had one or two run ins with him [Clough] about where I should be playing and what I should be doing. Then I started to go out on loan because Clough didn't want me. So I went on loan to Lincoln City for a month, which was great fun and it was great to build my confidence and then to Doncaster for another month, and by this time I'd had two good months where a lot of other clubs were starting to show interest. So Cloughie got me back and said "There's all these clubs enquiring about you. I'd better give you a chance to see if I'm wrong." In the reserves I was playing on the left wing as I'm a naturally left footed player. I went

SOMERSET NEWS
VOL. 7
NO. 10
10p
AYR UTD
VS
NOTTINGHAM FOREST
ANGLO/SCOTTISH CUP — SEMI-FINAL
WEDNESDAY, 3rd NOVEMBER, 1976
Kick-off 1930 hrs.

to see Clough and said, "I want to play up front," as I'd played up front for Lincoln; and he played me in the Anglo-Scottish Cup and then I played ever since.'

The boost gained by reaching a cup final, even if it was 'only' the Anglo-Scottish Cup, carried over into the league performances; a 3-0 home win over Blackburn (in which Peter Withe scored, *left*) was followed up by a much needed away win at Orient, who had also qualified for the Anglo-Scottish Cup Final in December.

The next home game was a big one and the BBC sent its Match of the Day cameras on a rare sojourn to the Second Division as Chelsea visited Trentside. The Londoners were leading the table at the time, with Forest six points behind in fifth place. The atmosphere was especially highly charged due to some disgraceful fighting inside and outside the ground before, during and after the match. The club had attempted to cut down on the violence, which had also erupted in home games against Wolves and Sheffield United earlier in the season, by putting the away fans in the Trent End and banning home fans from the stand. The reason for this seemingly drastic, and almost 'blasphemous', step, was that it was the only part of the ground where the crowd could be segregated as a season high of 27,089 attended. The other three stands were 'open' and fans could move freely between them once inside the ground. The game itself was tight and the teams evenly matched. Martin O'Neill capped a fine move between himself and Tony

Woodcock and scuttled a shot under Peter Bonetti (*pictured above*) to give Forest the lead and silence the blue and white hordes in the Trent End. Chelsea hit back when Steve Finneston beat Sammy Chapman wide on the right and swung in a long cross that Viv Anderson seemed to have under control. However the ball bounced strangely and ballooned off Anderson, right on to the head of the waiting Chelsea forward Ian Britton, who floated a header over the stranded John Middleton in the Forest goal.

The Woodcock-Withe partnership was really starting to blossom and both forwards scored in the 3-0 win at Cardiff and also in the next match, a 4-2 win at home to Bristol Rovers. Another 3-0 away win at Millwall signalled the start of four games in seven days leading up to Christmas.

The second and third games of this hectic schedule were the first and second legs of the Anglo-Scottish Cup final against Orient. The first match was played in London on Monday 13 December with the home leg just forty-eight hours later on 15 December. Though the Final had been slotted in amongst the supposedly more important league games, Clough ensured that a full strength team was put out for both ties. 'A lot of people thought that competition wasn't important,' says Frank Clark, 'but Brian didn't. He took it very seriously and he was absolutely right. For the vast majority of players in that team it was the first thing they had ever won. It's a nice feeling and the players thought, I'll have a bit more of this, so he was right: it gave a great boost to that particular group of players to win that competition.'

'We won it,' says Brian Clough, 'so that was the first thing. It didn't make life rosy but at least we'd got over the first hurdle. You can't get over the other nineteen hurdles if you don't get over the first one.' The first leg was close as the 1-1 score suggests but Forest blew the tie open with a 4-0 romp in the home leg, Colin Barrett grabbing two goals from a midfield role. Despite it being the club's first trophy in seventeen years, fewer than thirteen thousand turned out to see John McGovern lift the cup. 'I can remember thinking to myself after the final when we'd beaten Orient that this John Robertson could be some player,' recalls Frank Clark. 'I seem to remember that as John saying to the world, "Here I am."' For Tony Woodcock the trophy was just another step on his path to becoming an established first-team player. 'It wasn't about winning, it was about breaking into the team and about staying there,' he says. 'Or if I wasn't going to be staying there I was going to be playing somewhere else. I wanted to play first-team football.'

'I mean it was a big thing,' says Larry Lloyd. 'Forest had been reasonably successful way back in the 1960s but they'd had nothing for a while and basically the Anglo Scottish was quite a big step for them. I played in one leg in the final, because my deal was that I'd be paid extra the more games I played, and Clough being Clough he left me out because he wouldn't pay me any more money!'

Second Division Table – Top 6

	Pld	Pts	GD
Chelsea	23	32	+10
Bolton Wanderers	22	30	+12
Wolverhampton W.	21	27	+24
FOREST	**21**	**27**	**+21**
Blackpool	22	27	+9
Millwall	20	22	+6

(*after games of January 11th 1977*)

Following Forest's win English teams continued to do well in the tournament, with Bristol City (1978), Burnley (1979) and Chesterfield, who beat Notts County in the 1981 final, all being successful. The lone Scottish triumph saw St Mirren take home the cup in 1980. Following the Chesterfield win Scottish clubs withdrew and the tournament continued under the title of the Associate Members Cup, changing its name numerous times until its current incarnation as the LDV Vans Trophy.

Back to the bread and butter of the promotion race, Forest took four points from a possible six in the Christmas period. The 1-1 draw at Bolton would prove to be invaluable and the 3-1 New Year's Day win at Blackburn sent them to fourth in the table. The month of January was almost exclusively taken up with FA Cup

ties. The third round match-up with Bristol Rovers saw 1-1 draws at both clubs' home grounds before a second reply at Villa Park saw Forest triumph 6-0. The fourth round pitted the Reds against Southampton. The Saints had won the Cup in 1976, beating Manchester United in the final, and had been tipped for promotion from Division Two this time around but by late January they had slipped from contention. The game at the City Ground on 29 January brought in a gate of over thirty-eight thousand to see a six-goal thriller. John Robertson gave the Reds the lead after Alan Ball had tripped John O'Hare in the penalty box before Southampton hit back to take a 2-1 lead. Robertson equalized with a curling shot past ex-Red Peter Wells before Forest fell behind 3-2, and it was left to Tony Woodcock (*shown above*) to force a replay. After the City Ground excitement the replay was a harsh let down with a controversial Ted MacDougal goal proving to be the difference in a 2-1 defeat; the goal was later proved on TV replays to have been offside.

This cup exit seemed to deflate the team, and successive 2-1 defeats at Wolves and then at home to Luton (with Larry Lloyd scoring, *above*) looked like becoming an unwelcome hat-trick of losses when Southampton returned to the City Ground for a League encounter. The 16 February game looked bleak for Forest as the Saints took a 1-0 lead into half time on the strength of a Nick Holmes goal. Forest were really struggling and John McGovern admits that 'We wouldn't have scored if we'd played until midnight.' Luckily the Trent then took a hand in proceedings and during half-time a thick fog started billowing in from the river. By the time the teams returned, visibility was limited and two minutes into the second half the

game was abandoned and the score deleted from the records. Due to further weather cancellations and blank cup weekends the Reds found themselves with over two weeks between games. A team break in Spain was planned, but before flying out the club was in the news again. Derby County had undergone some changes with George Hardy taking over from Sam Longson as chairman. Having sacked manager Dave Mackay, Hardy wanted Clough and Taylor to return to the Baseball Ground. Much to the dismay of the Forest faithful Clough and Taylor actually entered into many hours of talks with Derby on 21 February, then announced that there would be a press conference at the Baseball Ground the following day. The writing seemed to be on the wall as Clough was photographed at the City Ground (*above*) setting off to Derby with Jimmy Gordon. The twist in the tale occurred when Clough arrived in Derby to tell the assembled board members that he'd changed his mind back again and would be staying at Forest! He'd made the journey simply because he wanted to tell them in person. Taylor who had been quite keen on going to Derby stayed out of the spotlight and left Clough to explain to the Derby press what had been going on.

Second Division Table – Top 7

	Pld	Pts	GD
Chelsea	32	43	+14
Wolverhampton W.	30	41	+32
Luton Town	32	40	+18
Bolton Wanderers	30	39	+17
Blackpool	32	37	+11
Notts County	31	37	+6
FOREST	**30**	**34**	**+19**

(*after games of March 19th 1977*)

Having dodged this bullet, the Forest squad flew out to Spain for a much-needed break in the sun. Colin Barrett remembers that they weren't alone on their trip: 'We went on to Torremolinos and Southampton were there at the same time. We trained fairly hard. We had to go to bed at the right time and had to do everything right. They were out with Alan Ball, drinking and having a right good time. We came back and continued to struggle, they went to Sheffield United and won. It was one of those situations where we couldn't believe that we'd worked that hard that week they went enjoying themselves and won. I think that through the season we thought we were good enough to go up and we didn't contemplate what was going to happen until it happened. But, as history says, we did OK.'

The first three weeks of March weren't much better than February had been. Two wins, a draw and two defeats left Forest with a mountain to climb if they were going to get promoted. Then they were facing the replay of the abandoned Southampton game on 22 March, and a win was absolutely vital. Notts County had overtaken Forest and even winning games in hand wouldn't be enough to reach third place – and games were running out. For the Southampton game Clough mixed things up a little. He moved John McGovern back into midfield and paired Chapman and Lloyd at the heart of the defence. O'Neill (*pictured bottom of previous page*) and Woodcock provided goals and Forest kept the slim promotion hopes alive with a 2-1 win. 'Things just gradually got better,' recalls John McGovern. 'I spent part of season at centre half with Sammy Chapman and then Larry Lloyd. It had affected my fitness because you don't do so much running and I can remember the first game that Clough put me back in midfield, Southampton at home, I'd taken up squash as extra training to keep my fitness up.' The race was back on, with McGovern pulling the strings in the centre of midfield, the

defence pulling out three straight clean sheets and Withe and Woodcock scoring for fun again (a spell of nine goals in six games followed) as three quick wins were reeled off within a week.

The 3-0 home win over Blackpool was a great example of the partnership that Peter Withe and Tony Woodcock had struck up. In the forty-second minute a long ball from Larry Lloyd was flicked on by Woodcock, was misjudged by future Forest manager Paul Hart, and Peter Withe converted the chance for a 1-0 lead (*pictured above*). Moments later, in first-half injury time, McGovern fed Withe who in turn played in Woodcock for a 2-0 lead and then late on the pair combined again for Withe to round out the scoring. Forest now had third place to themselves, but Bolton Wanderers were one point behind with two games in hand – and were the next visitors to the City Ground.

Despite a negative performance in which Wanderers were clearly playing for a draw, Forest managed to break them down and win 3-1. The key games were coming thick and fast now. Next up was the short trip to Meadow Lane for a game against another promotion contender, Notts County. The resultant 1-1 draw seemed to have done neither side any favours and a Forest loss at Chelsea made the next home game versus lowly Cardiff was a must win encounter. Cardiff shocked all concerned with a 1-0 win, however, which seemed to confirm Forest's instability when the chips were down. It was the first home league game that Forest hadn't scored in.

The Reds needed to show their mettle and they dug deep to answer any doubters with a convincing 3-0 win over Oldham who had slipped out of contention since Christmas. Forest had two away games to come before a last home match hosting Millwall who had also dropped away during 1977.

Top left: Peter Withe battles through the Second Division mud.
Top right: Viv Anderson goes close to getting a late equalizer against Cardiff at the City Ground.
Above right: Frank Clark continuing his ever-present record.

'Our last two away games, were they down in the West Country,' remembers Frank Clark. 'We stayed on Dartmoor in this country house hotel in the middle of nowhere. Also staying in the hotel was David Soul and a terrific English character actor called Jack Watson, big tall fella who played in a million films and was in *Zulu*. They were doing a television series and they were staying in the hotel and this Jack Watson used to be walking around.'

The first game of this double header produced a 1-1 draw at Bristol

Rovers and was followed two days later by a 2-1 win at Plymouth on bank-holiday Monday courtesy of goals from, who else? Woodcock and Withe. The bringing-forward of this game was an unheralded Clough masterstroke, but of course if they had lost at Plymouth it would have backfired badly. Forest won, though, and had sole possession of the vital third and final promotion place. As Clough always preached, it's better to have the points rather than games in hand. The pressure was on the chasing teams, and even more so if Forest could beat Millwall. If they lost they could finish as low as sixth, since Notts County, Bolton and Blackpool could all leapfrog them.

The decisive game with Millwall was as tense as predicted. Forest attacked in waves but Millwall, with nothing to play for but pride, held on. The only slip up was when Millwall full-back Jon Moore headed into his own net to give Forest a precious 1-0 win. But would fifty-two points be enough? Many fans didn't think so, and only 23,529 had come to the game. Promotion or not, it had been a memorable season with a trophy and some exciting attacking football to reflect on. All they could do now was wait. While Forest beat Millwall, Bolton had drawn, to leave them on forty-eight points with three games in hand. Due to Forest's far superior goal difference the task for Bolton was straightforward – anything less than two wins and a draw in the last three games would send Forest into the First Division. Wanderers' fortieth game saw them triumph over Cardiff 2-1, which left them needing three points from the last two games. Saturday 14 May was to be a critical day and it just so happened that Forest were flying to Spain for their annual end-of-season break.

Second Division Table – Top 6

	Pld	Pts	GD
Wolverhampton W.	40	54	+38
Chelsea	40	52	+16
FOREST	**41**	**50**	**+33**
Notts County	40	48	+8
Bolton Wanderers	38	47	+21
Blackpool	39	46	+14

(*after games of May 2nd 1977*)

The tension in the Forest camp mounted as they boarded their flight at East Midlands Airport at 3p.m., just as Bolton were kicking off against Wolves, who had already wrapped up the championship. Brian Clough had asked the pilot to try to keep in touch with the match by radio, and despite some poor reception the news filtered through that Wolves had taken the lead. A great roar went up, but Clough insisted that no one take anything for granted. Kenny Hibbitt had scored the goal and he would soon be called on to help in other ways, as John Robertson remembers: 'The Wolves goalie got

Let Bolton worry, says Clough

by JOHN LAWSON

LET BOLTON do the worrying. That was the message that beamed out from the City Ground today as Nottingham Forest wait for their Lancashire rivals to slip.

Ian Greaves' side need five points from three games to knock Forest out of the Second Division's vital third spot.

And Forest chief Brian Clough declared: "Although Bolton have it in their hands to beat us, there is no way I would

Bruges yesterday sealed the Belgian Championship

Team from:

Boulton, Moseley, Langan, Webster, Daly, McFarland,

Ground fears are 'premature'

NOTTINGHAM Forest have no immediate fears about their attendance being restricted to 25,500 if they win promotion to the First Divi-

apply to First Division and International grounds so we have not even got to the stage where it affects us."

"We have not actually been told anything yet, so there

Leigh sixth in golf

NOTTS county golfer Terry Leigh (Sherwood Forest) finished in sixth spot in the Midland Open Amateur Championship at Little Aston GC.

His four-round aggregate

injured and Kenny Hibbitt went in goal!' Bolton poured forward in the second half but couldn't find an equalizer. 'The pilot told us on the plane that he believed that Wolves were a goal up,' says Robertson. 'We were there on tenterhooks and it stayed that way until we got to the airport. Stuart Dryden made a phone call and sure enough Wolves had won.' Forest were virtually up, only a Bolton win by a cricket score in the last match could have changed things. In the end Bolton drew the last match and the celebrations began.

'We had to wait until we landed,' says Frank Clark. 'It was party time then. It was the first time I was ever drunk in front of Brian. I got such a bollocking the next day – he wasn't very happy at all. We used to go to Calla Mallor at the end of every season for a week and we had one rule. They used to stay in a different hotel – Brian, Peter, and they used to take the kids and sometimes the wife – and there was only one rule: don't get into trouble.'

CO-OP MEMBERSHIP REALLY PAYS! JOIN NOW AND SAVE AS YOU SPEND. DETAILS IN ALL OUR SHOPS. Greater Nottingham Co-operative Society Ltd.

EVENING POST 6

No. 30,750 NOTTINGHAM, MONDAY, MAY 16, 1977 PRICE 6p

I just want the best — fresh — and I get it from Pork Farms

Just great to be back!

Brian Clough
A lot of pleasure

MY FEELINGS—CLOUGH

'Thanks for everything'

BRIAN CLOUGH spoke for the first time today about his side's elevation to the First Division and declared: "I am happy for the people who have stood by me."

The Forest manager, holidaying with his players in Cala Millor, told me on the telephone:

"A lot of people have supported me during the last three-and-a-half years and it gives me a lot of pleasure to see them get joy out of the achievement.

"I am pleased for my family too, because there have been times over the last few years that their life has been anything but rosy."

Forest, back in the First Division after a five-year absence, are already planning ahead for the future but for the time being at least, the players are in a holiday mood.

Delighted

Added Clough: "Obviously, we are all delighted about going up but even though I have been with the players all weekend we have not talked about the First Division for two minutes.

"It's more important for me to see the players relaxing at the moment. The season has been a long, hard one and now we are getting the rewards.

"Having said that, it means a lot to me to be back in the First Division. I feel at home at places like Anfield and Old Trafford and when the time comes, I will be ready for the challenge."

Forest will return from their Majorca break to a civic reception that was confidently planned weeks ago.

As jubilant fans celebrated world-wide over the weekend, Coun. Jack Green, leader of Nottingham City Council, said: "We were so confident they would go up that we arranged this reception three weeks ago."

Now Forest have been invited to rub shoulders with Nottingham's Lord Mayor — an avid Notts County fan — at the Council House on May 31.

The Lord Mayor, Coun. Bernard Bateman, said today: "I'm delighted that at least one of our two clubs has gone up. It is an achievement for Nottingham."

A former soccer player himself, Coun. Bateman added: "And congratulations to Mansfield on winning the Third Division championship. They and Notts County can now keep

Continued on Back Page

JOY—12,000 MILES AWAY

SECONDS before the final whistle blew on the hectic Bolton-Wolves promotion battle, a Nottingham Forest fan rang the Evening Post sports department from Australia and asked: "Have the Reds gained promotion?"

It was 28-year-old former Long Eaton man John Lawrence who, after a night out had stayed up till 2 a.m. "Down Under" to make the call. When we gave him the news he said: "That's fantastic, just great. It was just the thing I've been waiting to hear.

"I tried to ring the Wolves ground this morning to wish them luck, but I couldn't get through."

HOLIDAY

John, who has been in Australia for nine years, has been a Forest fan since he was 14.

John, a Sydney bank officer, added: "I am sorry that Notts County did not go up with Forest because it would have been tremendous for both of them to go into Division I."

And he said: "I hope Forest stay up long enough for me to see them in Division I because I am making another trip back home in another couple of years."

Brian Clough: 'When we got promoted out of the Second Division, it's forgotten in the things that we achieved and yet it was the most important thing in some respects, because without that base we couldn't go anywhere else. We couldn't go and win the First Division Championship. We couldn't go and win in Europe if that wasn't there. So the first time, the first rung on the ladder, was the most important. Unless you get on that you don't get anywhere. Then the club took off, simple as that.'

Colin Barrett: 'It was a week of mayhem, celebrations, headaches – but it was all good fun.'

Ian Bowyer: 'It was nothing to do with Bolton failing, we'd played forty-two games to do it.'

Larry Lloyd: 'The majority of the party travelled from East Midlands Airport on Saturday afternoon but three of us – that was myself and Peter Withe, because we still lived in the West Midlands, and the director Fred Reacher – we had to come over on the Sunday. So as a matter of fact I was watching Coventry on Saturday afternoon when I heard that result from Bolton. We joined them then, obviously they had a big night out the Saturday that we'd missed it but it was a big week out!'

Central League, Final Table 1976-77

	Pld	Pts
Liverpool	42	69
Manchester United	42	56
Wolverhampton W.	42	54
Bury	42	51
FOREST	**42**	**50**
Manchester City	42	49

(*Top 6 of 22 only*)

Midland Intermediate League, 1976-77

	Pld	Pts	GD
W. B. A.	20	26	+14
FOREST	**20**	**25**	**+18**
Mansfield Town	20	25	+6
Shrewsbury Town	20	23	+8
Notts County	20	19	+9

(*Final table, top 5 of 11 only*)

Second Division, Final Table 1976-77

	Pld	Pts	GD
Wolverhampton W.	42	57	+39
Chelsea	42	55	+20
FOREST	**42**	**52**	**+34**
Bolton Wanderers	42	51	+21
Blackpool	42	51	+16
Luton Town	42	48	+19
Charlton Athletic	42	48	+13
Notts County	42	48	+5
Southampton	42	44	+5
Millwall	42	43	+4
Sheffield United	42	40	-9
Blackburn Rovers	42	39	-12
Oldham Athletic	42	38	-12
Hull City	42	37	-8
Bristol Rovers	42	37	-15
Burnley	42	36	-18
Fulham	42	35	-7
Cardiff City	42	34	-11
Orient	42	34	-18
Carlisle United	42	34	-26
Plymouth Argyle	42	32	-19
Hereford United	42	31	-21

Above: John McGovern and Martin O'Neill enjoy a trip to an away game in 1976.
Below left: Peter Taylor's message to the newly promoted side.
Below right: an end of season fundraiser for a future Red.

Dreams come true for McGovern

By JOHN LAWSON

CLUB captain John McGovern greeted his and Nottingham Forest's return to the First Division with the declaration: "My dreams just keep on coming true."

McGovern, who won First and Second Division championship medals under Brian Clough at Derby, commented:

"When I joined the boss at Forest it was not a case of 'if' or 'how,' but 'when' we would get promotion.

THRILLING

"Going up is just as thrilling as the success I had with Derby, but I don't like to think too much about the past. The future counts most of all and the lads just can't wait to get cracking in the First Division.

"Even though I expected us to go up at the beginning of the season, it's still a fabulous surprise when it comes along.

"I didn't really fancy Wolves very much at Bolton, but they won and that's the important thing. We've had a few drinks on the strength of it this weekend."

Forest players celebrated their success in an English-style pub in Cala Millor but there was still a slight anti-climax about it all.

Ian Bowyer explained: "We are really thrilled about it all, but it's a bit strange when you have to wait for someone else to clinch promotion for you.

"It's also a bit odd being out here in Majorca when everyone in Nottingham is celebrating.

"Going back to the First Division is very important for me. It's another chance for me to have a crack at the big time because I wasn't very old when I got into the Manchester City side."

And John Robertson commented: "I'm over the moon. It's been a marvellous season, but the big challenge is ahead for all of us. I know I have to prove myself in the First Division, but I am really looking forward to having a try."

TAYLOR TELLS FOREST—GET INTO EUROPE

Peter Taylor

NOTTINGHAM Forest, already looking forward to their First Division future, were given a European target today, writes JOHN LAWSON.

The man issuing the challenge to Forest's elated squad is assistant manager Peter Taylor.

He asserted: "I see no point in setting our sights low and survival in the ...

We could set the place alight.

"From the experience we had of Europe with Derby, I can say it is something special. You are competing at an exciting level and nothing but good can come out of it.

Derby show interest

Stags hope to

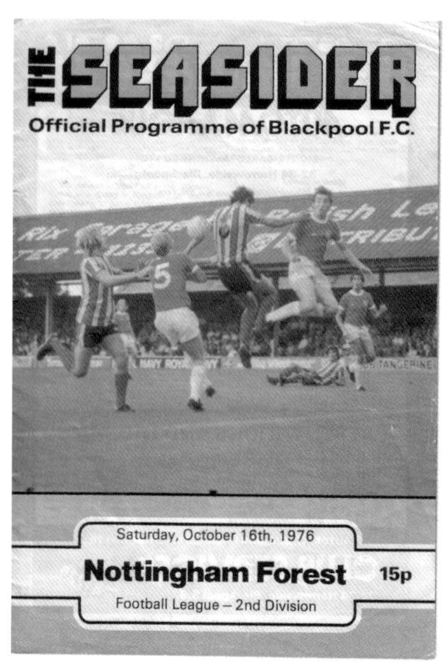

July 1976

27	SV Furth, West Germany	A	2-3	PSF
28	SV Jahn Regensburg, W.Ger.	A	5-0	PSF
30	FC Augsburg, West Germany	A	1-0	PSF

August

1	SC Furstenfeldbruck, W.Ger.	A	4-2	PSF
3	HSB Heidenheim, W.Germany	A	3-1	PSF
7	Notts County	A	0-0	ASC
11	West Bromwich Albion	H	3-2	ASC
14	Bristol City	H	4-2	ASC
21	Fulham	A	2-2	
25	Charlton Athletic	H	1-1	
28	Wolverhampton Wanderers	H	1-3	
31	Walsall	A	4-2	LC2

September

4	Luton Town	A	1-1	
11	Hereford United	H	4-3	
14	Kilmarnock	H	2-1	ASCQF, 1
18	Southampton	A	1-1	
21	Coventry City	H	0-3	LC3
25	Carlisle United	H	5-1	
28	Kilmarnock	A	2-2	ASCQF, 2

October

2	Hull City	A	0-1	
9	Sheffield United	H	6-1	
13	Grantham	A	3-0	F
16	Blackpool	A	0-1	
20	Ayr United	H	2-1	ASCSF, 1
23	Burnley	H	5-2	
26	Notts County	A	0-1	CCF*
30	Oldham Athletic	A	0-1	

November

3	Ayr United	A	2-0	ASCSF, 2
6	Blackburn Rovers	H	3-0	
13	Orient	A	1-0	
20	Chelsea	H	1-1	
27	Cardiff City	A	3-0	

December

4	Bristol Rovers	H	4-2	
11	Millwall	A	3-0	
13	Orient	A	1-1	ASCF, 1
15	Orient	H	4-0	ASCF, 2
18	Plymouth Argyle	H	1-1	
27	Bolton Wanderers	A	1-1	

January 1977

1	Blackburn Rovers	A	3-1	

8 Bristol Rovers H 1-1 FAC3
11 Bristol Rovers A 1-1 FAC3R
14 Charlton Athletic A 1-2
18 Bristol Rovers N 6-0 FAC3R2*2
22 Fulham H 3-0
29 Southampton H 3-3 FAC4

February

1 Southampton A 1-2 FAC4R
5 Wolverhampton Wanderers A 1-2
12 Luton Town H 1-2
16 Southampton H 0-1 *3

March

2 Hereford United A 1-0
5 Carlisle United A 1-1
8 Notts County H 1-2
12 Hull City H 2-0
16 Grantham Town A 2-0 F
19 Sheffield United A 0-2
22 Southampton H 2-1
26 Blackpool H 3-0
29 Orient H 3-0

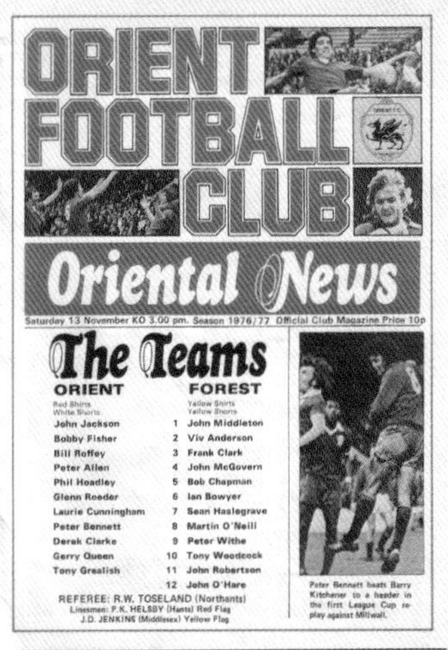

April

2 Burnley A 1-0
6 Bolton Wanderers H 3-1
9 Notts County A 1-1
16 Chelsea A 1-2
23 Cardiff City H 0-1
27 Oldham Athletic H 3-0
30 Bristol Rovers A 1-1

May

2 Plymouth Argyle A 2-1
7 Millwall H 1-0
9 Derby County A 0-1 F*4
10 Mansfield Town A 2-1 CCSF
12 Peterborough United A 5-2 F

* = final for the 1975-6 season
*2 = played at Villa Park, Birmingham
*3 = abandoned after 47 minutes due to fog
*4 = Kevin Hector Testimonial

	Pld	W	D	L	F	A	PTS	GD
Home	30	19	6	5	73	36	44	+37
Away	39	18	10	11	67	39	46	+28
League	42	21	10	11	77	43	52	+34
League Cup	2	1	0	1	4	5	2	-1
FA Cup	5	1	3	1	12	7	5	+5
Anglo Scottish Cup	9	6	3	0	20	9	15	+11
County Cup	2	1	0	1	2	2	2	0
Friendlies	9	7	0	2	25	9	14	+16
Total	**69**	**37**	**16**	**16**	**140**	**75**	**90**	**+65**

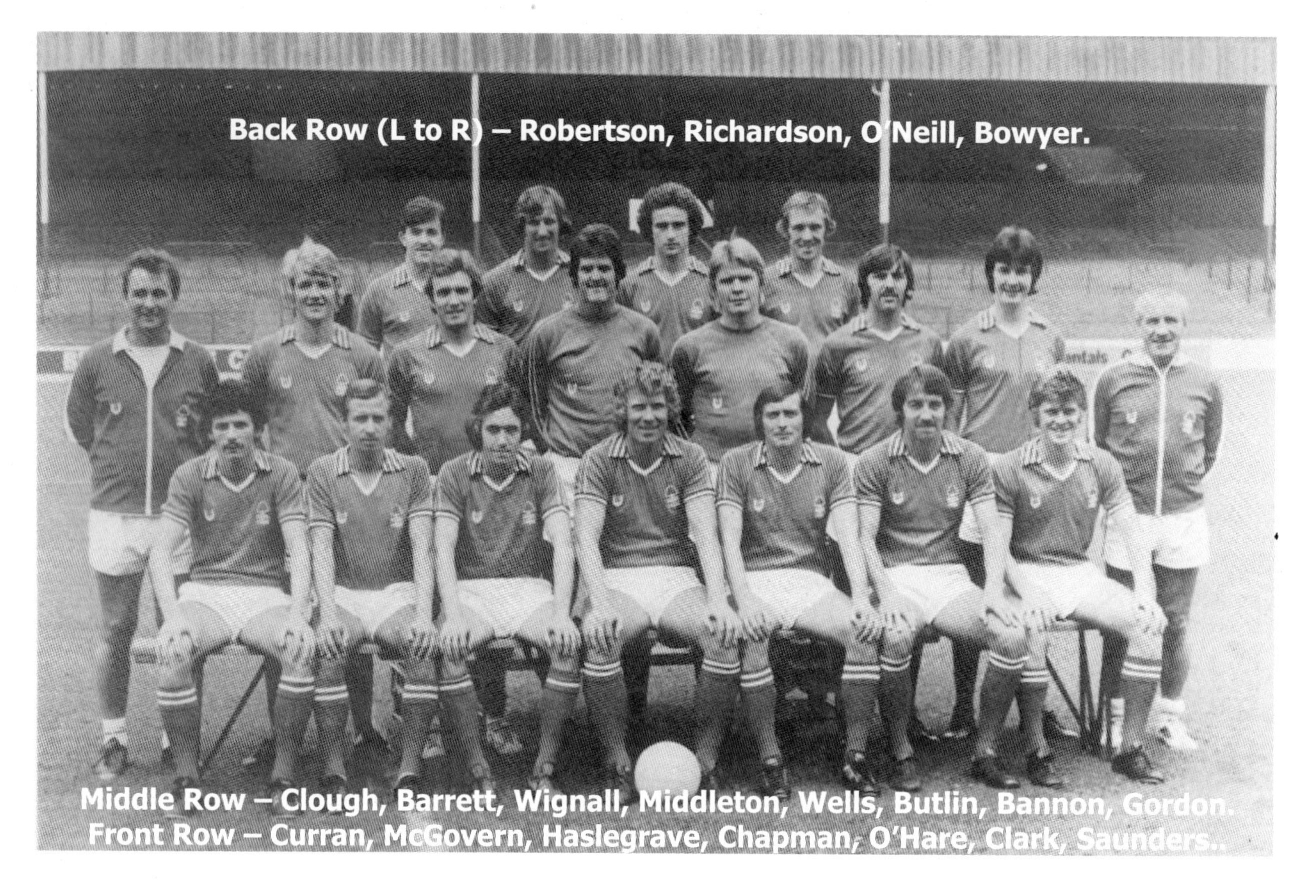

Back Row (L to R) – Robertson, Richardson, O'Neill, Bowyer.
Middle Row – Clough, Barrett, Wignall, Middleton, Wells, Butlin, Bannon, Gordon.
Front Row – Curran, McGovern, Haslegrave, Chapman, O'Hare, Clark, Saunders..

1976-77 Player Statistics

	Lge	FAC	LCup	ASC	CC	F	Totals
John Robertson	41-6	5-3	2	9-3	2	6(2)	65-12
Frank Clark	42	5	2	7	2	7	65
Ian Bowyer	41-12	5-1	2	9-1	2	5-2	64-16
John McGovern	39	3	2	7	2	7	60
Martin O'Neill	38(2)-9	5	2-2	6(1)	2	5(2)-2	58(3)-13
John Middleton	38	5	1	5	2	3	54
Viv Anderson	35(3)-1	5-1	0	6	1-1	2	49(3)-3
Sammy Chapman	31(1)-2	2	2	6(1)-2	2	6	49(2)-4
Peter Withe	33(1)-16	5-1	0	4-2	2-1	3-1	47(1)-21
Tony Woodcock	30-11	5-5	0	2-1	1	2-1	40-18
John O'Hare	19(3)-3	5-1	2	6-2	0	6-1	38(3)-7
Larry Lloyd	26-3	5	0	3-1	1	2	37-4
Terry Curran	13(2)-6	0	2-1	5-4	(1)	5(1)-3	25(4)-14
Colin Barrett	10(3)-2	0(2)	2-1	5(1)-2	2	5	22(6)-5
Barry Butlin	10(2)-3	0	2	5-3	1	4(1)-4	22(3)-10
Sean Haslegrave	5(2)-1	0	0	6	1	3(1)-2	15(3)-3
Peter Wells	4	0	1	4	0	4	13
Glyn Saunders	4	0	0	3	1	2	10
Paul Richardson	1(1)	0	0	0	0	2(2)	3(3)
Garry Birtles	1	0	0	0	0	1(1)	2(1)
Steve Wignall	0	0	0	0	0	2(1)	2(1)
Bert Bowery	1	0	0	1	0	0	2
Paul Bannon	0	0	0	0	0	2	2
Steve Burke	0	0	0	(1)	0	1(1)	1(1)
Bryn Gunn	0	0	0	0	0	(1)	(1)

Note: team versus Peterborough on 12/5/77 is unknown.
LCup = League Cup, CC = County Cup, ASC = Anglo-Scottish Cup, F = Friendlies

The 1977 - 78 Season

Back Row (L to R) – Gordon, Gunn, O'Neill, Bowyer, Withe, Anderson, Middleton, Birtles, Butlin, Barrett, Burns, Clough.
Front Row (L to R) – Lloyd, Haslegrave, Clark, McGovern, Robertson, Curran, Woodcock.

In the summer of 1977, if you asked anyone in Europe what they thought of when you mentioned the city of Nottingham the answer would invariably be 'Robin Hood,' or maybe 'Lace.' It wouldn't be 'Nottingham Forest.' The 1977-78 season would change all that. The summer had been dominated by the Queen's Silver Jubilee tour, which visited Nottingham in late July. The royal entourage drove through the city with tens of thousands lining the route; soon a similar crowd would gather in the streets to pay tribute to a very different party.

At the City Ground, the summer was spent implementing the ground improvements required for First Division acceptance. Commercial manager John Carter worked to hard to boost the merchandising side of things as money was tight and more would be needed from all areas to try and improve the squad. The likes of Clark, Bowyer, Barrett, McGovern and Lloyd had all played a significant amount of games in Division One before so it wasn't a team of total novices, though most Forest fans were hopeful of survival and little more. Disappointingly small initial season-ticket sales bore this out.

Clough continued to wield the axe and a trio of players were shown the exit door – Sammy Chapman crossed the Trent and joined Notts County; Barry Butlin was later shipped out to Peterborough for a cut rate £20,000; and Sean Haslegrave, having never made the grade at Forest, moved to Preston for £30,000. The major player move of the summer came on 11 July when the club announced that Scottish striker Kenny Burns had put pen to paper for a £150,000 move from Birmingham City. Though Burns had hit twenty goals the previous season, playing alongside Trevor Francis, the announcement caused the raising of some eyebrows because of his reputation for liking a drink and a bet. Surely he'd be too wild to fit into Clough and Taylor's strict, disciplined style? As usual, though, the duo hadn't made their move without doing a little homework first.

'Taylor followed me about the place,' reveals Burns. 'He stalked me to the dog track – I do like the dogs a wee bit. Afterwards he said that I wasn't a big gambler or drinker and I'd never even noticed him. I don't think I would have recognized him with his flat cap on and he blended in at the track. So then Clough phoned me – I was away with the girlfriend at the time – and he told me he had agreed a fee. So when I came back I met him in Tamworth and we went to a pub between Tamworth and Ashby called the Four Counties. When I got there he says, "That car you came in, is that stolen?" It wasn't, but the one before was! He would always refer to that. Then I met him on a Saturday morning, went to his house and had a drink, then he took me to a sweet pea flower show! Peter Taylor picked me up then and he says, "Don't forget we might want to sell you if you get fed up of winning things!"'

The pre-season schedule again included flying out to the Augsburg training camp in West Germany, just as they had when preparing for the Second Division campaigns. The 1 July flight to Munich was followed by an early morning start for the 150-mile drive to St Gallen in Switzerland for the opening game of the tour. Awaiting the party was a modern looking ground, not unlike the current

MacAlpine Stadium in Huddersfield, and a pitch that bore grass four inches long. The Swiss had let the surface grow in order to protect it for their upcoming league fixture against Grasshoppers Zurich – whom Forest would face the following season with rather more at stake. As the team came out for a warm up they were met by a sizeable group of Forest fans among the 2,300 crowd. The team's line-up no doubt took the travelling fans by surprise, as Larry Lloyd remembers: 'The point was we knew that, having got to the big league, he [Clough] had to improve the squad. So we were thinking, Who's going to be playing, who's he going to buy? I was pretty confident that I was OK because I had a lot of experience playing in the big league anyway, but then Kenny Burns signed and of course at the time was playing up front for Birmingham so that put Peter Withe under a bit of pressure; he thought That's me out then, that's me gone. But as it happened in the first practice match Cloughie said to Kenny, "Go back and play with the big lad at the back" and that's how our partnership was formed, which was very successful.' So in one of the stranger managerial decisions of all time at Forest, Brian Clough bought a twenty-goal-scoring centre-forward and immediately played him at centre-half. Forest went 3-1 up in this opening game, the Swiss pulled one back and then had an equalizer ruled out because the final whistle blew as the ball crossed the line. Apart from the Burns change, the team was pretty much the same one that had gained promotion, with Middleton, Anderson, Clark, McGovern back in his more customary midfield position, Lloyd, Curran, Bowyer, Withe, Woodcock and Robertson.

Two days later the Reds were on the road again, this time to Austria for their sternest test for some years, against the Austrian champions Wacker Innsbruck. The same eleven started the match and Forest put on a superb display to tame the hosts by a 2-0 scoreline. A 'friendly' match this was not. A hostile seven thousand-plus crowd and a home side fired up for the occasion saw the challenges fly, and Peter Withe was sent off for retaliation after getting an elbow in the face which broke his nose – he flew home for treatment after the match and played no further part in the tour. That wasn't the only breakage as Ian Bowyer recalls: 'Kenny took his teeth out just before kick-off and he ran over to Martin O'Neill, who was sub, and he gave Martin a bit of tissue with his teeth in. So Martin put them in his tracksuit. Later when we scored Martin jumped up and broke the teeth! Then at the end of the game he had to go up to Burnsy and say "sorry, Kenny...."' The style and ease of Forest's victory was later put in an even more favourable light when Wacker went on to reach the quarter-finals of the European Cup, seeing off FC Basle and Celtic before losing to Borussia Moechengladbach on away goals.

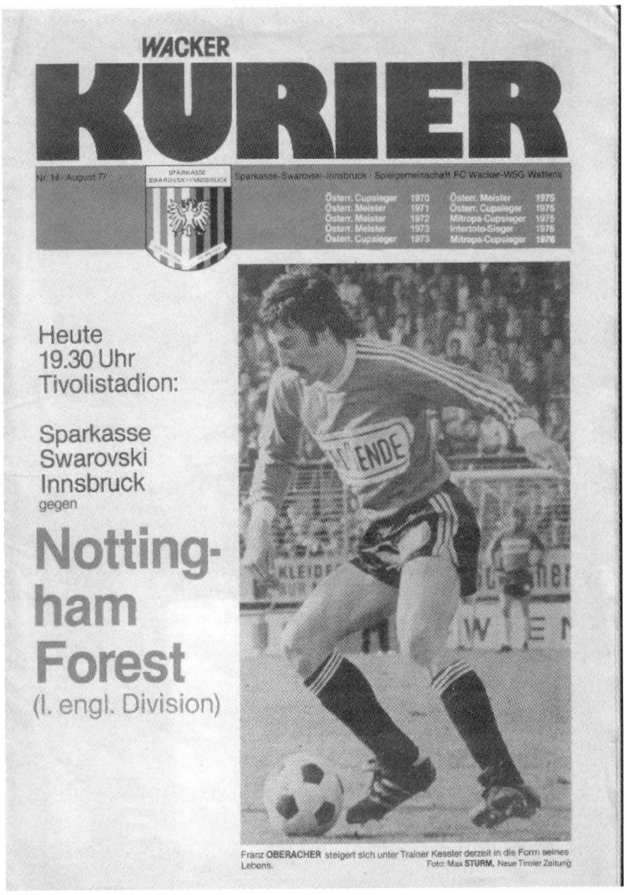
WACKER
KURIER
Nr. 14 · August 77
SPARKASSE SWAROVSKI INNSBRUCK
Sparkasse-Swarovski-Innsbruck · Spielgemeinschaft FC Wacker-WSG Wattens
Österr. Cupsieger 1970
Österr. Meister 1971
Österr. Meister 1972
Österr. Meister 1973
Österr. Cupsieger 1973
Österr. Meister 1975
Österr. Cupsieger 1975
Mitropa-Cupsieger 1975
Intertoto-Sieger 1975
Mitropa-Cupsieger 1976
Heute
19.30 Uhr
Tivolistadion:
Sparkasse
Swarovski
Innsbruck
gegen
Nottingham
Forest
(I. engl. Division)
Franz OBERACHER steigert sich unter Trainer Kessler derzeit in die Form seines Lebens.
Foto: Max STURM, Neue Tiroler Zeitung

The rest of the trip was taken up with a trio of games versus lower league sides and Forest won them all by a combined score of 13-1. Stephen Elliott who had stepped in to replace Peter Withe helped himself to four of the goals, including a hat-trick in one game. In all, eight different players found the net on the trip.

Back on home soil, the last week before the season-opening trip to Everton saw two more warm-up games. The first was a seaside trip to Skegness (for which each player was presented with a bottle of champagne). The 4-0 win would turn out to be Terry Curran's last match for the club. Two days later the County Cup Final for the previous season was played at the City Ground and, despite the high-scoring attacking play that had racked up the goals both in Division Two and during the European trip, the management duo decided to change things around and dropped Curran for the hard working Martin O'Neill. The game was a pretty dour affair and after being held to a 1-1 draw,

Forest won the cup on penalties. All thoughts now turned to the Reds' first top-flight game for five years.

By a twist of fate the opening league game was at Goodison Park against Everton, the site of Forest's last top flight game at the end of the 1971-72 relegation campaign. 'I remember sitting next to Martin [O'Neill] going to the ground from the hotel,' says John Robertson. 'I can't remember the exact details about how we went, but going up the road to Goodison with all the people around, it was a very nerve-racking feeling. But it was great to be going back to play in the First Division.' As kick-off approached Peter Taylor was keeping everyone loose with some funny stories and anecdotes, anything to keep the players from thinking too much about the task at hand and getting nervous. Then there was a knock at the door and a surprise guest made an entrance. 'Brian Clough let Bill Shankly come in the dressing room,' remembers John McGovern. 'Usually the dressing room was sacrosanct – no one was allowed in – especially after the game, unless it was under strict permission of the manager. Shankly knocked on the door and Clough said, "You give the team talk." He described the season as "a marathon, not a sprint" and the players were just in awe of Shankly and listened to every single word that he had to say.'

'I'd been great friends of Bill's when I was at Derby,' says Clough. 'I did a lot of television work with him. He was on the panel with Don Revie. There was Don Revie, Bill Shankly, and I was the minnow of the partnership but it didn't do me any harm because I listened. You'd be amazed how much I listened over the years. People thought I always did the talking but I didn't. I listened and listened and listened to them. Bill was very lonely when he left his job. He thought he could carry it and he was turning up at training grounds and things like that but, of course, going to Liverpool I didn't care where he was. Even if I'd had to go to one of the dock pubs I'd have invited Bill Shankly.' So as the bell rang the team ran out into the August sunshine with the words of Brain Clough, Peter Taylor and Bill Shankly ringing in their ears.

As they ran out they had no idea that they were embarking on what would be the greatest league season in the club's history to date and almost 30 years later it still stands as that. For the seven thousand Forest fans at the game it was a surprise to see Terry Curran out of the team again and Martin O'Neill wearing a new, shiny red Adidas-designed number 7 shirt. 'We'd played 4-2-4 against Notts County,' says Colin Barrett, 'but we reverted back to 4-4-2 at Everton and we were a real solid unit. That basically was the last of Terry Curran. I thought that Terry would be the big cheese, but it didn't turn out that way; it happened to be John Robertson on the other side who was the main man.'

'I can remember being at Goodison Park,' says Tony Woodcock. 'I'd never been there before and I think a few of the lads hadn't been there. I remember running out and it was really loud and I was thinking So this is First Division football and then Everton came out and it was like the whole place was collapsing in on us! I think we played very well in fact, and it came to be a normal thing for us; it seemed to boost us, not put us down, when we were playing in front of a packed house every week.'

'Even from the start there was no fear,' says Larry Lloyd. 'We had a bunch of lads with a lot of ability but were sort of wasted in there at Forest. They didn't have anyone who could bring their true ability out. Cloughie did. The likes of John Robertson, Viv Anderson, Martin O'Neill, people like that. Then they had the likes of me who needed desperately to prove myself again. Being only twenty-

seven I was at my peak, so I desperately needed to prove myself in the big league and of course Kenny was in the same position. There was no fear about us. It was quite strange really. We just went out, we played. There was none of this "Let's sit back, let's soak it up, let's get a point out of it." No, let's go and win the game!'

Forest certainly showed no fear in the early stages and went close on a number of occasions before Peter Withe opened his First Division account with a close range header at the ground he'd stood outside selling programmes as a boy. On thirty-eight minutes John Robertson drove in a second off the inside of a post and Everton were shocked into action, pulling one back against the run of play right on half-time. The second half was more of the same, with Woodcock using his pace to good effect and Robertson tormenting his marker Dave Jones. The game was finally won when Martin O'Neill hammered home a close range effort on seventy-seven minutes (*which the bench is shown celebrating, above*), his one fisted salute to the Forest fans would become a familiar sight. It was probably his finest ever game in a Forest shirt.

The players weren't given a chance to delight in the win too much though. Clough pointed out to McGovern some things that could have been better. 'I had a couple of shots,' says the captain. 'I should have passed and he said "Give it to someone who can shoot or you're out of the side" – and we'd just won 3-1. It didn't matter if you were the captain or not.'

The national press heaped the superlatives on the display. 'It was a classic

20 *Football Post, Saturday, August 20, 1977*

IT'S A THREE-GOAL ROMP

Flying start by Clough's men

JOHN LAWSON at Goodison Park

NOTTINGHAM FOREST sounded out a message to the First Division with first half goals by Peter Withe and John Robertson against Everton here this afternoon.

They came during a seven minute period of in-

their next attack Bowyer cut in from the right to release a

Forest were soon back on the offensive and Wood was

who lost his p
Thomas, and withd
winner Darracott.

O'Neill was penalised for a cha
Goodlass but Llo
commanding in
headed strongly aw
The Reds swept
and, after receivin
from McGovern, R
again beat Jones b
ing a shot into the
ting.
The action flo
mediately to the
goalmouth and a
run by McKenzie
have led to an
equaliser.

Forest were alwa
to punish Everton a
they did so with a t
in the 77th minute.

case of the First Division not knowing what we've got,' says Colin Barrett. 'It was a massive surprise to them and we caught them. We were on a good day, and if you look at results of most sides which get promoted over the years they often cause an upset in their first game.'

'That was a massive result,' says Frank Clark, 'because Everton were a "proper" team. We won well as a group and we thought, We're all right here.' After the game Bill Shankly was again invited to talk to the players. Ian Bowyer: 'Afterwards Shankly said, "You can win it, don't just be in the First Division, go and win it!" That was after one game! Very few people got into the dressing room but Brian had an enormous amount of respect for Shankly.' Frank Clark recalls 'The other people he'd allowed in were Jock Stein, Elton John and Geoffrey Boycott, which was great for me; he was my idol. I used to play cricket myself in the north east I packed in when I came down here.'

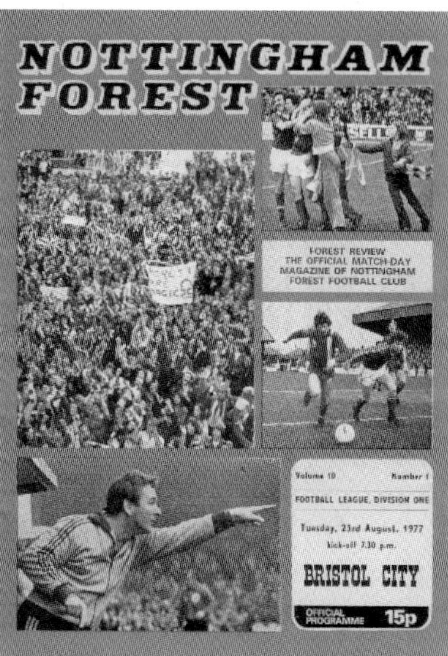

After such an encouraging start, the attendance for the opening home game against Bristol City on Tuesday 23 August was a somewhat disappointing 21,743. Brian Clough had drummed into his team the importance of keeping their feet on the ground: a win away from home was of little use of you didn't consolidate the points with a solid home performance. It was not going to be an easy night though as City, featuring ex-Forest favourite Peter Cormack, came and set their stall out to play for a draw. Marshalled by Norman Hunter, a leader of the anti-Clough movement among Leeds players two years earlier, the visitor's defence held firm for most of the game. Ian Bowyer had a shot cleared off the line and as the game wore down a goalless draw beckoned. Then with eight minutes to go Peter Withe rose to head home a John Robertson cross and secure both points. The big centre forward now had two goals in two games, and if assists had been recorded in the 1970s John Robertson would already have been top of that category with his third of the young season. Next up was Clough and Taylor's first meeting with the club where they had made their names – Derby County.

Derby had slumped in the years since the dynamic management duo had departed. Though they had won the league in 1974-5, using the largely Clough-assembled squad, they had only finished 15th in 1976-77 - just three points from the relegation places. ATV's *Soccer Special* cameras came to the City Ground and viewers got a glimpse of the exciting football that was to take the country by storm. In the very first moments of the game John Robertson was tormenting Derby full-back David Langan and causing panic as he swung in cross after cross, but the opening goal actually came from the right-side. Viv Anderson won a tackle and set Martin O'Neill away to force a corner. Tony Woodcock whipped the set piece in with his left foot, and it came off Larry Lloyd to Peter Withe. He took one quick touch and, as Roy McFarland rushed out to block the shot, the in-form striker volleyed it high into the top corner (*pictured bottom of previous page*). The City Ground erupted. Robertson continued to dominate in the second half and it was his long ball that sent Tony Woodcock away. Despite giving two Derby defenders a good head-start, he flashed past them and into the Derby area - eventually the ball fell to Withe and the game was over, 2-0. Commentator Hugh Johns was ecstatic over what he was seeing: 'That was some of the most electrifying football I've seen for a long time,' he enthused. When Robertson calmly placed a third into the bottom corner with just twelve minutes left, it capped both his and the team's fine start to the season. The first league table of the season showed Forest proudly looking down on the rest of English football – the only team with maximum points from three games.

In a break from League action, West Ham visited Nottingham in the second round of the League Cup. By the end of the night they wished they'd stayed at home. The Reds were rampant once again and ran out 5-0 winners as experienced Hammers full-back Frank Lampard was given a right old roasting by John Robertson. '[Robertson] is the best winger around,' lamented the Cockney defender. 'He goes either side which isn't really fair!' Many more full-backs would be crying the same story as the season unfolded.

Only three league games into the season and *The Sun* was already calling Forest 'the most exciting team in the First Division'. Most other national media outlets were less than convinced though and when the Reds visited Arsenal on 3 September, many were just waiting for Forest to fall. For once they were right. 'We always had a tough time at Arsenal,' says John McGovern, 'it was just one of those places. They had a great team and the 3-0 defeat brought us back to earth with a bump. In that era there were more teams that could win the league. Now you look no further than Manchester United and Arsenal, but there were more teams back then that could potentially beat anyone home and away, but we felt we could beat all of them, such was the feeling of confidence in the team.'

The game at Highbury was one of Forest's loosest of the year. Frank Clark was lost with a hamstring problem, and discipline was poor with both Burns and Lloyd getting involved in off the ball incidents. Burns was caught head-butting the Gunners' Richie Powling. 'They got a free kick right at the edge of the area,' Burns explains, 'I was standing behind Richie Powling and I, er, sneezed. And it was on camera, right in front of everybody. So I came in the next morning and the boys were saying "Hey Burnsey you're for it!" So I thought, Oh, sugar. We went training and then Jimmy Gordon comes in and says, "There's a meeting lads." So we all went into this meeting in the committee room and Cloughy comes in and says "Kenneth, this is for you." It was an envelope with a red tree on it – a sure sign that it was a fine. I opened it up and it was £50.' Lloyd was also fined.

Frank Clark's injury, meanwhile opened the door for Colin Barrett to get back into the first team on a regular basis. 'That was significant for me,' says Clark. 'It was the first time I'd ever had a hamstring and in a way it was the start of my decline at the club and I was never really first choice after that. The next game was the first game I'd missed since getting in the club. We only had about fifteen or sixteen players so they actually converted Colin Barrett. Colin had come as a centre back really and had played midfield a little bit and at right back but never really established himself in the team. So they stuck him to left back in desperation really – they had nobody else – and he was fantastic, from then on he was first choice really.'

The next game, at Molineux against Wolves, was the first league game that Clark had missed for two years and Barrett took his chance with both hands. 'They shoved me left back against Wolves,' he says, 'and from there I stayed in the side. We played the best football I ever played in during the first half of that season. We just destroyed sides by playing positive football.' Wolves were the next of these teams to be destroyed. Yet another Withe header, this time from a long Kenny Burns free-kick gave Forest a first half lead, and despite a lot of pressure it took until the last twenty minutes for the next goal. Woodcock's ability to turn defenders and then leave them with his pace started a move that ended when Robertson saw Ian Bowyer breaking into the area and his pinpoint cross was nodded in by the midfielder. Four minutes later Withe turned provider as his cross was glanced in by Woodcock for 3-0. Despite a late Wolves rally, Forest went home with a 3-2 win. Most managers would have been more than satisfied with the start to the season, but Clough and Taylor were already thinking ahead and had two transfer targets in their sights. The first was a player they had coveted for many years: the England goalkeeper Peter Shilton.

First Division Table – Top 4

	Pld	Pts
Manchester City	5	9
Liverpool	5	9
FOREST	**5**	**8**
West Bromwich Albion	5	7

(*after games of September 10th 1977*)

The Leicester-born goalkeeper had signed for his home-town team and progressed as the understudy to the great Gordon Banks, eventually playing over three hundred games for the Foxes after Banks moved on to Stoke City. Shilton's next move was also to Stoke City where he played another 110+ games, but when Forest were promoted to the First Division Stoke were relegated from it. It later became apparent that Forest had tried to sign Shilton in the pre-season but had a £250,000 bid turned down. In September they came back in with a £270,000 bid (a record for Forest); it was accepted and Shilton signed on the 13 September making his debut four days later against Aston Villa.

Shilton must have been pleased to get such an easy debut as Forest won 2-0 and he hardly touched the ball. Brian Clough was presented with the Manager of the Month award for August before the game and must have expected a harder match against the League Cup holders. Villa included PFA Player of the Year Andy Gray, Brian Little, Gordon Cowans and Dennis Mortimer as manager Ron Saunders was building a squad for a championship challenge of their own. That wasn't much in evidence on this occasion as Forest coasted to a 2-0 victory with an early Woodcock goal and a very late Robertson one (*pictured left*), both set up by Withe, book-ending the win.

'Shilton was arguably the best around at the time,' says John McGovern. 'I always thought his biggest strength was in one on one situations, because he had such quick feet, and he was a massive boost to the team. He was a great talker and the back four always knew what was going on; and it's a sign of a great player that even if he wasn't directly involved in the play he kept his concentration and was involved by always talking to the defence. His great concentration came through when he didn't have a lot to do in some games and then somebody would break and he was on his toes for that one shot.'

Larry Lloyd was happy to see that the Forest 'money men' were sensing the time was right for some investment in the squad. 'You have got to look at the Forest board,' he says. 'It wasn't a board of directors then it was a committee, and they were quite brave. It was a lot of money for a goalkeeper in those days. So you have got to admire the committee for sticking their necks out because they'd never been a wealthy club. So we felt good then. Being the main defender along with Kenny, we knew that with Shilton at the back it gave you a lot more confidence.'

Shilton soon made any doubters about the fee eat their words as he started to make the most amazing saves seem like routine ones. In his first twenty-two league games he conceded only nine goals and had seven clean sheets in his first ten away games, figures that still seem too good to be true. By the end of the campaign Forest would equal the Liverpool record of conceding only twenty-four goals in forty-two league games. His next league game was also an easy one as the Reds won 3-0 at Leicester. with the travelling support almost as big as the home fans' attendance.

Though Forest had now spent over £400,000 on Shilton and Burns, a massive amount for the club at the time, the shopping wasn't over yet. Another surprise was sprung when Archie Gemmill was unveiled as a Forest player, making the short move from Derby County. The deal also saw John Middleton, who was now expendable with the arrival of Shilton, and Terry Curran, who had never regained his place from the pre-season, going the other way. 'I didn't have to think twice,' says Gemmill. 'Knowing the boss from the Derby days I fully expected to win trophies at Forest. I knew that any of Clough's teams would have very good players individually and that ninety-nine times out of a hundred they would all gel as a team. We never felt any different playing at home or away we had a great belief.' Gemmill had made his Scottish League debut for St Mirren and had had a short spell at Preston North End before Clough signed him for the first time, for Derby in 1970. The hard running midfielder had broken through as a Scottish international and captained the national side. Clough wasn't just bringing good players in but making sure the team's 'vibe' wasn't upset. 'The three signings that they initially brought in – Archie Gemmill, Kenny Burns and Peter Shilton – if you could have picked anyone I don't think you could have picked better than those three,' says John McGovern. 'Signing Shilton was an absolute coup; Kenny Burns was transformed from a centre forward to the best defender in the First Division; and with Archie Gemmill it was the final piece in the jigsaw, which now had quality in every department. I was just hoping he didn't try and buy someone to replace me! Eventually he did try to replace me when he bought Asa Hartford but after a few games they found that the team didn't quite function the same with Asa in the side and though Asa was quicker than me and a little bit trickier, the end product of the team was compromised.'

It was McGovern who lost his place to Gemmill for the game at home to Norwich City on 1 October. The game saw two firsts – Kenny Burns' first league goal for Forest (*pictured right*) and the first goal that the Reds conceded at home, in their fifth home game. Though Archie Gemmill was to prove an invaluable member of the team he had a shaky debut and the team lost much of its attacking fluidity. City's Martin Peters admitted afterwards that Norwich had adjusted their system to stifle Forest, and his header thirteen minutes from time stole a point and stopped Forest from going top of the division. Gemmill was picked out for criticism by Brain Clough, who said he'd picked up bad habits recently at Derby and that he wouldn't put up with so much sideways and backwards passing. Gemmill was dropped for the next game at home to Ipswich, with the centre of midfield again being marshalled by McGovern and Bowyer.

For this midweek game Clough again had little to do in the way of motivation as Mick Mills was widely quoted in the press, calling Forest a team of 'has-beens'. The Trent End took great delight in barracking Mills at every opportunity and Forest, in the words of Martin O'Neill, 'absolutely murdered them!' The final score of 4-0 actually flattered the visitors; Lloyd had a goal disallowed and several other chances were spurned. Peter Withe netted all four for Forest, giving him a total of ten goals in ten games. 'Clough quoted Mick Mills in his team talk,' recalls Kenny Burns. 'That *was* his team talk. He didn't usually say that much, he always said let them concentrate on you. So we went out and scored four goals. Peter Withe scored the four and normally when you score three or more you get to keep the ball and Clough says to Withe "When you can learn to play with it you can have it!" He wouldn't give him the ball, but I think he finally gave him it on the Friday morning.'

First Division Table – Top 4

	Pld	Pts
FOREST	**10**	**16**
Manchester City	10	15
Liverpool	10	15
West Bromwich Albion	10	14

(*before the games of October 15th 1977*)

One of the most significant things to come out of that night was that Forest went clear at the top of the First Division as Manchester City lost 4-2 at Coventry City. It was a position that the Reds would not relinquish for the rest of the season. A 0-0 draw at West Ham consolidated the lead and when Manchester City visited Nottingham on 15 October it was a case of first versus second.

BBC's *Match of the Day* was drawn to the City Ground and the game didn't disappoint the nation-wide audience. Unlike Forest, City were considered as bona fide championship challengers with a star-studded line-up including Dennis Tueart, Mick Channon, Peter Barnes, Joe Corrigan and Brian Kidd, who opened the scoring on twenty-one minutes. A right wing corner fell at the strikers feet and he swivelled to volley a shot high over Shilton's shoulder. Forest were stirred into action and regularly sent three players forward to chase down City's back four who were happy to play the ball back and forth. After thirty-three minutes Woodcock, Withe and Robertson all pushed up to challenge and Robertson intercepted an attempted clearing pass from Willie Donachie and set off on a mazy run. After twisting and turning three defenders inside out he rolled the ball into the six-yard box, where Woodcock was on hand to side foot the equalizer. The game ebbed and flowed until Robertson found space late in the second half and put in a low cross to Woodcock. Just as he was about to shoot Peter Withe took the ball off his foot, carried out a virtual pirouette and then placed the ball under Joe Corrigan for a famous winner. As the Forest players celebrated Ian Bowyer was clearly picked up on camera running back to the centre circle with his hand over his mouth, laughing like a mischievous school boy at an unidentified City player. 'I was laughing at Asa Hartford,' he admits. 'There's always little bits of banter going on. I can't remember exactly what had been said but I was having a few words with Asa. When he came here [to Forest] we had a laugh about it, it was a bit of mickey-taking on my part.'

A trip to Sheffield two days later illustrated the professionalism that Clough instilled into his players at all times. The occasion was a testimonial at Sheffield United for John Harris, as Colin Barrett remembers: 'Brian Clough wasn't there on the team bus and we thought, This is great. He wasn't there, nobody was there – Jimmy Gordon was taking it. So we all thought it was a nice easy testimonial match and it was 1-1 at half time. We were laughing and joking in the dressing room and all of a sudden Cloughy walked in. He went ballistic, I don't know whether he'd been watching or not but he went ballistic. He said, "I want six here this second half!" and walked out. Consequently we played the second half like a cup final, Sheffield United couldn't believe what had hit them and we smashed in five goals in the second half at this testimonial, which was supposed to be a nice friendly. We walked back into the dressing room, he never came in, so we don't know whether he'd gone home at half time, but that's the hold he had over the players in terms of making them realize they are professional footballers and they have to do everything right."

The following Saturday was another trip to the capital for a game against Queen's Park Rangers, but this time Clough didn't need to say anything to motivate the team – *Football Focus* TV pundit Bob Wilson did it for him. Wilson famously claimed that he thought Forest were little more than a flash in the pan and 'a bubble that will soon burst.' In answer, the Reds dispatched QPR 2-0 and stayed top of the table. 'People in the journalistic industry don't do themselves any credit at all,' says Brian Clough, 'then that bloody Bob Wilson, who's never been a manager in his life, committed the cardinal sin of saying our bubble had burst or something like that. Poor old Bob, one of the nicest men you could ever meet in the game, saw me ages afterwards, maybe a year, and he said, "I got more post about that remark than...." I said, "Are you feeling sorry for yourself, Bob? Well don't. You should have kept your bloody mouth shut. If you don't know what you're talking about don't talk!"'

Forest had been drawn at home again for the third round of the League Cup, which provided a chance for a renewal of the Forest–Notts County rivalry. Because Peter Shilton and Archie Gemmill had already played in the competition, for Stoke and Derby respectively, they were 'cup-tied' and therefore could play no part in Forest's attempted cup run. Gemmill's loss was not too difficult to balance as the Reds had a number of midfield options, but the absence of Shilton and the earlier sale of John Middleton meant that seventeen year old Chris Woods was given his debut. After playing schoolboy football in his native Lincolnshire Woods had caught the eye of several scouts. 'I was going to sign for Derby, actually,' says Woods. 'Brian Clough and Alan Hill were at Derby and just before I was signing they left. I obviously got on very well with Alan Hill and so I went across to Forest with them. I'd skipped the youth team and was playing in the reserves from the age of fifteen with the likes of Bryn Gunn, Steve Elliot and Stuart Gray. For me to be working with someone like Peter Shilton could only help me. Needless to say I didn't know that I was going to like see him as someone who was later going to stop me getting in the England team but I really enjoyed working with him. He was a great help to me. I didn't even realize that he was cup tied or that I'd be playing.' Like Shilton's debut earlier in the season, Woods had a relatively easy start to his Forest career as they won out comfortable 4-0 winners. Ian Bowyer, in for Gemmill, notched two goals (*one of which is pictured on right*), Tony Woodcock helped himself to his sixth goal of the season and was then felled by ex-Forest captain Sammy Chapman to enable John Robertson's penalty. Forest were into the fourth round for the first time since 1969-70 and only the second time ever.

Bowyer's two goal cup show enabled him to keep his place for the next league encounter and Gemmill came back in for Martin O'Neill. Despite the changes Forest rattled off another 4-0 win over Middlesbrough, who couldn't stop the rampant Reds even with Graeme Souness and his afro hairstyle rushing around the midfield. The game was capped by two spectacular Viv Anderson goals (see left). The composed full-back had been playing some excellent but largely unheralded football in what would later be termed a wing-back role. 'Any opportunity to get forward was encouraged,' says Anderson. 'Myself and whoever played the other full-back position were encouraged to go all the way and get in the box, which was quite unique in those days.'

The goal spree came to an abrupt end at Chelsea on bonfire night as the poorest display of the season led to a 1-0 defeat. It was also the day that the FA announced their intention to interview Brian Clough for the England manager's role. The side's lethargy seemed to spill over into the next match, at home to Manchester United. In the long shadows cast from some strong autumnal sunshine, the visitors took a fifth minute lead through Stuart Pearson and held it until half-time. By the time the teams came out for the second half the sun was long gone and the City Ground was enveloped in a murky gloom before the floodlights were switched on. Minutes into the second period Forest won a free kick which John McGovern fooled everyone by taking short to Archie Gemmill, who unleashed a long range shot that deflected from a defender and into the path of Kenny Burns, who had gone up for the set-piece. Burns calmly used his striker's instinct to wait for United keeper Roche to commit and then blasted his shot low into the corner. Forest now had United on the back foot and flooded forward while the weather completed its 180-degree about-turn and a torrential downpour began. In the last fifteen minutes a Peter Withe cross was powerfully headed home from sixteen yards by Archie Gemmill, who seemed almost to launch his five-foot-five frame into orbit in order to meet the ball. Sixty seconds later Brian Greenhoff bundled Woodcock over in the area but Robertson's spot-kick was saved by Roche to prevent an even heavier loss. United would have no such luck in the return game five weeks later.

The visit to Elland Road proved to be a landmark: it was the last league game Forest lost all season. 'That was one of the best games of football I've ever played in,' recalls John McGovern. 'It was wet on the day, which suited us, but it also suited them because they were a good footballing side and it was one of the games where Clough actually paid me a compliment! Because I'd suffered at Leeds along with him, when I came off the pitch he said, "You didn't put a ball wrong today", and I knew that I'd played exceptionally well because I had something to prove at Leeds before a full house. It was fast, it was furious and was end to end stuff for ninety minutes, the pace never faltered. Unfortunately we lost 1-0 when Leeds scored after Peter [Shilton] had been in a collision with Ray Hankin and was on the ground. There was a scramble and the ball was put in while he was still suffering a little bit. I think in the modern game someone would have kicked the ball out so the goalkeeper could receive treatment but it didn't work like that on that day.'

In typical Clough and Taylor fashion, something out of the ordinary was called for to get the team's mind off a defeat – this time a midweek trip to Isreal, something that would be unheard of today. A friendly against Maccabi Tel Aviv was arranged and a full strength Forest side travelled and won the game 6-1. 'It was something we got used to under Clough and Taylor,' explains John McGovern. 'They liked any excuse to keep the players together, whether we went down to the national training centre or to the coast for a walk on the beach and a paddle in the sea. All the players were together, which helped the team spirit. All the trips we made abroad we never really had any time for any sightseeing. We'd arrive, have a rest and a meal and then go for a light training session or even a warm-up session, then play a match the next day.' Colin Barrett adds that 'Another thing you have to give Brian Clough and Peter Taylor credit for is whether it was a testimonial for someone or a benefit of any shape or form, the whole team played.'

The return from Isreal brought a 0-0 draw at home to fellow top four side West Bromwich Albion, followed by another West Midlands opponent in Aston Villa. Villa, as League Cup Holders, visited in the fourth round of the tournament but were duly dumped out of it 4-2. Chris Woods again took his place in goal but made his first error: 'I always remember letting a stupid goal in,' he says. 'I think it might have been Frank Carrodus, that one slipped through my arms and legs and rolled across the line, hit the post and went in. I was absolutely devastated but all the lads were brilliant at that particular time. I mean obviously I was young, they were helping me through it. Brian Clough would always be the one that give you the rollicking but Peter Taylor walked round after him and would say, "Hey, but you know you can do it. We believe you can do it."' Woods wasn't on the end of many rollickings and was picked out to take a prestigious role at the club – Brian Clough's Friday morning squash partner. 'I even got in trouble once for going training on a Friday morning rather than playing squash with him,' says Woods. 'I don't remember how it came about but I played squash from being quite young. It was funny because all the lads used to come back after Friday training and we used to have a meeting afterwards and they'd know as soon as he walked in whether I'd beat him or whether he'd beat me by his mood!' Another surprise bonus had been the form of Kenny Burns (*pictured above right*). The transformed centre-forward played like a natural at centre-back, showing a strong bite in the tackle and domination in the air as well as an ability to bring the ball forward and spray it around when required. His improvement continued as the season progressed.

In early December the news came through that Brian Clough had been passed over for the England manager's job in favour of Ron Greenwood. This naturally came as a big relief to Forest fans who had collected a twelve-thousand signature petition asking the manager to stay. It was widely accepted that if Clough was given the England position then Forest would soon fade back to relative obscurity. The popular, and probably accurate, opinion was that the FA were scared stiff of Clough, despite his being the public's number one choice, so decided to go for the 'easy' option of appointing Greenwood. '[Greenwood] was a nice man,' says Clough; 'he didn't want trouble. They [the FA] thought I was going to take over the FA, and I would have!' In the years following the appointment England pretty much did nothing – they failed to reach either the World Cup finals in 1978 or the European Championship finals in 1984 and were disappointing at the 1982 World Cup and 1980 European Championships. On the other hand Clough and Forest went on to greater things. Clough's sides achieved more at club level than 1970s England managers Revie's and Greenwood's sides had done. Successive England managers like Bobby Robson, Graham Taylor and Kevin Keegan had equally poor club records afterwards which can only leave one asking what might have been, if Clough been given a chance at national team level.

It was business as usual in the First Division, as a 2-0 away win at Birmingham and a 2-1 win at home to Coventry (*with McGovern scoring, left*) kept the Reds a point clear of Everton, who had put a good run together to overtake Manchester City and Liverpool. In the Coventry game Larry Lloyd broke his foot against his former team and was ruled out for ten weeks, giving Forest their first injury worry of the season. One option was to play John McGovern at the back, but instead Clough decided to delve into the transfer market and in short order he had signed ex-Notts County centre-half David Needham.

Needham was well known in the East Midlands having started out in the Leicester schools system before moving to Notts County in 1966. He spent eleven years with the Magpies, appearing in 465 games for them. There had been rumours that Forest had moved for him the previous summer, but Notts didn't want to sell to their neighbours and he ended up going to Queen's Park Rangers for £90,000. He'd been there for just six months and was still living in Nottingham when Forest came calling. He'd contributed three goals to the Rangers' relegation battle and Clough saw the big defender as the perfect replacement for Lloyd. He was even happy to give Rangers a quick profit on the player by paying £150,000 for him – taking the season's total spend to almost £700,000. 'I heard it through the grapevine that Forest were interested,' says Needham, 'and then they came in for me within a week. It was nearly Christmas and my wife and I were at home and we got the phone call from Brian Clough saying, "Come round to Forest and have a word." It was quite a shock. It took us all of twenty-five minutes to get over there and we went for an Italian meal. We had a good chat and sorted things out.' Needham's debut was in a pivotal game for Forest, a pre-Christmas trip to Old Trafford.

All good teams who become great ones normally have a defining game where they make the step up. It's usually a game where all the players hit top form on the same day and steamroller the opposition, no matter where the game takes place or who the opposition are. Real Madrid had made the step in public consciousness at the 1960 European Cup when they thumped Eintract Frankfurt 7-3. The game that saw Forest capture the imagination was their 17 December 1977 game at Old Trafford. Manchester United at the time weren't a bad side; they were the FA Cup holders, were in a comfortable mid-table position and had earlier beaten Liverpool 2-0 at Old Trafford and only lost 2-1 at the City Ground. On this day though they were, in the words of *Match of the Day* commentator Barry Davies, 'buried in their own back yard'.

The home side ironically ran out to the sound of Queen's 'We Are The Champions', which was little more than wishful thinking. The Stretford End seemed to continue this theme by greeting the Forest team with a chant of 'You're going down again!' A healthy fifty-four thousand-plus crowd had crammed into Old Trafford to see a full strength United side for one of the first times of the season, as Dave Sexton's side had had its share of injury problems and they started quite brightly. Irish international Sammy McIlroy shot wide early on and Kenny Burns had to be alert to snuff out a Steve Coppell run, but soon Forest began to find their feet and take control of the game.

Peter Withe was playing as the perfect target-man with Tony Woodcock making effective runs off him. This partnership was helping the midfield to join the waves of yellow shirts that were increasingly playing some lovely one-touch flowing football. On twenty-three minutes Withe brought Archie Gemmill into the play and his little lob sent Woodcock scampering into the United area (*pictured above*). He twisted and turned to get an acute-angled shot in; it hit the post and then United's Brian Greenhoff before crossing the line. United were rattled and Forest poured forward. Five minutes later John Robertson's measured pass to Withe was flicked first time to Woodcock, who thumped it home in front of the Stretford End. A split second of silence followed before an eruption of noise cascaded down from the opposite end of the ground where the away fans were housed. Within moments Viv Anderson blazed high and wide from the corner of the six-yard box, totally unmarked, and Woodcock's sharp-angle volley was palmed away by Paddy Roche in the United goal. Before the half was over Anderson could have scored again when his shot from the edge of the area almost sailed over the keeper. 'Manchester United look pedestrian when compared to Forest,' gasped Barry Davies, and they did. It could easily have been 4-0 by half-time; luckily for United, it was just half that.

The second half kicked off as rain started coming down, but it didn't hinder the Yellows' crisp one-touch passing. First Robertson broke free, but was bravely stopped by Roche at the edge of his six-yard box. Moments later United had a free-kick at the edge of the Forest area. The shot was charged down and Forest were away. Archie Gemmill's shortest legs on the field seemed to be going a mile a minute as he chased the ball towards the halfway line. There he nutmegged the onrushing United defender Nichol and sent Robertson away with a delightful pass from the outside of his foot. Robertson calmly moved in and rounded Roche before killing the game with Forest's third goal in the fifty-third minute. The floodgates were open now – McGovern had a shot deflected wide for a corner from ten yards and Anderson should have scored again (and could have completed a hat-trick) when he was again unmarked with just the keeper to beat but blasted it over again.

Forest's dedication in all areas of the field was epitomized by Martin O'Neill chasing back forty yards to tackle United's winger in the last minute while 3-0 up. There were many empty seats by the time Gemmill's never-ending running sent Woodcock away one on one and he calmly slotted in number four. It could, and perhaps should, have been seven or eight though.

'That was the absolute pinnacle, if we had realised it at the time,' says Brian Clough, 'but we took it step by step. There was a spell between us getting the third and the fourth and I said, "I'm glad that's gone in just to let people know we could have had ten" – and we could have had ten! That's how much Manchester United were inferior to us.' For David Needham it was an even easier debut than the ones that had been afforded to Peter Shilton and Chris Woods. 'We played absolutely fantastically and it was like birthday and Christmas all in one. How lucky can you get? I was fighting a relegation battle at QPR and then to go straight into a side that was playing the sort of football Forest were was pretty special.'

'Years before I had played there in the reserves,' says Tony Woodcock. 'I'd played left back in the reserves, and then after we beat the reserve team I ran up to the back of the Stretford End just to have a look at the goal, and a year later I'm playing there with the first team! In fact I can remember Ian Bowyer saying to me before the game, because I'd had a good season, he said if you want to do it anywhere this is the place to do it. He said that to me just before we went out and it went well for me – apart from Robbo who should have slipped me in for his goal! (*see below*) But I got a hat-trick, you see the first goal was mine, it hit the post and the defender and went in so I claimed it. Some papers gave it me, some didn't, so for me it was three.'

20 Football Post, Saturday, December 17, 1977

4-0 ROUT BY LEADERS

Forest rip United to tatters

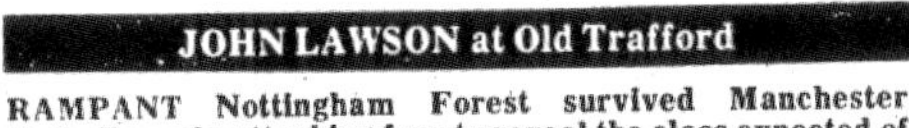
JOHN LAWSON at Old Trafford

RAMPANT Nottingham Forest survived Manchester United's early attacking fury to reveal the class expected of

SCOTTISH (Premier Division)

Clydebank 0 Ayr
Dundee U 2 Partick
Hibernian 2 Aberdeen
Rangers 3 Motherwell
St Mirren 3 Celtic

'They caught us on a very good day,' adds John McGovern. 'Everyone hit form and the 4-0 scoreline was a little bit fortunate for Manchester United. We literally ran them ragged. I can remember being interviewed on the BBC after the match and I said,"We had a fantastic day, fantastic performance" and Dave Sexton looked very sheepish having to go on and explain why a Nottingham Forest side had run his side ragged and scored four and could have had ten on the day. We looked on a different planet, not in a different league – but that was possible when we all hit form.' Dave Sexton: 'They don't play with eleven men. They seem to have sixteen or seventeen. When they are attacking they have about seven of them coming at you and when they are defending there are about nine of them!'

First Division Table – Top 5

	Pld	Pts
FOREST	**20**	**31**
Everton	20	29
Liverpool	20	25
West Bromwich Albion	20	25
Arsenal	20	25

(*after games of December 17th 1977*)

The way Christmas fell that year meant that Forest now had nine days off before their next game. As usual Clough wanted the team to stay together for some of the time and so the day after the United game Forest flew out for a few day's break in Benidorm. 'At the start of the season we were flying,' says Colin Barrett: 'We had a good League Cup run, we're at top of the table, and then we smashed United 4-0. We went to Benidorm the next day, flew from Manchester to Benidorm and had a real team bonding time. I think then we realized hold on a minute, we had something special if we could just keep it going.' John Robertson agrees: 'I think I knew we had a very good chance of the league title when we went to Manchester United and won 4-0. Then we went to Benidorm and that was when John O'Hare said we had a great chance. His was an opinion I really respected: he'd already won it, and he thought we were ready.'

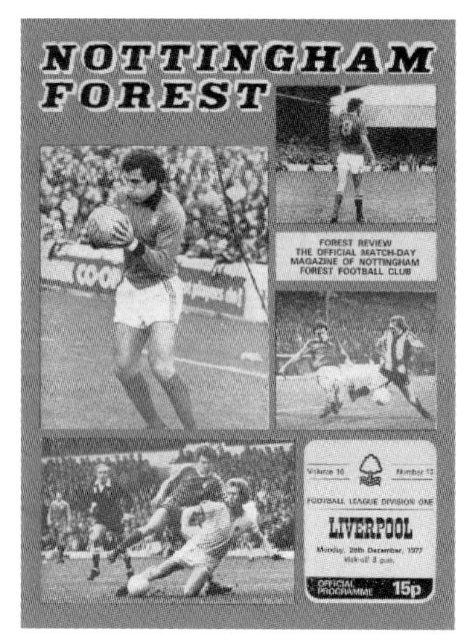

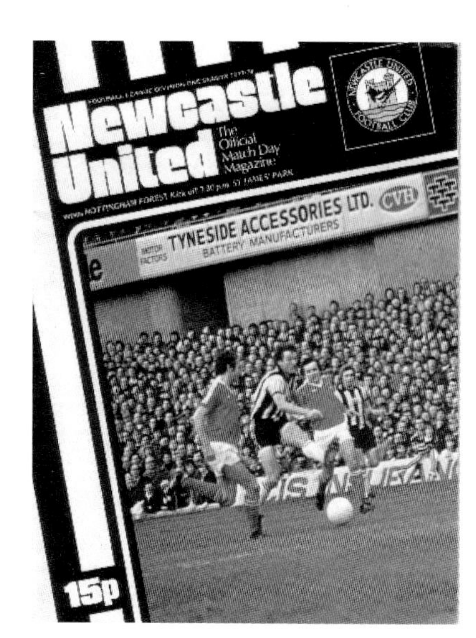

The break came at a good time for Forest: a busy holiday schedule was lined up, with four games in seven days, including two home league games against the Merseyside giants Liverpool and Everton, both of whom were hanging on Forest's coat-tails, waiting for the first sign of a slip. The Boxing Day match against current European Champions Liverpool was a prelude to some of the mammoth clashes between the two that would follow later. Gemmill gave Forest the lead (*pictured left*) but the 47,218 crowd saw the Reds pegged back for a 1-1 draw. Two useful away wins at Newcastle (2-0) and Bristol City (3-1) put Forest five points clear of Everton, who occupied second place. The Newcastle win was so emphatic that afterwards Brian Clough commented, 'When we play away we give Shilton the match ball afterwards because he never sees it during the game!' Scotland boss Ally MacLeod was at the game running the rule over possibilities for World Cup selection. At Bristol David Needham scored for the second consecutive game, Tony Woodcock made it two and Martin O'Neill secured the win with a solo effort for the third. When Everton arrived in Nottingham on 2 January 1978 a crowd of 44,030 packed the City Ground to give a total of over ninety thousand for the two Christmas home games. The resulting 1-1 draw kept Forest's lead at the top of the table intact. Cup wins in January included a 4-1 FA Cup success over Third Division side Swindon Town, and a safe negotiation of the potential banana skin of a League Cup quarter-final at Bury which Forest won 3-0. It took some believing, considering where Forest had been less than twelve months earlier, but now they were in a major cup semi-final.

In the league, the big games were still coming thick and fast, with Arsenal in Nottingham on 21 January and the home side had a score to settle after the 3-0 reverse they'd suffered earlier in the season. On an atrocious City Ground pitch, which was mostly covered by an inch or two of mud with little grass on view, the much vaunted Arsenal midfield of Graham Rix and Liam Brady were outworked by John McGovern and Martin O'Neill. Archie Gemmill was getting forward so much it was almost a 4-3-3 formation and several times Pat Jennings had to be at his best to deny the Scotsman. 'One thing I would have liked to have done a bit more in my career was get more goals from midfield,' says Gemmill. 'Usually, if I went near post the ball went far post so I was always grateful to get a goal.'

In the first half Arsenal had a couple of chances, the best of which was an Alan Sunderland shot on the run that was sharply turned away by Peter Shilton. After thirty-two minutes a David Needham near post header from a Woodcock corner beat Jennings and gave Forest the lead. 'That's been one of my fortes throughout my career,' says Needham. 'I always scored quite a few goals. I think I got about sixty goals altogether from centre-half so it wasn't a bad record. In the First Division when you're playing for the team top of the league they're all-important, aren't they?'

'Dave could always jump higher in the opponent's box than in his own box,' quips Kenny Burns. 'He's a big lad and he did well. He was a bit more mobile than Larry [Lloyd]. If you came up against Larry you treated him like a roundabout – you went left, onto Larry's right foot, and that's not his best.' It stayed 1-0 until midway through the second half, when a Brady pass was intercepted by Gemmill just outside the Forest area. Gemmill pushed it wide to Withe on the left wing and set off up the field. As Withe carried the ball forward, Tony Woodcock made a diagonal run to pull the last defender, Sammy Nelson, out of position. As TV pictures memorably showed, Gemmill continued his run to appear at the bottom of the screen and slide in Withe's cross – 'Withe hasn't seen him, he has now!' said commentator David Coleman.

'Archie's goal was the highlight,' recalls John McGovern. 'It was typical Forest at the time. We withstood a period of Arsenal pressure then we got possession with Archie, being twice as quick as I was, managing to get up to the other end and put it in. His endeavour typified everything about Forest.' This second goal broke open the game and, like others in which Forest battled to gain the upper hand, it soon became like a scene from the Alamo around the Arsenal goal. McGovern had a cross shot cleared by Pat Rice; Gemmill, Woodcock and Robertson all forced stellar saves from Pat Jennings; and the Trent End gleefully sang, 'If you hate Bob Wilson clap your hands!' Afterwards, Arsenal boss Terry Neil was gracious in defeat and conceded, 'Good luck to them, they deserve to win the championship.'

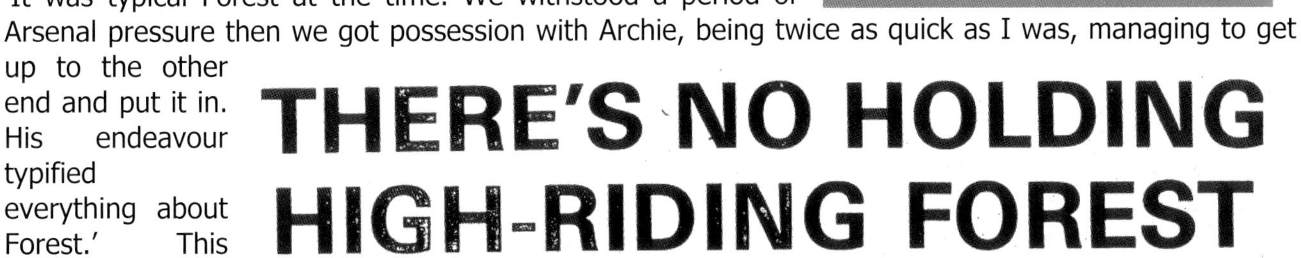
THERE'S NO HOLDING HIGH-RIDING FOREST

JOHN LAWSON at the City Ground

THE skill and commitment of Nottingham Forest proved too much even for the considerable defensive qualities of title rivals Arsenal in another thrill-packed game, here this afternoon.

Attendance: 35,743

'If you look at today's game, they play on bowling greens,' says Colin Barrett; 'they never have to worry about the ball bouncing, they never play in mudbaths, they call a game off if it's wet, and we played in ankle-deep mud! We were still trying to play good football, trying to do the right things. Whereas we played in mudbaths, by the end of the season there was just a diamond-shape of mud and the wings used to be the grass bits. You used to try to get the ball out to the wings, the old fashioned way of playing, but they wouldn't play on that today – well, they would do, but maybe not as well.'

With a couple of days left in January the Forest squad embarked on a different kind of team-building exercise – they travelled to Birmingham to record a single. The Nottingham band Paper Lace (of Billy, Don't Be A Hero fame) provided the backing for a song penned by Barry Mason. Mason had written for several big names, including Tom Jones, and based the Forest tune on 'He's Got The Whole World In His Hands', renaming it 'We've Got The Whole World In Our Hands', and rewriting the lyric to include the whole Forest Squad. Some singing from the Trent End was added to the mix and Warner Brothers released the single. Like everything else Forest seemed to do at the time, the single sold well and reached number 24 in the national charts, and spent a total of six weeks in the charts.

'John O'Hare, Archie Gemmill and myself had all played at the Baseball Ground, so playing in six inches of mud came naturally to us and we all loved playing in it. Some of those games would never even start nowdays. We did so well away from home because it was a pleasure to play on better surfaces. Playing on that muddy pitch at home helped us to be more of a footballing team when we went away and we often outplayed the home team.' - John McGovern.

Back to business and a 2-1 fourth round FA Cup win over Manchester City (featuring a wonderfully curled John Robertson goal) left the possibility of a unique treble still on the cards. The players, though, weren't even thinking about winning anything yet. It really was the stereotypical case of taking one game at a time. '[The championship] wasn't even discussed,' says John McGovern. 'To a degree we were just enjoying it so much, we couldn't wait for the next training session or the next match. I don't think we ever discussed the championship or the possibility even of us winning it.' Everyone else was discussing it though. At the start of February a poll of managers was taken, with Liverpool's Bob Paisley saying there was a long way to go and that 'Nobody has won anything yet'; Everton's Gordon Lee was hoping for some help in catching Forest, commenting that the Reds may drop points on away trips to Manchester City and Liverpool. Forest put all the discussions behind them and continued to roll on, with a 2-0 win over Wolves. The match highlighted what a difference a year had made. Wolves had won the Second Division as Forest sneaked into third place and now, while Forest topped the First Division, Wolves were fighting against relegation.

The rest of February was pretty much given over to various cup ties and battling against the weather to get these games played. First up was a crucial League Cup semi-final, first leg at Elland Road. Around ten thousand Forest fans were present to see the game against Leeds, who were in form and came into the match on the back of four straight wins. With David Needham cup-tied (along with Archie Gemmill and Peter Shilton) and Larry Lloyd still injured, John McGovern was moved into the back four and John O'Hare was called in for just his second start of the season. It proved to be a sweet return for the ex-Leeds trio of O'Hare, McGovern and Clough. Forest were on the attack right from the kick-off and breached the Leeds defence twice in the first half. A Martin O'Neill cross was flicked on by Colin Barrett and Peter Withe stretched to poke in the first. Two minutes later the bearded centre-forward towered above the Leeds goal to powerfully head a second. It could have been 3 or 4-0 before Leeds pulled one back through

Eddie Gray to give the home side a glimmer of hope. The score 2-1 score remained until thirteen minutes from time when O'Hare played a neat one-two with Peter Withe and rifled a low drive for the third goal and a commanding first-leg lead.

'Everyone thought it was the end of it,' says Peter Withe, 'but the management kept our feet on the ground, saying that there was a lot of work to do yet.' John McGovern recalls that 'I played alongside Kenny Burns, found out an hour before kick-off. I got a couple of rollickings off Kenny for not being in the right place at times, but the end product was a great win and left us red-hot favourites to go through at home.'

It had been another competent outing for Chris Woods who, like Shilton in many league games, had to keep his concentration for long periods while seeing little of the ball. 'I can remember that I made a save from Arthur Graham when it was a one against one and I pushed it round the post,' he says. 'Little things like that obviously helped us on our way and that just was the one thing that really stood out to me because it was at the Leeds supporter's end.'

The whole country was in the grip of a cold snap and games were being postponed left, right and centre due to the frozen pitches. Forest were thus left with a ten day break before their next game. All the players could do was train and wait.

Training at Forest was something that the players have a lot to say about; it was simple designed to make them keep to the basics and get them right while allowing them the freedom to express themselves in games without having too strict a regime to follow. 'Training was a case of "John Robertson takes the set pieces and that's it"' says John McGovern. 'If he needs a quick free kick he'll take it quick, if he needs a short corner he'll take it short. He used to like to take short corners because on lots of occasions you could catch the opposition sleeping. We'd take quick free kicks all over the field because we tried to break quickly. With the assets of the speed of Tony Woodcock and Viv Anderson we could break very, very quickly and later with Archie Gemmill we really had a team that was adapted for quick breaks and they knew what to do with the ball when they did break, they didn't run offside every two minutes.'

'Jimmy [Gordon] would do most of the training,' says John O'Hare. 'In the early days Brian Clough would come down quite a bit and everyone would jump a bit, do things a bit quicker. Pete Taylor used to come down and walk his dog but I never saw him in football gear or anything! Clough used to join in the five-a-sides and the tackles would really go in!'

'You talk about the difference Brian Clough made when we did the warm up!' says Colin Barrett. 'We used to run down the Trent and Jimmy Gordon would be the trainer and we'd all be taking nice and easy and then you'd see Cloughy's car come. You'd set up a five-a-side and all of a sudden the pace of that five-a-side quickened. When he started to walk by the touchline, the pace was like a cup final. I spoke to Denis Law, who I'd played with at Manchester City, he said, "What's your training like, what do you do? What's this bloke [Clough] like?" I said, "We don't do anything, all we do is five-a-sides." He said, Matt Busby was the same - all he did was five-a-sides. It was really interesting, he said Busby never practised a corner or free kick, the whole of the time, it was off the cuff.'

'No, we never ever practised a free kick, or a corner,' says Kenny Burns. 'First thing when we got a free kick was to have a shot at goal, or touch it to the side for a shot at goal. At corner kicks we sent two out for a short corner kick or if they sent two out it was a near-post one for a flick on and that was it. It's a very hard ball to defend against. We did that and no team could really defend us and it was all so simple.'

'If you were looking at today, it's all scientific,' adds Colin Barrett. 'They are on diets now, which we never did. A typical week when you played a match midweek, you'd play Saturday, have Sunday off, go in Monday, he would give you Tuesday off, play Wednesday, have Thursday off, come in Friday and Saturday. Clough's belief was two games a week were enough, you didn't need to run millions of miles, all you needed to do was tick over. On Monday, if you knew you had a game on Wednesday, you weren't going to do anything heavy. Sometimes you'd have Tuesday off, not all the time, Wednesday was light training on the morning of the match; Thursday off; then again Friday, light training because you have the game on Saturday, and that's how it was all the way through the season. Lots of five-a-sides but nothing strenuous.'

'In those days the goalkeepers would do most of the warm up and running with the rest of the players,' says John McGovern. 'Nowadays the goalkeeper goes straight into the specialist work and doesn't really train with the rest of the players unless it's some kind of shooting work. Peter Shilton would be able to do cross-country runs and sprints with the best of us. He was so fit and the amount of times he could go down and make a save, get up and then save another one and the length of time he could keep that going for was probably greater than anyone else in the game. He was a supreme athlete and along with the masses of ability that he had he was always at his best.'

When the cold weather finally broke, if only slightly, a fifth round FA Cup tie at Queen's Park Rangers was allowed to go ahead despite the pitch being partially frozen. When Forest weren't struggling to keep their feet on the treacherous icy pitch they found themselves under the cosh, and Martin Busby gave Rangers a first half lead. Despite a long range effort from Archie Gemmill that Phil Parkes kept out while at full stretch, Forest didn't really threaten until the late stages of the game. When the Reds did manage to get forward, they went for it as though their lives depended on it. At one point John Robertson was taking a free-kick and all nine other outfield players were in the Rangers box! Martin O'Neill went close from twelve yards and then in the last moments of the match Gemmill crossed for O'Neill to glance a last gasp header for the equalizer. He then went on a half-pitch lap of honour, to the delight of a massive Forest following. The treble was still alive, if only just.

The following Wednesday Forest played the rearranged second leg of the League Cup semi-final. Leeds were in no mood to roll over and let Forest progress, and were in a fighting mood right from the start. The highly tense atmosphere went up a notch when Leeds' Frank Gray's twenty-five yard rocket hit the top corner of the Forest net after twelve minutes, bringing the aggregate score back to 2-3. Though Peter Withe prodded home a Forest goal from five yards, it took just a further sixty seconds for Arthur Graham to rob Larry Lloyd of the ball (in his first game back from injury) and plant it behind Chris Woods. Two–one to Leeds on the night, 4-3 to Forest on aggregate. The 38,131 on the ground sensed that the tie was balancing on a knife edge – the next goal could prove vital. United almost stole it right on half time when Tony Currie hit the bar from well outside the area, but it luckily bounced away to safety for Forest.

Half-time came not a moment too soon for the Reds, and Clough and Taylor had some harsh talking to do during the break. Whatever they did say worked wonders, and Forest rattled in three second-half goals. Two minutes into the second half a collective sigh of relief was issued when Ian Bowyer restored the home side's two goal margin (*pictured on next page*).

Twenty minutes later Bowyer set up O'Neill for another, and the rout was complete when Tony Woodcock joyfully hammered home another for a 4-2 win on the night, 7-3 overall. For the first time in twenty years Forest were back at Wembley. 'It was another end to end game and was a shoot-out,' recalls John McGovern. 'When we went 2-1 down, unlike some other teams we didn't let any negative thoughts enter our minds. We didn't like losing any game, especially at home. Chris Woods did a magnificent job as a youngster. He got a lot of help from the experienced players, but we knew pretty early on that he was a capable player.' Referee Clive Thomas added that 'Forest are a credit to the game. This is Clough's greatest achievement, even if Forest go onto win the treble.'

Forest's next match, away at Norwich City, was also a six-goal thriller, but Brian Clough didn't see it as he'd taken a short holiday in Spain. If he had been present he wouldn't have been too pleased, though. Forest raced to a 3-0 lead in just twenty-one minutes through Withe, Barrett and O'Neill, but in the end they had to settle for a 3-3 draw and were lucky not to have been beaten. 'All I ever wanted to do was see Brian Clough walk through that door,' admits Colin Barrett, 'if I saw Brian Clough walk through that door I was happy. It didn't matter what Peter Taylor said to me, Cloughy was the main man. It was proved when Clough had one of his mid-term breaks and went away while we went to Norwich and drew 3-3. We came back for QPR in one of the FA Cup games on the Monday and again we drew, so there was another replay and Clough came back in and said, "Don't you think I've come back off my holiday's just because you've not been winning games, I've come back, because I've had to come back!" He was a one off and the only thing you could copy from him would be his thing about the game being pretty basic. Coaches make it complicated and managers make it complicated but it's not that complicated." The games that Barrett refers to are the fifth round FA Cup replay which ended in a 1-1 draw after extra time and then, with Clough on the bench, Rangers were brushed aside in the second replay by a 3-1 scoreline. 'They were tough, tough games,' says John McGovern. 'We couldn't knock them over. We didn't want the extra games, but we had to go through them.'

Back for the first home league game in a month, Forest dispatched struggling West Ham 2-0 to

maintain a four-point cushion at the top of the table. Two goals in the last ten minutes were required including a twice taken John Robertson penalty (*pictured below*). In all competitions Forest were now on a twenty-two game unbeaten streak, but just what did Brian Clough and Peter Taylor say to the players to get such consistency? 'The team talks were pretty simple,' says John O'Hare. 'You knew what was expected of you. You head it, you tackle, you cross, you score. At half time, they had a great memory for all the little things that had happened. Clough's man-management and motivation were great but he also really knew his football, no doubt.'

'In the dressing room at half time he'd say, "Right, you do this and I want you to do that and you should have done this,"' adds Colin Barrett. 'He would pick out certain things, but again nothing complicated. Every now and again, he would rant and rave and teacups would fly! But it was very basic. He wanted his defenders to defend, his midfielders to create and his goal scorers to score goals. It wasn't a matter of "coaching", he'd say, "You're a defender, you can't do this you can't do that, so you get the ball you give it to him – John Robertson he'll do it." He'd say, "When the ball comes in your box as a defender, you head it, you get it clear." Everything was very, very basic, and around that was a team spirit, team ethics, where you were all in it together and you defended from number 1 to 11 and you attacked the opposite way and that was the way we built our sides up.'

Frank Clark agrees that the team's togetherness was a big part of the success, and he did his part to promote it. 'We would train on Friday at the training ground, then we would all go in the guest lounge and sit there and wait for Brian and Peter to come. Sometimes you waited an hour. They'd come in tell you to have a drink, you could have beer if you wanted – and sometimes they wouldn't say anything, just have a drink and go, while sometimes he would take about anything other than football sometimes he would talk about football but nothing to do with the match tomorrow, sometimes Peter [Taylor] would do the talking. So you never knew what they would talk about. If we were at home on the Saturday six or eight of us would go round to Bill McKay's café and have chip butties. When I was at Newcastle I never used to go home for my lunch, I always used to go into town. Sometimes I would go on my own, sometimes there might be four or five of us, it varied. When I came to Forest the first thing I noticed when we finished training every day was that everyone went home. So I started going round to Bill's Café, round the corner, couple of days a week in the first season. I tried to get people to come round; gradually Colin Barrett used come round and then there'd be anywhere between eight and nine. Then Colin and I started going to this wine bar called Uriah Heep's for lunch and again that would be anywhere between two and a dozen and we'd

be there all afternoon, but only if there wasn't a midweek game. I'm sure Brian knew, but he didn't mention it, it was never a problem.'

The chip butty for Friday lunch was no doubt gobbled up before setting off for a sixth round FA Cup tie at West Bromwich Albion on 11 March 1978. With a week to go before the League Cup Final, Forest were now quoted by the bookies at 11/2 for the treble of League, League Cup and FA Cup. For this game 38,500 crammed into the Hawthorns. Viv Anderson was suspended and Ian Bowyer yet again showed his versatility by fitting in at right back. 'Archie [Gemmill] and I both picked up knocks against West Ham,' reveals John McGovern, 'but because the manager wanted to retain the shape of the side we both played at West Brom and I had to hold my hand up and say I was well below par. I was

BANG GOES TREBLE – REDS OUT OF CUP

JOHN LAWSON at The Hawthorns

OPPORTUNIST goals by Mick Martin and Cyrille Regis headed Nottingham Forest off their other route to Wembley, here this afternoon.

carrying an injury and Archie was too so there wasn't as much industry going on in midfield as there normally was.' Despite his injury, Gemmill started brightly and forced Albion's Tony Godden into an early save, as did a Martin O'Neill header. Then in the eighteenth minute Mick Martin poked out his foot which connected with the ball and looped over Peter Shilton. Martin's look of astonished bemusement confirmed that he hadn't even meant it. Forest weren't quite at the races, and two minutes into the second half they were caught cold. A long punt beat the defence for the first time all season, and the onrushing Cyrille Regis hit it very early on the volley and it flashed into the corner of Shilton's net. The Reds did stage a mini rally and forced a save from a Withe header, then Needham hit the bar and it clearly wasn't to be Forest's day. The sense of disappointment that they would miss out on winning all three major domestic trophies illustrated how far the club had come. 'I can remember the manager saying, "We only had one player playing in midfield today called Martin O'Neill - it would have been nice if someone else had joined him,"' says John McGovern. 'It was a little reminder to Archie and myself that even though you were injured he expected you to play a lot better than that.' Things did improve, but not spectacularly in the next league game against Leicester City. Hapless City had just three wins and only thirteen goals to their name in thirty-one games, but Forest laboured for a 1-0 win thanks to a John Robertson penalty. Next up was the small matter of a date with the mighty Liverpool at Wembley.

Peter Withe and Phil Neal battle it out at Wembley.

Route To The Final

Forest	5	Round Two	Liverpool	2
West Ham	0		Chelsea	0
Forest	4	Round Three	Liverpool	2
Notts County	0		Derby County	0
Forest	4	Round Four	Liverpool	2*
Aston Villa	2		Coventry	2
Bury	0	Round Five	Wrexham	1
Forest	3		Liverpool	3
Leeds United	1	Semi-Final 1st Leg	Liverpool	2
Forest	3		Arsenal	1
Forest	4	Semi-Final 2nd Leg	Arsenal	0
Leeds United	2		Liverpool	0

March 18 1978 was the date that Forest really got back on to the national stage with their first Wembley appearance since the 1959 FA Cup Final win. The club invited the 1959 team to accompany them as guests of honour, and many travelled to London for the game. Though the club as a whole had limited Wembley experience, several individual players had been there before. Larry Lloyd and Frank Clark had previously played on the hallowed turf while Ian Bowyer had won a League Cup medal with Manchester City in 1970. Peter Withe had been there with the Wolves squad in 1974 but didn't play against Manchester City, who had Colin Barrett in their squad.

Neither Liverpool nor Forest had ever won the League Cup, which was held in higher esteem then than it is now. There were no byes for top-level clubs, and the playing of reserve teams in the competition was unheard of. European places were limited in those days and this final provided a valuable entry to the UEFA Cup for the 1978-79 season.

Forest's route to the final must surely have been one of the most spectacular in any domestic cup competition, as the scores of 5-0, 4-0, 4-2, 3-0, 3-1 and 4-2 attest. The twenty-three goals that they scored were almost double the thirteen that Liverpool had notched up enroute to Wembley.

Forest were allocated a total of thirty thousand tickets for the final out of the hundred thousand capacity. The fourteen thousand seat tickets they were given ranged in price from £5 to £8, while the sixteen thousand terrace tickets were just £2.50. Though the team and management approached the game as 'just another league match', the fans made a full day (or in some cases, weekend) of it – especially as they didn't know they

Forest fans on the way to Wembley. Including, in centre, Paul Jones, Pat Guerrin, Steve Tring, Jeff Reynolds, Douggie Hackett, Nick Boland and Chris Mills.

would be paying regular visits to the Twin Towers in the coming years. For all they knew it could be another two decades until yhe next visit.

On the day Liverpool were pretty much at full strength and were well used to the showpiece occasions. Goalkeeper Ray Clemence and the entire back four of Phil Neal, Tommy Smith, Phil Thompson and Emlyn Hughes were all England internationals. Kenny Dalglish was a British record transfer when he moved from Celtic for £440,000 in 1977 and Ian Callaghan had been around for so long he had already been awarded an MBE. Steve Heighway and Ray Kennedy were also England internationals. Forest on the other hand were already without some of their most experienced players before a ball was kicked – Peter Shilton, Archie Gemmill and David Needham were all cup-tied and Colin Barrett was injured. 'I had a stress fracture of the leg, about a week or ten days before the final against Liverpool,' recalls Colin Barrett, 'and they told me I couldn't play in that game. I'd missed two finals while at Manchester City so I thought I'd never play in a final.' Graeme Souness was cup-tied for Liverpool, having moved to Anfield from Middlesbrough in January.

For Chris Woods this would be just his sixth first-team appearance, on the biggest stage in the country. 'Believe it or not, I wasn't too nervous,' he says. 'I'll always remember Ray Clemence saying the first time he went there that he was really nervous and he froze. It was just him trying to get at me a little bit. But we went down and, I mean, I didn't particularly sleep well the night before but we got there early, we all went out, had a walk on the pitch, and after that I seemed to sort of feel OK. Obviously I was a little nervous but once we got out there I didn't think of it.'

Bob Paisley and Brian Clough led the teams out, after the league had rejected a request from Forest to allow Clough and Peter Taylor to lead Forest out together. As the packed crowd greeted the teams, Clough stopped the Forest team and made them turn and wave to the Forest faithful at the Tunnel End. Paisley walked on a couple of steps before realizing that Clough had stopped, and patiently waited for the Forest manager to catch up with him.

Martin O'Neill is covered by both Phil Thompson and Emlyn Hughes.

After the usual formalities, introductions and national anthem, referee Pat Partridge blew his whistle for Liverpool to kick off. The Merseysiders were immediately on the attack, with Dalglish shooting wide early on. Jimmy Case then shot wide from distance: Forest were happy to let Liverpool keep possession as long as they were going to shoot from way out. Forest were confident enough that Chris Woods would comfortably deal with that kind of pressure. Tony Woodcock caused a couple of problems at the Liverpool end as he shot wide when well placed and then had a chase with Ray Clemence for a long through ball which the Liverpool keeper just won when well outside his area. Ian Bowyer came closest for Forest with a dipping shot that grazed the top of the crossbar. At the other end, Terry McDermott's disallowed goal was the closest Liverpool came and Forest got to half-time safe in the knowledge that they'd matched the European Champions for the first forty-five minutes.

Forest opened the second half defending the goal in front of their fans at the Tunnel End as Liverpool picked up the pace. They continued to have the lion's share of possession as they flooded the midfield to cut off the supply to John Robertson, but most goal attempts were long-range ones again. Woods had to move smartly to get his chest behind a long Ray Kennedy effort and then dived at Kenny Dalglish's feet, getting a kick on his bare hands for his trouble (*pictured top right of opposite page*).

Left: Larry Lloyd dispossesses Kenny Dalglish.

In the Forest midfield, John McGovern was still not fully fit from the groin injury he'd carried through the West Bromwich Albion F.A. Cup game the previous week. Midway through the second half he was withdrawn and replaced by John O'Hare. 'I was my first time at Wembley,' says O'Hare. 'I'd only played for Scotland against England at Hampden. I can remember going on, I wasn't nervous about it at my age but I didn't want to be responsible for doing anything silly while it was 0-0.

The pattern of the game stayed the same after O'Hare's introduction as a long range Emlyn Hughes drive whistled wide. As the ninety minutes came to an end Forest managed their first period of sustained pressure. First a Larry Lloyd header caused a Clemence fumble and then Tony Woodcock forced another save that fell to Martin O'Neill. The Irishman pulled the ball back to Peter Withe from a sharp angle and the big striker hooked it wide as normal time expired.

Extra time came and went with astonishing speed. Liverpool 'super-sub' David Fairclough was introduced, but it was Steve Heighway who came closest to breaking the deadlock. At half-time in extra time Clough and Taylor stayed on the bench rather than speaking to the players, and sent a hobbling John McGovern out with a message instead.

Finally the teams that had combined for thirty-six goals in reaching the final had to settle for none in two hours at Wembley. Peter Taylor also spoke about the decision to stay on the bench in extra time: 'We play it off the cuff,' he explained, 'I fancied us in extra time, they were in good order and there was nothing we could do to help them.' Peter Shilton was interviewed afterwards and commented on Chris Woods' performance: 'He proved a point today about what a good goalie he's going to be.' Chris Woods reveals that his big day is not one that he's gone back to over the years. 'To this day I've not actually seen like any television clips or video clips at all,' he reveals, 'but I remember making like the odd save and the one where I fumbled it and it came out to Dalglish and I had to throw myself and block it. The biggest thing that stands out in my mind nowadays is the fact that the grass was a little damp and I played with no gloves on. I wouldn't dream of doing that in this day and age.'

'I've got to say we were probably a bit lucky to get away with the game at Wembley' says John Robertson. 'Chris Woods kept us in the game that day with some brilliant saves and he was only a kid.'

'With all the experienced players cup-tied and Chris Woods in goal, he did very, very well at seventeen or eighteen or whatever he was. Nobody gave us much of a chance really,' recalls Viv Anderson. 'Liverpool were household names and we were up against the best team around at the time. They were the team to beat.'

'John Robertson was brilliant, you could give the ball to him and he would give it you back. He could beat players. He could pass it with either foot. It surprised me when a lot of people thought he was left footed, but he's right footed. Look at him take a penalty – it's always his right foot. I thought he was two footed. He wasn't the quickest on the block, but he was quick over a couple of yards and a really intelligent footballer.'
– Colin Barrett

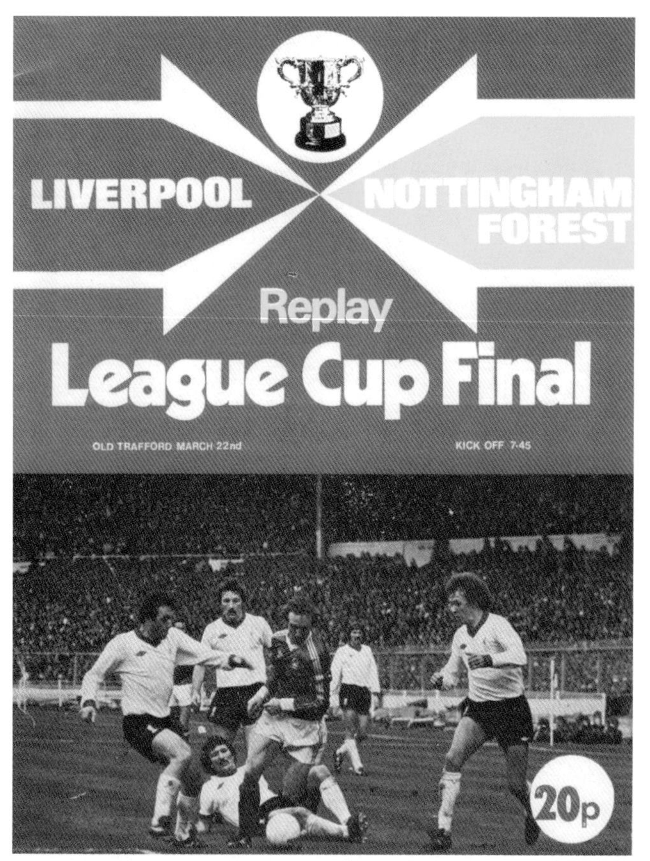

Manchester United F.C. Ltd.
FOOTBALL LEAGUE CUP FINAL
REPLAY
at OLD TRAFFORD
LIVERPOOL
v.
NOTTINGHAM FOREST
WEDNESDAY, 22nd March, 1978
Kick-off 7.45 p.m.
Secretary
Issued subject to the Rules, Regulations and Bye-Laws of the Football Association.
No Ticket exchanged nor money returned.
This portion to be retained

PADDOCK
UNITED ROAD
Nº 3900
Admission
£1-50
As a capacity attendance is expected, it is strongly recommended that patrons ENTER THE GROUND not less than 30 minutes before kick-off.

With replays, rather than penalty kicks, being used to settle cup ties in the late 1970s, the two teams prepared to meet again at Old Trafford four days later. The previous year's final had required two replays before Aston Villa managed to beat Everton.

Forest had been due to play a league game at Middlesbrough on the Tuesday, and a training trip to Scarborough had been pencilled in to prepare for this. With the advent of the replay, the league game was cancelled but the trip to Scarborough was kept, as preparation for the replay instead. John McGovern's groin problem ruled him out of the game, so the Forest team that had finished the game at Wembley started the one at Old Trafford. 'At Wembley John McGovern was captain and he got injured,' explains Kenny Burns. 'Larry [Lloyd] took it upon himself to be captain and he went up for the toss up for extra time. When it came to the replay everyone was thinking it would be Larry but the gaffer says, "Hey Burnsey", well he didn't call me Burnsey he called me Kenneth. He says, "Kenneth," he threw the ball at me and then said, "take them out." So it must have annoyed Larry, if it was the other way it would have annoyed me; but it was a great honour.'

Pat Partridge was again in charge and would soon become the centre of attention. The first half was relatively quiet as both teams seemed quite tense, aware that one mistake could make the difference. Forest wore the same yellow away kits that they had on the last trip to Old Trafford when they'd humbled Manchester United. Peter Withe had Forest's best chance: he beat Ray Clemence to a cross but his header drifted wide of the gaping net. Phil Neal's cross-shot was Liverpool's best effort but Woods got his hand to it. Still no goals after 165 minutes.

Early in the second half Liverpool were buzzing around the Forest goal, as Chris Woods

recalls: 'Someone cut in inside and hit across to my right hand side. It was one of those where you make a save and you think Is that an opening for us to go down and score at the other end? I mean its amazing how many times throughout my career I pulled off a really good save and then we've gone down the other end and scored.'

In the fifty-second minute, Frank Clark's long ball from left-back was nodded down by Withe to Woodcock, who fed a streaking John O'Hare as he made an intelligent run down the middle towards the edge of Liverpool's penalty area. The swiftness of the move caught Phil Thompson off balance and he was a half step behind as the Forest forward moved in one on one with Ray Clemence to shoot. Just as he pulled his foot back Thompson brought him down and he fell inside the area. Then all hell broke loose. The linesman had indicated a penalty. Pat Partridge later said he knew it was a foul and just needed confirmation from his linesman of where it had taken place. Liverpool players surrounded Partridge and it was a good few minutes before Robertson stepped up and beat Clemence low to the keepers right-hand side.

'Phil Thomson hacked John O'Hare down well inside the box and Robbo didn't usually miss from twelve yards,' says Kenny Burns. Afterwards Thompson tried to say that he had committed the foul outside the box. 'There was no way I could get to him and John O'Hare would of scored and I had to kick him.' In today's game he would also have been given a straight red card for the cynical nature of the foul.

'I've never dived in my life,' says O'Hare. 'A lot of people still remember it. At the time I didn't know if was a penalty or not; I think it was deserving of a penalty because it was a clear enough foul and I couldn't help but fall in the box. Years later I went to Liverpool when I was scouting for Martin [O'Neill] at Leicester City and I didn't have an official parking pass but I went up to the guy at the gate and said, "John O'Hare, Leicester City, can you give me an idea about a good place to park?" and the guy said, "You can f*** off, we don't like you here!" and that was over fifteen years later!' Would O'Hare have scored anyway if Thompson hadn't hacked him down? 'I would have liked to have thought so,' he laughs, 'but we'll never know about that will we?'

The game became more open for the last half hour as Liverpool pushed forward and left some gaps at the back. Robertson found some room at last for the first time in the two games and almost sealed it with a curling shot from the edge of the area that Clemence just managed to get a hand to and tip over. At the other end Woods made saves from Dalglish and Kennedy before being beaten by

McDermott. However the whistle had already gone for hand ball by the Liverpool midfielder, and the goal was disallowed.

'In the stand there was Peter Shilton, Archie Gemmill, myself, David Needham and Colin Barrett,' recalls John McGovern. 'We absolutely hit the rafters when the final whistle went, it was kind of a race to get down to the dressing room and join in the celebrations. Kenny received the cup; he was delighted to be the first one of us to get a major trophy. Like all games, some decisions go your way and some don't. I think that they must have known that, over the two games, with five of us sat in the stand we deserved to win. If you'd taken out five of their players, they would have been the underdogs. Because it was midweek and we had a game on the Saturday the celebrations were short-lived. We didn't really get elaborate with the celebrations. We were always reminded by the manager that we could celebrate in May, when the season finished.'

Left to right: O'Hare, Woodcock, O'Neill, Robertson and Lloyd celebrate at Old Trafford.

Kenny Burns collected the cup on the pitch and led Forest on a lap of honour. No matter what else the season would bring, they had already qualified for the UEFA Cup. 'It was a bit sweeter being against one of my old teams.' says Larry Lloyd, 'although I've always had a reasonable relationship with all the fans that I've played for because I was sort of a "fan's man" if you want. So I was lucky in that way, I didn't take too much stick from them. But it was sweet, yes.'

In a strange twist of fate this proved to be the last game Chris Woods ever played for Forest. At the end of the following season he moved to Queens Park Ranger's and went on to have a successful career with Everton and Glasgow Rangers as well as winning many England caps. 'When my contract was up they wanted me to stay,' says Woods, 'but I just said I wanted to play first team football and obviously they couldn't give me that opportunity with Peter Shilton in the team.' He left a great little legacy at Forest though and was a key member of the team that brought the first major trophy to the City Ground for twenty years. He'd also faced one of the most explosive attacking forces in Europe and kept them out for 210 minutes, not a bad record to be remembered by.

Souvenir brochures (*left*) were printed and an LP featuring commentary of the games was released (*below*), but this was just the tip of the iceberg as far as Forest were concerned. They would have bigger games to contend with over the next few years and the rivalry with Liverpool would continue in the league as well as presenting the two teams with new battles to fight in no less than three major cup competitions in the next two years.

First Division Table – Top 5	Pld	Pts	GD
FOREST	**32**	**50**	**+39**
Everton	35	48	+27
Arsenal	35	44	+22
Manchester City	34	43	+17
Coventry City	34	42	+16

(*after games of March 25th 1978*)

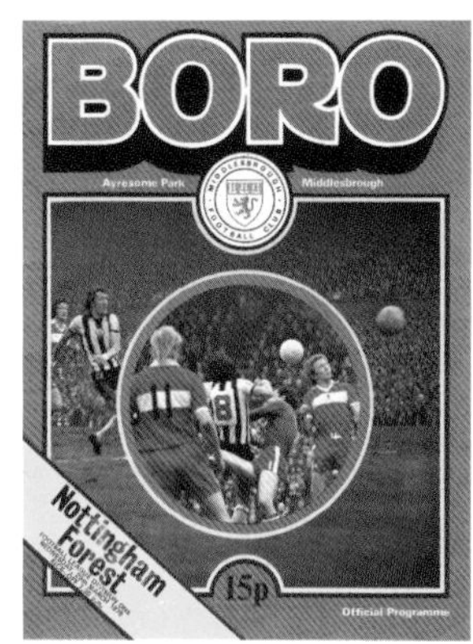

Clough and Taylor made sure that the players were soon concentrating on the bread and butter of the league campaign. Forest had twelve games left, but seven of the last ten would be away from home, with a potentially vital last match of the season at Anfield. Because of postponements and cup commitments Forest had two games in hand over the chasing pack and both were against north-east opposition. The first was a home game against Newcastle United; a healthy 35,552 turned out in pouring rain to greet the newly crowned League Cup winners, quite a good turn out considering that large parts of the ground weren't under cover. The conditions weren't really conducive to flowing football, but Forest got a break in the first half when Alan Kennedy knocked over Tony Woodcock and John Robertson converted the spot kick. Newcastle were involved in a relegation battle and pushed the Reds all the way. Peter Shilton was called upon to make two wonder saves after which the Newcastle player's heads visibly dropped. Forest gradually regained control in the second half and after sixty-seven minutes Viv Anderson scored when he was the first to react after Archie Gemmill's shot hit the bar. A midweek trip to Middlesbrough for the rearranged game brought a 2-2 draw leaving Forest in a healthy position going into the last ten games.

Teams were now coming to the City Ground and playing for a draw, making it harder to break them down. Chelsea managed to stay into the game until late on before Forest pulled away for a 3-1 win, capped by John Robertson (*pictured right*). Despite being the most important run of league games in the club's history, Brian Clough found time to take a full strength team to play a testimonial for Henry Newton at Derby. 'Clough was very generous to causes, like testimonials,' says John McGovern. 'He wouldn't take half the reserves, he took the whole side. He'd say, "We're going as Nottingham Forest Football Club." We thought we were mollycoddled but compared to the modern players where teams have squads of about thiry-five and half the players are left out for big chunks of the season, how they can get tired I don't know. It's a fallacy that players can get tired in the modern game, because of the better surfaces they play on, the boots are lighter, the ball is lighter, they train harder so they're supposed to be fitter; how they can get tired, I don't know. They don't play in six inches of mud like we used to. If they played in that they might need squads of sixty! Being tired is just an excuse that modern managers use like they use referees as an excuse. Clough was very big on that – "How many mistakes have you made today? You've made four mistakes and the referee only made three, so he's doing his job better than you!" It's just common sense. We weren't allowed to talk back to referees we weren't allowed to argue with them, and there was quite a lot of respect between players and referees. If you did speak back, even if you weren't booked Clough would fine you.'

A tight 1-0 win at Aston Villa (on the same night that Everton lost at home to Liverpool) followed and then a 0-0 draw at Manchester City ended the home side's last lingering hopes of the title. Almost forty thousand crammed into the City Ground in the spring sunshine when Leeds visited for the clubs' fourth meeting of the season. Again Forest seemed nervous, and a Frank Gray penalty gave the visitors a half-time lead. The second half saw a better Forest performance and Peter Withe broke his goal drought in the league (one League goal in twenty-five matches!). If Forest were sick of playing Leeds they must have been even more tired of seeing Queen's Park Rangers. On 18 April they visited the City Ground for the teams' fifth game of the season. Forest were right on the verge of being crowned champions for the first time and put in another nervous display which required a Robertson penalty to gain both points.

First Division Table – Top

	Pld	Pts	GD
FOREST	**37**	**58**	**+44**
Everton	39	52	+27
Arsenal	38	48	+24
Liverpool	37	48	+21
Manchester City	37	46	+22
Coventry City	39	46	+15

(after games of April 15th 1978)

That penalty was almost as important as the one that won the League Cup. The Reds could now only be topped by Liverpool on goal difference, and Forest's was twenty-three goals better off with five games to go. One more point would make it mathematically certain. In light of this the club announced that a testimonial would be arranged for Brian Clough and Peter Taylor even though they'd only been at Forest for three years.

20 Football Post, Saturday, April 22, 1978

KEEPER IN GREAT FORM

Reds' title thanks to Shilton

JOHN LAWSON at Highfield Road

A BREATH-TAKING save by Peter Shilton finally tipped the First Division title conclusively Nottingham Forest's way in an absorbing tussle with Coventry here this

SCOTTISH
(Premier Division)

Aberdeen.. 4 St Mirren. 2
Half-time: 1—2
Ayr .... 2 Hibernian. (
Half-time: 1—0
Celtic....... 5 Partick T. :
Half-time: 3—0
Motherwell 0 Clydebank 1
Half-time: 0—0
Rangers.... 3 Dundee U. (

The first chance Forest had to gain that elusive point was on 22 April at Coventry. *Match of the Day* sent their cameras to see Forest fight a rearguard action for much of the game. The Reds were again under strength with Lloyd suspended and McGovern and Woodcock injured. 'It was a red hot day,' recalls Frank Clark, who also missed the game. 'The management made everyone have a [alcoholic] drink, which is the worst thing you can do for dehydration, but he thought it was a good idea. We were very poor on the day; Peter Shilton played out of his skin that day.' Shilton made two amazing saves from City's striker Ian Ferguson to preserve the draw. The most memorable one came when diminutive Scotsman Ian Wallace hooked over a cross from the right corner of the six-yard box. Shilton was covering his near post and as the ball floated across to Ferguson at the far post he seemed to have an empty net to place his powerful header into, but Shilton appeared from nowhere and palmed it over for a corner. Forest finished the season with a whopping twenty-five clean sheets in the forty-two League games.

The massive away following stayed behind long after the final whistle as masses of red and white scarves were held aloft, flags and home made banners waved. FOREST ARE MAGIC said one, WE'RE PROUD OF YOU was written on another; and sprayed on what looked like someone's bedsheet was the simple message CHAMP-IONS. Brian Clough became only the second manager to win the title with two different clubs (Herbert Chapman had been the last one to do it with Huddersfield and Arsenal between the First and Second World Wars).

FOREST
v. BIRMINGHAM CITY
Football League
Division One
Volume 10, Number 30
Saturday
29th April 1978
Kick-off 3 p.m.
OFFICIAL MATCH-DAY MAGAZINE
PRICE 15p

Back in 1974 Clough and Don Revie had famously clashed on national TV, after Clough had ended his forty-four day stint at Leeds. Revie attempted to grill him about why he'd gone to Leeds after attacking them in the press so much beforehand. 'I want to win the league,' Clough had said, 'but I want to win it better than you – and there's no reply to that!' Revie was having none of it: 'You can't win it better, oh no, no, no, no, no, no - we only lost four matches!' Well, it had taken a few more years but Clough had now won it and lost only three!

'You wouldn't believe this, would you, but I missed that one at Coventry,' says Larry Lloyd when asked about winning the title at his old club. 'I was sat in the stand again with my dodgy ankle,' he says. 'I remember seeing Jimmy Hill in the reception at Coventry afterwards and he was talking to somebody and saw me coming and he said words to the effect of "Oh, we spent a lot of money on him, didn't do anything and we give him away" and I said, "Oh, Jimmy I must thank you for that by the way. I should have written you a letter thanking you for letting me go so cheaply." He didn't like that!'

John McGovern also had to watch from the sidelines. 'I was sat on the bench,' he says, 'and when the final whistle went I shook Clough's hand and said, "congratulations." He said, "Thanks", but again there were no elaborate celebrations. I remember a press reporter knocking on the dressing room door and he couldn't understand why we weren't going mad, but the season wasn't over and it was a remarkably low-key celebration at Coventry when we won it. The following week we played Birmingham at home and I was declared fit and I thought, Kenny isn't getting his hands on this one; and I was presented with the championship before the game. I remember that the realization had sunk in to everyone and I think there was a little bit of shock that we'd done so well. I think the concentration throughout the season had been so high and then when we'd done what we set out to do it was strange because we still hadn't finished the season. It was a case of well, we should really be celebrating like mad but we couldn't. I think it was a credit to everyone's professionalism at the club – especially the management.'

'If you're successful you're going to play a lot of games,' adds Archie Gemmill. 'I don't think any of the lads would say they were tired. If someone said at the start of the year that you're going to play seventy-five games you'd be delighted because it would mean you'd be there or thereabouts to winning trophies. We put in a very hard pre-season, then sometimes the gaffer would give us a day off in the week. It would be very interesting to see how current teams would fare against a Clough team and how they would cope.'

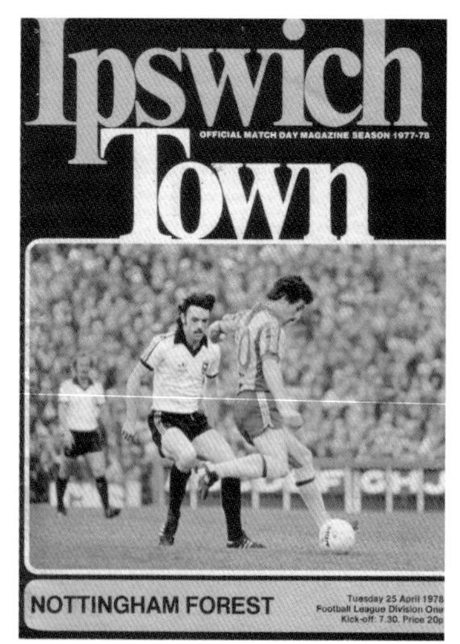

Before the official presentation of the trophy at home to Birmingham, Forest had a trip to Ipswich, who had beaten West Bromwich Albion in the FA Cup semi-final and were preparing to take on Arsenal at Wembley. Forest took the lead through a Paul Mariner own goal. Frank Clark takes up the story: 'It was a nothing game. We had won the title, I think Ipswich were in the cup final, so they weren't too bothered, it was a poor game. Clough could have pulled anyone off really, in those days of course you only had one sub, so he told Withey to get in the bath at half time. So, I'm getting warmed up and I'm looking at the team and I'm thinking, He's going to shuffle the team around a bit here, maybe put Ian Bowyer up front, Ian was playing left back that day. Everyone was looking at each other, the bell goes to go out and he still hadn't said anything and then he says, "Just go and play centre-forward, you can't do any worse than that big bugger in there!" Larry Lloyd started laughing, it was the only time I had heard anybody laugh really when he was trying to be serious. So the front two that day ended up being me and Archie Gemmill, I don't think there were any other strikers in the team, and we had a corner and it happened to drop at my feet in the six-yard box and bang, I scored! Peter Taylor went to see Bobby Robson [Ipswich's manager] to get the ball for me after the game, Bobby wouldn't believe him that I'd played five hundred games and never scored a goal.'

The next home game, versus Birmingham, saw the championship trophy presented on the pitch before the game. 'People used to say, "You don't smile much when you collect a trophy,"' says John McGovern. 'Whenever I received a trophy my thoughts always went to my dad and I'd wish he could have been here to see me achieve this. He'd never even seen me play football. I was delighted for my mum, I knew she'd be watching on television. But that's why I perhaps didn't show as much emotion as other people it was just a very personal thing.'

The season was completed undefeated with two away draws at West Bromwich Albion (2-2) and Liverpool (0-0). The latter saw Kenny Burns miss the game as Clough allowed him to travel to London to collect his sports writer's Player of the Year award. 'Clough tried to change the match to get the kick off early,' says Burns. 'It was the only game I missed that season. Our chairman was there, Brian Appleby QC, he was the main speaker and Billy Connolly was a speaker as well.' Burns was also the Forest fans Player of the Year. As well as winning two of the three major domestic team trophies Forest cleaned up on the individual front as well. In the PFA awards Peter Shilton and John Robertson were named in the First Division Team of the Year. The Player's Player of the Year also went to Shilton (with Archie Gemmill being the runner-up). Tony Woodcock was presented with the Young Player of the Year award and not surprisingly Brian Clough was the Manager of the Year.

One thing that hadn't been planned for at the season's start was actually winning the league. 'We never thought we were going to do it, you're promoted and we thought Well if we can stay in this division or towards to top half of this division we'll have done really well,' says Colin Barrett. 'To go and win it out right straight off – it was a shock and I think the whole of Nottingham thought it was a shock to be honest. I think a lot of things in that period of time happened too quickly for everybody and it's only ten years down the line you think, Hold on a minute what a good team that was. It just happened too quick"

'The bonus system that the management wanted us to have was based on our position in the league,' says John McGovern. 'There was no bonus for winning the championship because there was nothing in the contract relating to that, something which people might find incredible now, but the expectation wasn't there that you would waltz into the First Division and win the championship by seven points!'

'When we got promoted they came round with the bonus sheet and on the bonus page we never even bothered looking at it. In terms of "To win the League you get x amount of pounds" – there wasn't anything like that, so we never got a penny for winning the League. Clough said, "I'm not paying you for failure. I'll only pay you if we're in the top six. Bottom six you'll get nothing, top six you'll get bonuses." That's how it worked.'

With Forest now qualified for the European Cup, the whole country was starting to take notice of them. All year long Forest had had to fight against the doubters in the national press. First it was that they were an 'early-season fluke' after the good start; then some said, 'I told you so' after the loss at Arsenal. Then came 'You haven't played the big boys yet' before they went unbeaten against Everton, Liverpool and Manchester City; then it was 'Winter will sort them out' before they beat all comers on the muddy City Ground pitch. The cry of 'Three competitions will be a

distraction' didn't ring true either as Forest won two of them and only lost in the quarter-finals of the other when key players were injured. Eventually the press had to eat their own words. On *Sportsnight* Brian Clough said to John Motson: 'We go out to win every match. We go out to entertain the public. We go out to make people want to come to football matches. We play with discipline. And one day John, you and your profession might just recognize that we are a good side!'

A large part of the success could be put down to the close relationship that the players built up. 'We went for a chip butty and a cup of tea and talked about things and I think that helped tremendously,' says Larry Lloyd. 'The players did everything together en masse and that galvanized the team spirit and we all respected each other,' adds John McGovern. 'I think in those days there was a lot more pride than there is now. Also a lot of players were on appearance money so if you don't play you don't get that money. All the players we had had great footballing brains but you had no idea about the financial state of the club, you didn't know what the guy next to you was earning, but now everyone knows what everyone else is on. I don't think that's right, it should be a private contract between the player and the club. But it didn't bother me what I earned as long as I was in the side. We were strong at the back, we had a great goalkeeper, we had a bit of everything. Good running power, craft, pace, skill and we were all good mates as well, which helped. There was a great team spirit among us all socially as well as at work that whenever we had a night out nearly everybody came.'

On top of the great skill and commitment in the side, the strong team spirit and the mental toughness, the icing on the cake was the best management duo in the country. 'We're brothers,' said Peter Taylor at the time. 'Together we can have success quicker than individually.' Many of the players remember that Clough and Taylor could act like a good cop, bad cop routine, but the catch was that you didn't know from day to day which one would be the good one and which the bad. There was always a lot of humour around, more often than not coming from the mouth of Taylor. 'Clough loved Taylor, he really did,' says Martin O'Neill. 'He understood him, he could be annoyed by him really quickly but he knew that the two of them together were very good for each other.'

'We were so engrossed with the goings on week to week,' says Brian Clough 'and the excitement building up that you never really sat down at any particular time and said, "Well this is going to be it." We knew were in with a chance right from the time we went to the top. We knew we were full of ourselves. We knew ourselves; it was the other people who didn't know. We knew we were on the same wavelength. Some idiot journalist said that "Cloughie rules by fear" and I took exception to that because nobody rules anything by fear. You can't perform if you're frightened and our lads went free as birds, free as butterflies. Fear never entered their heads. They'd never been in a position where they were experienced enough to be frightened. You've only got to be experienced to be frightened. Then another idiot said we were lucky - I took exception to that as well. You know you can be lucky once, twice, three times, four times. You certainly can't be lucky forty-two times!'

'At the end of that season,' recalls Ian Bowyer, 'after Liverpool won the European Cup at Wembley. Bob Paisley said after the game that, "Forest will be our biggest threat to retaining it next season."' How right he was!

First Division, Final Table 1977-78

	Pld	W	D	L	F	A	Pts
FOREST	**42**	**25**	**14**	**3**	**69**	**24**	**64**
Liverpool	42	24	9	9	65	34	57
Everton	42	22	11	9	76	45	55
Manchester City	42	20	12	10	74	51	52
Arsenal	42	21	10	11	62	53	52
West Bromwich Albion	42	18	14	10	62	53	50
Coventry City	42	18	12	12	75	62	48
Aston Villa	42	18	10	14	57	42	46
Leeds United	42	18	10	14	63	53	46
Manchester United	42	16	10	16	67	63	46
Birmingham City	42	16	9	17	55	60	42
Derby County	42	14	13	15	54	59	41
Norwich City	42	11	18	13	52	66	41
Middlesbrough	42	12	15	15	42	54	40
Wolverhampton W.	42	12	12	18	51	64	39
Chelsea	42	11	14	17	46	69	36
Bristol City	42	11	13	18	49	53	36
Ipswich Town	42	11	13	18	47	61	35
Queens Park Rangers	42	9	15	18	47	64	35
West Ham United	42	12	8	22	52	69	33
Newcastle United	42	6	10	26	42	78	32
Leicester City	42	5	12	25	26	70	22

August 1977				
1	St. Gallen, Switzerland	A	3-2	PSF
3	Wacker Innsbruck, Austria	A	2-0	PSF
5	S.V. Platting, West Germany	A	5-1	PSF
6	Neuburg, West Germany	A	5-1	PSF
9	S.W. Bregenz, Austria	A	3-0	PSF
13	Skegness Town	A	4-0	PSF
15	Notts County	H	1-1	CCF*
20	Everton	A	3-1	
23	Bristol City	H	1-0	
27	Derby County	H	3-0	
30	West Ham United	H	5-0	LC2
September				
3	Arsenal	A	0-3	
10	Wolverhampton W	A	3-2	
12	Leicester City	H	0-0	F*2
17	Aston Villa	H	2-0	
24	Leicester City	A	3-0	
October				
1	Norwich City	H	1-1	
4	Ipswich Town	H	4-0	
8	West Ham United	A	0-0	
15	Manchester City	H	2-1	
17	Sheffield United	A	6-1	F*3
22	Queen's Park Rangers	A	2-0	
25	Notts County	H	4-0	LC3
29	Middlesborough	H	4-0	
November				
5	Chelsea	A	0-1	
12	Manchester United	H	2-1	
14	Hartlepool United	A	2-2	F
19	Leeds United	A	0-1	
22	Maccabi Tel Aviv	A	6-1	F
26	West Bromwich Albion	H	0-0	
29	Aston Villa	H	4-2	LC4
December				
3	Birmingham City	A	2-0	
10	Coventry City	H	2-0	
17	Manchester United	A	4-0	
26	Liverpool	H	1-1	
28	Newcastle United	A	2-0	
31	Bristol City	A	3-1	
January 1978				
2	Everton	H	1-1	
7	Swindon Town	H	4-1	FAC3
14	Derby County	A	0-0	
17	Bury	A	3-0	LCR5
21	Arsenal	H	2-0	
24	Manchester City	H	2-1	FAC4

February

4	Wolverhampton W	H	2-0	
8	Leeds United	A	3-1	LCSF1
18	Queen's Park Rangers	A	1-1	FAC5
22	Leeds United	H	4-2	LCSF2
25	Norwich City	A	3-3	
27	Queen's Park Rangers	H	1-1	FAC5R

March

2	Queen's Park Rangers	H	3-1	FAC5R2
4	West Ham United	H	2-0	
11	West Bromwich Albion	A	0-2	FAC6
14	Leicester City	H	1-0	
18	Liverpool	N	0-0	LCF*4
22	Liverpool	N	1-0	LCFR*5
25	Newcastle United	H	2-0	
29	Middlesborough	A	2-2	

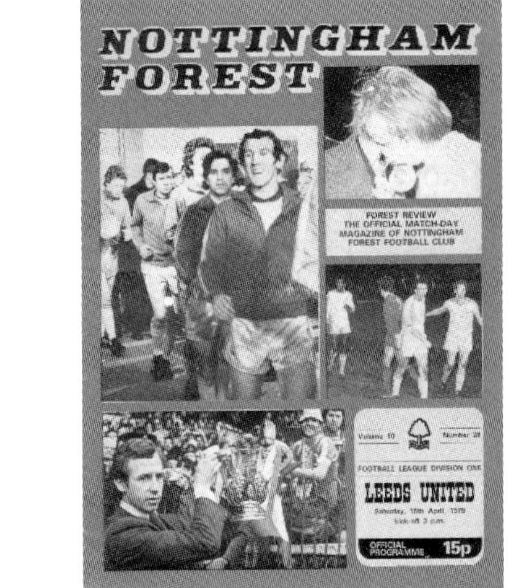

April

1	Chelsea	H	3-1	
3	Derby County	A	2-1	F*6
5	Aston Villa	A	1-0	
11	Manchester City	A	0-0	
12	Notts County	A	1-0	F*7
15	Leeds United	H	1-1	
18	Queen's Park Rangers	H	1-0	
22	Coventry City	A	0-0	
25	Ipswich Town	A	2-0	
29	Birmingham City	H	0-0	

May

1	Derby County	H	2-1	F*8
2	West Bromwich Albion	A	2-2	
4	Liverpool	A	0-0	

	Pld	W	D	L	F	A	PTS	GD
Home	32	23	9	0	67	17	55	+50
Away	38	23	11	4	79	30	57	+49
League	42	25	14	3	69	24	64	+45
League Cup	8	7	1	0	24	5	15	+19
FA Cup	6	3	2	1	11	7	8	+4
County Cup	1	0	1	0	1	1	1	0
Friendlies	13	11	2	0	41	10	24	+31
Total	**70**	**46**	**20**	**4**	**146**	**47**	**112**	**+99**

* = won 3-2 on penalties. For the 1976-77 season
*2 = Liam O'Kane Testimonial
*3 = John Harris Testimonial
*4 = at Wembley
*5 = at Old Trafford
*6 = Henry Newton Testimonial
*7 = Les Bradd Testimonial
*8 = Brian Clough and Peter Taylor Testimonial

1977-78 Player Statistics

	Lge	FAC	LCup	CC	F	Totals
John Robertson	42-12	6-3	8-3	1	11-4	68-22
Kenny Burns	41-4	6	8	1	11-2	67-6
Peter Withe	40-12	6-2	8-5	1	7-6	62-25
Martin O'Neill	38(2)-8	6-2	8-3	1	7(1)-2	60(3)-15
Tony Woodcock	36-11	6-4	8-4	1	9-8	60-27
Viv Anderson	37-3	5	8-1	1	9-1	60-5
John McGovern	31-4	4	7	1	9-2	52-6
Peter Shilton	37	6	0	0	5	48
Ian Bowyer	25(3)-4	3	8-6	1-1	7(1)-4	44(4)-15
Larry Lloyd	26-1	2	6-1	1	8-2	43-4
Archie Gemmill	30(2)-3	4	0	0	5	39(2)-3
Colin Barrett	31(2)-1	3	5	0	9(1)-1	38(3)-2
Frank Clark	12(1)-1	3	4	1	6	26(1)-1
Dave Needham	16-4	6	0	0	2	24-4
John Middleton	5	0	1	1	7	14
John O'Hare	10	(1)	2(1)-1	0	1(2)-2	13(4)-3
Chris Woods	0	0	7	0	(1)	7(1)
Terry Curran	0	0	0	0	5	5
Steve Elliott	0	0	0	0	4(1)-5	4(1)-5
Garry Birtles	0	0	0	0	2(1)-1	2(1)-1
Bryn Gunn	0	0	0	0	2(1)	2(1)
Sean Haselgrave	0	0	0	0	2(1)	2(1)

Also played once in friendlies: Duncan Mackenzie, Liam O'Kane, Colin Todd

The 1978 - 79 Season

The 1978-79 season was played through the 'Winter of Discontent'. As the Labour government struggled against a rising tide of industrial unrest, the Conservative party pounced on the turmoil and forged ahead to a General Election win which gave the country its first female prime minister, Margaret Thatcher, in May 1979.

Forest's preparation for the season was more evident in the work being done at the City Ground rather than in any transfer market activity. The Bridgford End was revamped, with new exit staircases and relaid terracing; the East Stand was also reterraced and a new state-of-the-art electronic scoreboard was installed. The new capacity was a reduced 41,930, but this would still be ample for the coming season even though the attendance figures had risen greatly over the last two seasons. Over a million people had attended home games for first time at City Ground in the championship season. Crowds had been swarming over Trent Bridge ever since Brian Clough had taken charge. From an average of around eight thousand, Clough had helped to drive attendances up to an average of almost thirteen in 1975-76, then further to eighteen thousand in 1976-77 and finally to 32,500 in the championship year. An increase of over 400 per cent in three seasons!

The summer of 1978 had seen the World Cup played out in Argentina and two Forest players – Archie Gemmill and Kenny Burns had played in it. 'I had good time in Argentina,' recalls Kenny Burns. 'I played in the first two games and I always remember [manager] Ally McCloud saying, "I want you to play like you play with your teams." So we did that and Alan Rough, in the games against Iran and Peru, got beat about three times at the near post. It's a cardinal sin for a goalkeeper to get beat at the near post. Anyway Archie [Gemmill] comes in at the end of the match, I think it was the Iran game, and he says, "Hey boss he never plays like that at Forest." Anyway I was dropped for the third game and Archie played in the third game, when he scored that great goal against Holland and I thought Thanks you little so-and-so! One thing I remember about Argentina was we when arrived in Cordoba. The officials were in the first bus, the team and coaching staff were in the second bus and we were coming up this hill and everybody was out waving Scottish flags to welcome us. The clutch went on the first coach, and the second coach had to push it up the hill. It was like arriving on Fred's Tours or something!'

Despite a loss and a draw in the opening two games, Scotland had a chance to progress from the initial group stage if they could beat Holland by three goals. They managed to get a 2-1 lead and then Archie Gemmill scored a memorable solo effort for a 3-1 lead and a chance of getting through until a late Dutch goal pulled the final score back to 3-2. Again Scotland were on an early plane home. By the end of the 1978-79 season the Forest squad had nine full and B internationals in its ranks – Shilton, Burns, Lloyd, Gemmill, Robertson, Woodcock, Anderson, Needham and O'Neill.

For the first time in several years Forest didn't have a pre-season camp in Augsburg, but followed up the initial fitness training in Nottingham with a tour of Yugoslavia and Greece. Unlike the previous summers the opposition was all against First Division teams; there was no chance of running up the score against relatively easy opposition this time. Frank Clark recalls the tough opening game against Red Star Belgrade: 'I was on the bench and they had this big defender who picked the ball up forty yards out and was lining up a shot. With Shilton in goal I thought Go on hit it (you've got no chance) and then *whoosh* it flew into the top corner!' Forest lost that game 3-2 and followed it up with three 1-1 draws, the last one being in Athens against AEK. 'I came back early,' continues Clark. 'One of my daughters had to go in to hospital. I flew to Athens, but then flew back myself to England. I remember the taxi ride to the airport was the most frightening experience of my life!' In retrospect Peter Taylor admitted that the preparation for the new season was a mistake. 'All our opponents wanted to beat the English Champions,' he said. 'It was as if every match was a cup tie instead of a good work out.'

The club had ten days back in England before the Charity Shield match against Ipswich Town at Wembley. The traditional curtain raiser for the season where the league champions play the FA Cup winners.

Bobby Robson's Ipswich team had won the FA Cup with an upset 1-0 win over Arsenal and despite Forest's slow start to the season, they were no match for the Reds. Brian Clough led the team out; again the league didn't allow Peter Taylor to join him. Taylor admitted he was so upset that he didn't even go to the game. Instead he went to see Bolton and Oldham battle out a 0-0 draw in the Anglo-Scottish Cup.

Forest pushed forward from the start. Mick Mills gave the ball away at edge of his own area, and after a scramble it fell to Martin O'Neill, who buried it to give Forest the lead (*pictured below*). This lead was doubled after Colin Barrett's header into the Town box was run on to by Peter With, who looped a header over the stranded goalkeeper Paul Cooper. No one knew it would be Withe's last competitive goal for Forest. 'I really enjoyed myself' says Colin Barrett. 'It was my first time at Wembley and I thought, Well this is it, I've fulfilled one of my ambitions. In those days the only time you could play at Wembley were League Cup Final, FA Cup Final, Charity Shield or for England, so your chances were slim, but these days they'll play any Mickey Mouse tournament at Wembley. So the chances of playing at Wembley each year were less and less, I thought, I'm not going to do it, and then I finally played in the Charity Shield.' The Reds put the game

beyond reach with in seconds of the second half kicking off. 'The only thing that disappoints me is that my goal was seconds into the second half and a lot of people were still coming back to their seats' laughs Larry Lloyd. 'It was a free-kick out on the left. Robbo took it, Peter Withe got there first, I shouted. "Leave it!" He jumped over it and I just volleyed it in. I do remember it very well, I didn't score that many.'

Peter Withe celebrates his Wembley goal.

Bobby Robson takes defeat on the chin.

The game turned into a rout when Martin O'Neill scored his second from another Robertson cross. Soon afterwards Brian Clough turned to Jimmy Gordon on the bench and said, 'If he doesn't lay it off next time he gets the ball, he's off.' Gordon thought Clough was joking – after all O'Neill was on a hat-trick – but sure enough when he didn't lay it off the next time he was in possession, Clough pulled the winger off and replaced him with David Needham. The scoring was completed by John Robertson with a beautifully crafted goal in the last seconds. It was no more than he deserved after tormenting the Ipswich defence all afternoon. The performance, and scoreline (which equalled the biggest ever win in the competition), sent out a chilling message to the rest of the First Division that Forest were not one season wonders.

Although the league season was due to start the following Saturday, Forest's pre-season games were far from over. The day after the Charity Shield, they flew out from Heathrow to a four team tournament in Spain, hosted by Celta Vigo. Forest's opening game was a 1-1 draw with the hosts on the Monday night. Larry Lloyd limped off after twenty-five minutes and would miss the first seven games of the season. His replacement, David Needham helped Forest get a last minute equalizer when his header came back off the bar for Peter Withe to score. Forest eventually lost 4-3 on penalties. Two days later they played a third/fourth place play-off against the other losing semi-finalists, Porto. The Forest side saw a number of changes, including a run out for young reserve team striker Steve Elliott. The Reds went down 1-0 to late goal while Brazilian side Cruzeiro, the South American club champions won the final 2-1 versus the hosts.

Forest finally got home less than forty-eight hours before the season opener against newly promoted Tottenham Hotspur. Tottenham had been relegated the year that Forest were promoted, and only slipped back into the top flight on goal difference ahead of Brighton & Hove Albion. They had immediately strengthened their ranks, though, and made the summer's biggest transfer coup. Argentina's World Cup triumph had given everyone a boost with the skilful attacking football they displayed in sweeping to the championship (ignoring the fact that they fixed a match against Peru) with the likes of Mario Kempes and Daniel Passarella leading the way. Spurs manager Keith Burkinshaw (who had been a team mate of Frank Clark at Newcastle four years earlier) was caught up in Argentina-fever and swooped to sign two of the World Cup winning squad for a combined £750,000. Ricardo Villa and Osvaldo Ardiles opened the door to overseas footballers coming to England and their league debut at the City Ground was eagerly anticipated. The away fans' enclosure on the Bridgford End had a capacity of three-thousand, but an estimated nine-thousand visiting fans crammed into the 41,223 crowd and gave their new stars a traditional Argentinean tickertape welcome. The ground now had steel fences all around the sides to prevent anyone getting on to the pitch, but these didn't stop the away fans fighting with the home ones. Ugly scenes were witnessed before, during and after the game. On the pitch Forest took a first half lead through Martin O'Neill and Peter Withe hit the bar, but Ricardo Villa squared the match and Forest had to be content with a point.

After the Spurs match the news broke that Peter Withe had put in a transfer request before the game. He'd been a key member of the team for two years, had formed a formidable partnership with Tony Woodcock and had top scored in both the promotion and championship seasons. The initial problem had been a dispute between Withe and the management over a new contract, but now the big forward had escalated the situation by handing in a transfer request. Of course Clough and Taylor were never going to be held to ransom by anyone and they shopped Withe's name around right away. Newcastle manager Bill McGarry was looking to prepare a promotion challenge back to the First Division after being relegated in May 1978 and had worked with Withe at Wolves in the mid-1970s; he put in a £250,000 offer which Forest accepted. When Withe realized that perhaps he had gone too far he asked to be taken off the list but it was too late. Within days he was gone. Clough pointed out that the club had made a profit of £208,000 on the player and had two great year's service from him. He'd also only scored two goals in his last thirty league appearances. The problem was that the only other striker at the club, Steve Elliott, was untried at first team level. Elliott made his debut at Highfield Road and was unlucky with a shot that came back off the post; but like the championship clinching game a few months earlier, it ended 0-0. Two more away games followed, giving two more 0-0 draws, one at Queen's Park Rangers and one in the League Cup at Second Division Oldham Athletic. Though Elliott (*pictured below*) was struggling to find the net, he wasn't alone. Tony Woodcock had just one goal in fourteen matches stretching back to the end of the previous season. The next game at home to West Bromwich Albion was yet another 0-0, but this time it was case of hanging on for a draw rather than missing a series of good chances as had been the case in earlier games. Albion caused problems all afternoon, especially the wing play of Laurie Cunningham, and Shilton had to make a point blank save from Ally Brown right at the death to preserve the point. It was the first game of the season that the West Midlanders hadn't won and they would stay in the top five all season long. Forest had now drawn their first four league games and scored just one goal.

The indifferent start to the campaign was reflected in the attendance for the Oldham replay at the City Ground – fewer than nineteen thousand paid to see the Reds finally hit goal-scoring form. When the goals came, though, it wasn't from the forwards. The two centre-halves David Needham and Kenny Burns both scored from corners early in the second half, and full-back Colin Barrett then finally set up Tony Woodcock to get his first competitive goal in five months, and a John Robertson penalty capped four goals in twenty minutes. A couple of late Athletic goals failed to change the outcome of the tie. For Steve Elliott it was the last chance to make his mark. Though he'd scored regularly for the reserves in the Central League he'd gone six games without a goal and the management decided it was time for a change.

'Peter Taylor secretly travelled to see me in a [Forest] reserve game,' says Garry Birtles. 'He paid to get in and hid himself away in his flat cap and he saw me do one thing, this drag-back that I used to do, and that convinced him to give me a chance in the first team.' Birtles had come to Forest from Long Eaton United back in 1975. 'I played for Long Eaton at Burton Albion,' Birtles recalls. 'We got beat 4-0 and Ian Storey-Moore was there scouting for Manchester United. Brian Clough heard about it and came to see me himself, because he didn't want United pinching someone out from under his nose. He said the half-time drink was better than my performance, but he gave me a trial.' He impressed enough in the trial to get a full-time contract but had played just once in the Second Division. He was currently in the reserves, playing as a midfielder. 'I hated it but it worked,' says Birtles. 'I was scoring goals from midfield.'

'I remember the first game of the season' says Frank Clark. 'I wasn't even in the squad, I was playing in the reserves, and at that time the reserves used to play on a Saturday afternoon as well as the first team. We played Sheffield Wednesday away with Garry Birtles in the team, and on the coach coming back Garry was absolutely down and distraught because he can't get a sniff [of the first team].'

'They had gone with Stevie Elliott and as luck would have it, for Garry not for Stevie, he couldn't get a goal for the team. The team wasn't scoring goals and really they stuck Birtles in out of emergency, they had to try something. They stuck him in and never looked back.'

Birtles' First Division debut came at home to Arsenal. 'I was petrified' he admits. The Gunners included big names like Frank Stapleton, Liam Brady and David O'Leary and provided a stern test as usual. Birtles wasn't the only new face though: Gary Mills was given a right-wing starting place at the age of just sixteen to become the youngest ever Forest player in a league game. Forest got a helping hand for their first League goal since the opening day when Steve Walford knocked Ian Bowyer down and John Robertson converted the penalty past Pat Jennings. Bowyer himself added a second and the Reds won 2-1. The relief at getting a league win was immense, and it came at just the right moment because the next game was Forest's debut in the world's greatest club competition: the European Champions Cup.

Tony Woodcock battles for possession with West Brom's Brendan Batson.

The draw for the European Cup had been made during the pre-season. Unlike the modern day competition it truly was the 'champion's' cup, with only one team from each country plus the holders being invited to play. There were thirty-two member countries, in the days before the USSR, Czechoslovakia and Yugoslavia broke into many different federations, and the holders made a total of thirty-three clubs, so a preliminary round was required before the first round proper. Club secretary Ken Smales and Peter Taylor flew out to Zurich for the draw and shared a plane with the representatives of Everton, Manchester City, West Bromwich Albion (all playing in the UEFA Cup) and of course Liverpool, who were the defending champions. After picking out the UEFA and Cup Winner's Cup draws, the main event was begun. 'We had visions of into going off into Europe, obviously,' says Brian Clough. 'Skegness was Europe to Nottingham Forest. We were going to somewhere where we might see the sea, and bloody Skeggy was the nearest one to Nottingham!' Ian Bowyer: 'We had our passports ready!', John McGovern: 'We were looking forward to going somewhere we hadn't been to before.' Larry Lloyd: 'We just wanted to stay away from Liverpool.' Liverpool were seeded in the draw, Forest were not. And sure enough the two were drawn together, with Forest being given the first leg at home. 'Some of us were playing golf at Wollaton Park' says Colin Barrett, 'and we got off the golf course and someone said we've drawn Liverpool. We all looked at each other and said, 'We can't draw Liverpool we're in Europe, that's incredible!'"

'We were deflated initially,' adds Archie Gemmill, 'but we had a good record against them so we were confident.' Kenny Burns adds: 'We got Liverpool, and I don't think we wanted them. We'd never been in Europe, not many of us had of played in Europe and we wanted to really go abroad and play. So we got Liverpool but we were champions and we were one team that could beat Liverpool. They didn't want us and to be fair we didn't mind them, but we didn't really want them.'

'I remember when I was told I was with Tony Woodcock in Barbados,' recalls John Robertson. 'Someone phoned us up and told us. I thought it was the worst possible draw and was thinking Well, what a great European run. But then of course we'd not lost to them in the four games we'd played with them. So we were reasonably confident but it was the worst possible draw you could have got and not even a trip to Europe.'

Brian Clough was typically unbothered by the draw 'If we have to meet them sometime – and we probably will – it may as well be now as later,' he said at the time.

The Liverpool tie immediately had ramifications for the players' bonus scheme that was traditionally agreed before the season started. Players would get a basic wage, a bonus for playing in the first team, a bonus for reaching a certain League position and bonuses for getting to certain rounds of the knockout competitions. The drawing of Liverpool suddenly meant that reaching the second round of the European Cup would be more difficult than might have been expected – and a bonus to reflect this was required. 'I had the job of negotiating bonuses,' says Brian Clough. 'In fact it's fair to say I did everything from A to Z at Forest. We had to discuss it and I sat down with them and I was conscious of the fact of how small a club we were. It was a small club when you could only draw twenty-odd thousand when you win leagues and get into semi-finals of European Cups and things like that. Manchester United were drawing the forties and the fifties at halfway up the First Division and we were having to play a month's worth of games to get their gate of one match. I said, "Come on, then its incentive time. Let's get thee in, let's get it worked out." We used to sit down, agree on everything all of us. I'd put my side, the club side as well, but I'd still got one foot in the player side and they put their side and we came up with a simple thing and it was all done in an hour. It was never a long drawn out negotiation. I put them on barely nothing for playing Liverpool in the first round of the European Cup and then put them on what was astronomical for the second round which was if we beat Liverpool - something like a thousand quid and there was groans round the boardroom table: "A thousand pounds if we beat Liverpool!" I said, "What are you cribbing at? We'll get two full gates. We'll get one full gate against Liverpool at our place. If we don't get through you don't give them a penny and if we get through you're going to give them a thousand quid [for which] you've already the gate in the bank [from the Liverpool game] and you're going to get another one because we're through to the next round." They didn't argue with me too much and of course our lads thought it was great. Our lads said, "Well, if we beat Liverpool then gaffer you've really done us proud." I think I put them on £1,000 but they earned every penny – and we got buttons for winning the European Cup.'

Liverpool had had a blistering start to the season, including a 7-0 mauling of Spurs at Anfield, and were concentrating on 'doing an Ajax' and winning the European Cup for the third straight year. The national press certainly thought Liverpool would manage the task and went as far as saying that the only chance of the European Cup staying in England would be if Liverpool knocked off Forest in the first round. Forest approached the game like it was a normal league encounter. 'We just went out to try and win the game' explains John McGovern. 'We had no thoughts of We need this score or that score.' In the championship year the Reds, despite having a really solid, strong defence, had attacked with an almost cavalier approach. 'We had no fear,' Martin O'Neill told Pat Murphy. 'We attacked away from home, there was none of this stuff about soaking up pressure, we just ran them off their feet. At home we were straight at them, just paralysing sides.' But Forest had learned a lot from the two League Cup games against Liverpool earlier in the year: they couldn't go all-out on the attack, they had to bide there time and play a cagier game. On the other hand Liverpool couldn't wait to get at Forest, they were doubly enraged having lost in the League Cup Final and having 'their' league title taken away. The last thing they wanted was to be dumped out of the European Cup in the first round against these upstarts called Forest as well!

Almost thirty-nine thousand forced their way into the City Ground to see the team that Clough had picked for what was arguably Forest's biggest ever game. The defence was the predictable line-up of Shilton, Anderson, Barrett, Lloyd and Burns; Archie Gemmill returned to take Gary Mills' place on the right side, McGovern and Bowyer patrolled the centre; John Robertson, of course, was wide on the left.

Up front Garry Birtles kept his place alongside Tony Woodcock. He'd gone from the Central League to the European Cup in a week.

Unlike in the previous League Cup games, Forest called the tune almost from start to finish. They attacked swiftly and in numbers, and they defended similarly. Both Forest full-backs were encouraged to get forward and the two very mobile strikers offered a different type of threat than the Woodcock-Withe combination. Whereas Withe was the consummate hold-up man and Woodcock made darting runs off him, Birtles could also do the hold-up role and was strong in the air (while looking rake-thin), but he also made penetrating runs at the heart of the Liverpool defence. Brian Glanville, writing in *the Times*, pointed out that the Forest forwards running directly at Liverpool's defence exposed the individual weaknesses that were usually papered over by their strong team ethics. This was evident early on when Birtles turned Phil Thompson inside-out and forced Clemence to tip over from a sharp angle. The pace of Forest's attack struck home midway through the first half. Kenny Burns brought the ball out from defence and chipped a pass over the head of Graeme Souness into the path of Ian Bowyer whose flick-on fell to an on-rushing Tony Woodcock. As he left the Liverpool defenders in his wake and advanced into area down the inside-right channel, Ray Clemence sensed the danger and rushed out to meet him. Woodcock, however, squared the ball for Birtles, who had the relatively simple task of side-footing the ball into the empty net, just ahead of Phil Thompson (*pictured on previous page*). The City Ground erupted. Promotion, the championship and now Forest were beating the European Champions! How good could things get?

The game progressed in a cat and mouse manner. As the second half proceeded Liverpool grew increasingly bold about pushing forward in an attempt to get an equalizer and the all important away goal. The visitor's best chance came when Kenny Dalglish shrugged off Viv Anderson inside the box and Shilton had to tip over the vicious shot to preserve to slender lead. Time was ticking down now. Would 1-0 be enough for Forest? Could Liverpool grab a vital goal? The Liverpool players obviously thought 1-0 would be a decent result for them: Phil Thompson ran past Garry Birtles late on and snarled at him 'One-nil won't be enough you know – you'll be going out!' This attempted intimidation blew up in his face though just moments later. As the game moved into injury time Colin Barrett charged down a pass from Jimmy Case at the halfway line. The ball fell to Phil Neal and his pass was again charged down by Barrett, and the ball rebounded into the Liverpool half. Garry

Birtles ran on to the loose ball and despite an attempt by Case to foul him he was away. After skipping around Phil Thompson's flailing challenge Birtles crossed to far post, where Tony Woodcock had pulled away from Alan Kennedy. He nodded it back across the six yard box to Barrett, who had continued his run from his own half, and volleyed an unstoppable drive from six yards before Emlyn Hughes could do anything about it. For a split second the ground was silent, then the ball rippled the net behind Clemence and the ground erupted for the second time that night. It was not only one of the most important goals in Forest's history, but also one of the most spectacular. 'I think I would have been fined if I hadn't scored' laughs Colin Barrett, 'I think by all accounts the fine was on its way. Apparently Peter Taylor was going mad in the dugout: 'What's he doing up there! Get back, get back!' It gave us a golden opportunity at 2-0.'

Moments later the game was over. 'I don't think we realized how good we were' says Tony Woodcock. 'It was the first time that Brian Clough had said that exactly where I should play. I'm

naturally left footed and I did a lot on the left hand side, but he said, "Play from a little bit deeper on the right hand side today." It was the only time in the all the years that he said it. Then as it happens I played the first ball from the right hand side to Garry, who put his first goal in and then for the second goal the ball came in and I headed it back, as I was coming in on the right, and the goal was in.' After the second goal Garry Birtles ran back to the centre circle. As he passed Phil Thompson he shouted, "Will two-nil be enough then?" The hatred was being turned up a notch. 'I shouldn't have said it really' admits Birtles; 'I was only a whippersnapper!' As Tony Woodcock walked off at the final whistle he didn't get many handshakes or congratulations from the opposition (but then again the tie was only halfway over), instead he got a few choice comments. 'I can remember one or two of the Liverpool lads saying, "Wait until we get you back up to Anfield, it's not over yet, it's not over yet".' He also recalls seeing (and hearing) the anger coming from the away dressing room after the game – walls were kicked, doors were slammed. The pressure cooker of the second leg would continue to boil for two weeks until the momentous second leg at Anfield.

'If you analyse it from start to finish its one of the best goals from any of the games I've played in,' says Viv Anderson. 'It was just a phenomenal goal from start to finish. He broke it up on the halfway line and went on a run and ends up putting it in from inside the box. It was a fantastic goal.'

ROYAL LIVER AS

Garry Birtles' first week in the first team was capped by a trip to Old Trafford. Arsenal, Liverpool, Manchester United: quite a baptism of fire. 'For my own personal game it was probably better [having Birtles in the team]', says Tony Woodcock. 'Garry came and we were a little bit similar sort of players and of course I'd had a little bit more experience. He was coming from non-league football; it was up to me then to take a little bit more responsibility having played a little bit longer than him. So we both played with our backs to goal, which was a new thing, but in the long run over the years that stood me in good stead for international football and football abroad, where you get man-to-man marking all the

time. The ball is being knocked into you and you've got to hang on to it. One of Clough's favourite sayings was, "Get hold of it" – particularly centre forwards, you've got to hang on to it. Particularly if the ball is being played up to you, hold it and no flicking it here and there.' The United game ended in a 1-1 draw, despite John Robertson being in inspired form and creating a host of chances. Birtles grabbed his first league goal (*see below*) in the next game at home to Middlesbrough with a splendid solo effort as Forest went 2-0 up. Worryingly they let the lead slip and had to settle for yet another draw, the sixth in seven league games, not the kind of defensive performance that gave much of a boost before the midweek European return at Liverpool. Even worse was the news that the hero of the first leg, Colin Barrett, had picked up a serious injury. 'You just never know do you?' muses Barrett. 'I think football for me, was summed up in that ten day spell. The ecstasy of scoring the goal against Liverpool and the heartbreak of smashing my knee ligaments on the Saturday against Middlesbrough. I ended up in a hospital bed and missed the second leg against Liverpool. In that ten days I was right up and then right down.' Barrett had torn his knee ligaments and would be out for six months. 'John Mahoney [Middlesbrough

midfielder] hit me right on side of my leg, I thought it was a dead leg' says Barrett. 'I tried to get up and walk and I thought It's not too bad and I tried a little jog. I remember John McGovern passing me a ball, I put the ball from my right to my left and fell over. I didn't understand why I'd fallen over but my knee was unstable and it had gone. It was only when I'd gone off the Doctor said, "You'll be in hospital tonight." They stitched all my ligaments back up and then it was just a long rehabilitation to try and get back.'

September 27 was the all important date for the fate of the 1978-79 European Cup. Despite having over twenty-five clean sheets the previous season, most people still though that Liverpool could score three to overturn their first leg deficit. A poll of the twenty First Division managers not involved in the tie was taken to see who they thought would progress and amazingly seventeen of them expected Liverpool to make it. Only Alan Dicks (Bristol City), Ken Shilleto (Chelsea) and John Neal (Middlesbrough) said Forest would prevail. This overwhelming faith in Liverpool was probably due to their recent European record at Anfield as they were on a streak of seven consecutive wins, and they'd all been pretty convincing, 2-0, 3-0, 3-1, 3-0, 5-1, 4-1 and 3-0. Brian Clough knew that his side had the skill and determination to get through, it was the mental side that would the biggest test. On the way up to Merseyside Clough stopped the bus and took the players on a short walk. Then at lunchtime, once they'd reached a hotel near Liverpool, he sat them all down for lunch and ordered a few bottles of Chablis; all the players then had a solid afternoon nap. At teatime the players were ready to go, but there was no sign of Clough or Taylor. Time ticked on and still no sign. It reached 6.30, an hour before

Colin Barrett (left) and Kenny Burns take a break from the long road back to fitness.

kick-off, and still no sign! Then the pair bustled in and ushered the players on to the coach. The idea had been to miss the crowds swarming to the ground, and it worked: the bus got to the ground in about ten minutes, unimpeded, and the players changed and went out for a warm-up.

The Forest players were doing some stretches and passing a few balls around in front of the Kop, but not too close. The atmosphere was tense already and some of the language aimed at the Reds players was colourful, to say the least. 'I was really nervous in front of the Kop,' recalls Garry Birtles. 'Then someone threw a tennis ball at John Robertson. He flicked it up and volleyed into the top corner of the net!' The Kop gave him a round of applause and some of the tension was broken, but by kick-off time it had doubled again.

'I loved going to Anfield, the atmosphere was incredible,' says Ian Bowyer. 'It was one of the most intimidating places to play at,' counters John McGovern. There was no live TV coverage in those days, so back in Nottingham tens of thousands of fans were huddled around their radios listening to the commentary. Like all commentaries on radio the crowd noise in the background gave an indication of what was happening before the commentator could actually describe it, which made listening almost unbearable. Everyone expected Liverpool to come out flying, and they weren't disappointed. Right from the kick-off they were on the offensive with the Kop screaming, 'Attack! Attack!' Forest were left to defend a corner after just forty seconds, it was taken short and Steve Heighway buzzed a twenty yard effort just over Shilton's bar and the Kop surged forward.

Though Clough was well known for not worrying about the opposition, he did tweak things here and there to gain an advantage over certain teams. Just as he'd told Tony Woodcock to play inside-right in the first leg, at Anfield he played Archie Gemmill on the right wing to help Viv Anderson defend against the forward runs of Liverpool left-back Alan Kennedy. With John McGovern playing a defensive role just in front of Burns and Lloyd. It made Forest a hard nut to crack. 'Clough wanted me as a first line of defence,' explains McGovern, 'so when we lost the ball the opposition didn't just go straight through the middle of our team. I covered in front of the back four because I could run all day. I'd chase one man down, then the next man down, and eventually he said, "Don't get so far forward." Now they call it the holding roll. I wasn't too bad at tackling so as soon as I won it I just gave it to someone like John Robertson.'

Liverpool's best opening in the first period came when Shilton and Dalglish clashed and the ball bounced goalwards, but Viv Anderson cleared from under his own bar. The commitment from both sides was 100 per cent. Frank Clark required seven stitches in a shin injury at half-time but he just quietly got on with doing his job. It was his first game of the season. 'The night they played Liverpool in the first leg, you could have five subs and I wasn't in the squad for the first leg' recalls Clark, 'I remember sitting at the back of the stand on my own, watching the game and going home very depressed. It was about the only time I was ever depressed in the whole of my time at the club. I seriously considered packing it in. I actually spoke to Colin Murphy and Dario Gradi, they were at Derby by then, and they wanted me to go there to be the reserve team coach, and I was really thinking seriously about it. Then Colin [Barrett] got injured on the Saturday while I was playing away with the reserves. Colin and I were probably best friends at the club, I was very upset for him obviously, but I got back in. My first game of the season was Liverpool away, so you can imagine what that was like. I'd had a lot of experience, but playing three or four reserve games wasn't exactly the best kind of preparation to go to Liverpool and they obviously tried to cash in on it. They threw everything but the cup down my side, but we managed to hang on.'

Liverpool's frustration grew in the second half. Again it was Dalglish that had the best chance when he turned in the area, but Shilton got down to the shot. Time ran out and Forest had done it. They'd got a 0-0 draw at Anfield and dumped the home side out of Europe. Liverpool's dream of a European treble was over. 'We'd proved when we won the league that we could defend,' says Kenny Burns. 'We didn't treat any teams differently, we paid them respect, but the bottom line is they are only as good as you let them be. And we didn't let them be, and that's it.'

'I remember Clough saying, "We're not gloating here. Let's get off. You've done the job, you've got rid of the European champions."' - Tony Woodcock.

Peter Taylor described it as the best performance by Forest in his time there. 'I remember Bob Paisley after the Liverpool game' says John Robertson. 'He was really kind. I remember him saying that Forest could go on and win it which was really, really, nice of him and actually brave really.' In fact Paisley went on record later as saying that the next day he went out and put a bet on Forest winning the cup. 'Well a famous quote came from Bob Paisley,' recalls Brian Clough. 'When we'd drawn them in some competition. I don't know what it was. It might have been the European Cup or something and we had to spin up for change of strip and my son, who eventually went on to play for Nottingham Forest, he was in the dressing room. I don't know how old he was, nine or ten maybe. Bob came into our dressing room and said, "We'll spin up". I said to Nigel, "Right spin the coin then, use the double-headed penny" and all that, and he spun up and we won. It was the only time I saw Bob Paisley lose his temper, and that was unique for him because he was a gentleman to the upper brackets. He said, "I can't even win the bloody toss against you lot!" Then he turned round, walked out and he nearly slammed the door off its hinges!' Forest made a hasty exit. Liverpool were left to concentrate on the league, which as it turns out, they did quite successfully.

The result obviously lifted everyone's spirits, and Forest set off on a goal-scoring run. From a team that couldn't score at all, they were suddenly transformed into one that rattled in thirteen goals in four straight wins. The spree saw Birtles score in three games, Robertson bagged four goals and Martin

O'Neill celebrated his return to the side with a couple in away wins over Aston Villa (2-1), Bristol City (3-1) and Oxford United (5-0 in the League Cup) and at home against Wolves (3-1). Before they knew it the second round of the European Cup had come around. Ironically Forest had been drawn against AEK Athens – a team that they'd played on their pre-season tour. In that encounter the result had been a 1-1 draw, this time Forest would go one better as they travelled to Greece for the first leg on 18 October. As Forest arrived, most local papers were boldly predicting a 3-0 home win, despite Forest having just knocked out the defending champions. AEK had knocked out Derby and Queen's Park Rangers in previous European competitions but their coach, the Hungarian great Ferenc Puskas, said that his side would need a two goal lead to take to Nottingham if they wanted any chance of progressing.

Forest took it easy for the two days they had in Athens before the game, with no formal training as such. They stayed at the same hotel they'd used in August, a complex of chalets near a sandy beach on the coast. 'I remember playing a kind of tag rugby on beach,' says Ian Bowyer. 'It was light-hearted until Lloydy got the ball. Then someone tripped him up and we all piled on! He got up and was looking around saying, "Who

did that? Who did that?" Garry Birtles also recalls the stay, 'We had a power cut at the hotel the night before the game. There were thunderstorms going off all over the place.' To get to the stadium for the game the players had to endure a hair-raising bus journey through the centre of Athens during rush hour, but they arrived unscathed.

'We didn't even know their players' says Larry Lloyd. 'I suppose we had someone out watching them but when they come back with a report they couldn't pronounce their names so they didn't mean an awful lot! I think the main thing was we played the way we played and we let the others worry about *us* and it worked.' The game started in a hostile atmosphere, an extremely loud mass of black and yellow screaming for the home side in searing heat. Forest needed an early goal to calm things down and they got one. Frank Clark took a quick free kick to John Robertson, his cross was flicked by Garry Birtles at the near post and John McGovern followed up to poke it home for a crowd quietening 1-0 lead after eleven minutes. The Greek side was filled with internationals, but their most influential player, Mimis Domazos, had been dropped after a public row with Puskas. His replacement, the Uruguayan international Milton Viera had an influence on the game too, but not in a positive way for his team: in the twenty-first minute he punched Kenny Burns in the face and was sent off! 'He thumped me and I went down,' says Burns. 'I could've stayed up, but I thought, You're gone pal!' Just before half-time Forest got a second goal when Frank Clarks' well timed run beat the off-side trap and John Robertson played him in to set up Birtles for an easy goal. 'They were operating a very clever offside trap, pushing right up to the halfway line' says Clark, 'and Robbo's got the ball on the halfway line. I ran from quite deep and I knocked it across and Birtles stuck it in. The atmosphere there was frightening really intimidating atmosphere, very difficult, we coped with it but it was difficult.'

In the second half Forest sat back a little and allowed the ten men to get into the game. A fifty-eighth minute penalty-that-never-was (TV replays showed that Burns cleanly won the tackle) made it 2-1. Late on both Birtles and Woodcock had goals disallowed, but Forest still returned home with a lead. The return journey didn't pass without incident though. As the players assembled in the hotel lobby to board the bus to the airport, Larry Lloyd came down without his club blazer on, while the rest of squad were wearing theirs. Brian Clough asked Lloyd to go and change but Lloyd refused, saying

there had been no official announcement that they had to wear blazers and also that his was packed in the bottom of a suitcase and on the bus. Clough fined him £50 on the spot and warned that it would double if Lloyd protested any more. Lloyd protested. The fine went up. And up. And up. Back in Nottingham Clough told Lloyd that he'd been dropped for the next game at home to Ipswich; Lloyd retaliated by demanding a transfer. Forest beat Ipswich 1-0 and Clough flew off for a short holiday, leaving Peter Taylor to sort the mess out. Eventually Lloyd paid the fine and all was forgotten.

After a 0-0 draw at Southampton (a game that Clough missed), AEK arrived in Nottingham hoping to overhaul the Reds' first-leg lead. Clough was back by now and had a couple of changes to make. John McGovern had come off injured at Southampton and Kenny Burns was suspended after being booked in Greece, so David Needham and John O'Hare were drafted in as replacements. In view of recent events, the biggest surprise was when Clough named Lloyd captain for the night. The Forest team had a real attacking look about it. As well as the obvious threats of Robertson, Woodcock and Birtles, the midfield trio of Bowyer, Gemmill and O'Hare were all expected to get forward when the chance arose. It was Athens that had the first chance of the night though; Mavros screwed a shot wide from eight yards in the third minute. Soon afterwards O'Hare played in Birtles one on one, but the keeper saved it for a corner. Anderson and Woodcock played it short before Woodcock clipped a ball to the near post for a flying Needham header to make it 1-0.

From them on it was one-way traffic. In the first thirty minutes alone, O'Hare got forward again and his shot was deflected to the goalkeeper; Birtles ran forty yards and fed Woodcock who rounded the keeper but saw his shot cleared off the line; Archie Gemmill got in on the act when he nutmegged one defender, left a second on the seat of his pants and then ran 30 yards before firing one just past the post. It was almost an elongated version of his famous World Cup goal. Then John Robertson got more involved, and showed why he would soon be considered the best winger in Europe. First he dribbled inside past three defenders then set Gemmill in free on the right but Gemmill took it back on his left foot and shot straight at the keeper. Then Ian Bowyer carried it forward and played a measured ball to Robertson whose pinpoint cross on to Woodcock's head made it 2-0 on the night and 4-1 on aggregate after thirty-six minutes.

The first half scoring was completed yet though. Viv Anderson intercepted a clearing pass, beat one man, then unleashed a twenty yard screamer into the top corner after thirty-nine minutes. 'It was just a toe punt from outside the box,' he says modestly. 'Toe punt' or not, it won the BBC Goal of the Month competition. Woodcock was clearly upended in the area, but the referee must have felt sorry Athens and waved it off. Then right before the interval Gary Mills came on for his first taste of European football as Clark went off injured. The Trent End was loving every minute of this one. 'There's only one team in Europe!' they sang, followed by 'Are you watching

Liverpool?' and a new variation on it that went 'Are you crying Liverpool?' The second half opened with a consolation goal for the visitors when Mavros' cross to Bajevic pulled back the score to 1-3 on the night. Normal service was soon resumed however. Robertson almost curled one in from distance; Needham misheaded a Gemmill free kick and Birtles to buried a volley for number four after sixty-six minutes; Robertson beat four then his right foot shot was tipped over from twenty-five yards, the ensuing corner on seventy-two minutes lead to Birtles near post header to complete the scoring. It was 5-1 on the night, 7-2 on aggregate. Forest were in the quarter-finals of the European Cup at the first attempt, along with Rangers, Cologne, Austria Vienna, Dynamo Dresden, Grasshoppers Zurich, Wisla Krakow and Malmo from Sweden. 'We need a breather now until March [when the quarter finals were played]' said Clough after the game. 'We have a small squad and we've had a few injuries. I think we'll have to go for two years undefeated before someone says were a good team' he added in reference to the fact that Forest still weren't getting the national recognition for their run of just one defeat in fifty-eight league and cup games.

Four wins and a draw had lifted Forest up the league table, they were still unbeaten, but he total of five wins and seven draws left them four points behind Liverpool and two behind the next visitors to the City Ground, Everton. John O'Hare continued to fill in for John McGovern, and Ian Bowyer had to play at left back because both Clark and Barrett were out injured. The small squad was close to breaking point. Everton looked the more likely side to take both points, but Micky Walsh squandered the best two chances of the match, one in each half. Afterwards Brian Clough admitted that he'd been unsuccessful in trying to strengthen the squad.

The two teams met again on the Tuesday night at Goodison Park for a League Cup fourth round clash. Everton were the favourites but Forest pulled out a gritty performance to keep hold of the trophy for a while longer.

Kenny Burns had a particularly unhappy night though. First he pulled up with an injury in the fifth minute and then he scored an own goal to give the Blues the lead. Burns limped on until the second half, even though David Needham, his natural replacement at centre-half, was already on the pitch, playing a midfield role as both Martin O'Neill and John McGovern were ruled out. Somehow, against the odds, Forest managed three second half goals from Lloyd, Anderson and Woodcock before a late Bob Latchford consolation goal. It was only after the game that it was learned that Burns had torn his cartilage and would be out for months. 'I just jumped something like eighteen inches and my knee went crack' recalls Burns. 'So Jimmy Gordon carried me off and put me down at the side of the bench, put some water on it. I went back on and ambled about a bit. When I came in at half time it was hurting, so we got a doctor down and he gave me a cortisone injection in my backside. As I was walking out the gaffer says, "Kenneth, don't let them see you limping", and I went, 'Thanks very

much!' I just collapsed about ten minutes from the end.' The small squad was really down to the bare bones now with Barrett, Clark, Burns, McGovern and O'Neill all ruled out. The unbeaten run continued though.

One of the best away results of the season came at Tottenham with the weakened side. Anderson, Robertson (with a Goal of the Season contender) and Birtles fired Forest to a 3-1 win. A 0-0 draw at home to Queen's Park Rangers and a 1-0 win at newly promoted Bolton stretched Forest's unbeaten league run to an unprecedented forty-two games. After a break of international games (during which Viv Anderson became the first black player for England, against Czechoslovakia, in a team that also included Woodcock and Shilton) Forest had a league visit to Anfield on 9 December to contend with. On top of all the other injuries, Tony Woodcock came back from England duty with a badly gashed ankle and was ruled out of the Liverpool trip. The red side of Merseyside had been counting down to this game ever since the European Cup games in September. Forest went into the game six points behind but with two games in hand. Liverpool wanted revenge and they wanted it badly: they didn't care if Forest had a weakened side or not, they hadn't beaten them in six attempts since Forest's promotion and it was becoming an obsession.

A first half Terry McDermott penalty after Dalglish tumbled in the box and another goal from the same player in the second half was the catalyst for scenes that might have come from a World Cup final such was the relief on the faces of the Liverpool players. They'd finally beaten Forest and the forty two game league run was over. Twenty five years later it's a record that still stands as the ultimate sign of consistency in the English game – the equivalent of going a full season undefeated. 'If Manchester United had done it' says Kenny Burns, 'you would hear it everyday in the paper, but they'll never do it.' For Brian Clough it was the highlight of his managerial career. 'Somebody had the bloody audacity to turn round and say 'Well it was over two seasons'. I don't care if it was over 22 seasons!' says Clough, 'if that had been any other club apart from Forest I'm telling you that the Royal Mint would have knocked the Queen off the coin [and put the team on it] and I'm not kidding either!'

'Well that's the thing I think annoys most of us more than anything' says Larry Lloyd, 'It'll never, ever, be beaten. Manchester United they've come close, Arsenal's come close but they will never ever beat that and its never mentioned in records. I think the unfortunate thing about it was that it was done over two seasons. It doesn't matter because it was all in the top flight. It wasn't as though half was in the Second Division, half in the First. It was all in the top flight. I for one would have liked a lot more recognition for that.'

'These days people get excited because Arsenal went 25 or whatever it was games unbeaten,' says Ian Bowyer. 'Going 42 League games in what was, and still is, one of the toughest leagues in the world, going a whole year unbeaten is incredible. What it does say is that each week we were ready to play, and over the course of a season you can get bad decisions from referees, you can get a bad run of the ball, injuries. We overcame whatever was put in front of us. The team spirit was fantastic if you were in or out of the team everyone got along. Unless they start changing the rules I can't see it being beaten.'

Brian Clough was also very strict about playing the game through this run in the right way. 'We never criticized referees in our lives,' he says. 'We'd commit the same fouls as anybody else, we got the same injustices as anybody else. It's been suggested in the newspapers in the last six months that clubs now should be punished if players get sent off. Clubs and managers. I proposed that to the Durham referees when I was the manager of Hartlepools and they're all on about it now! I said, "Fine the manager. He'll soon stop the player getting sent off." If he losses his months wages he'll say, "Hey, you're not going to cost me a months wages. You're not playing next week!" I think there's a few managers today who'd be a bit upset if they were being fined. The Arsenal fellow wouldn't have a penny!'

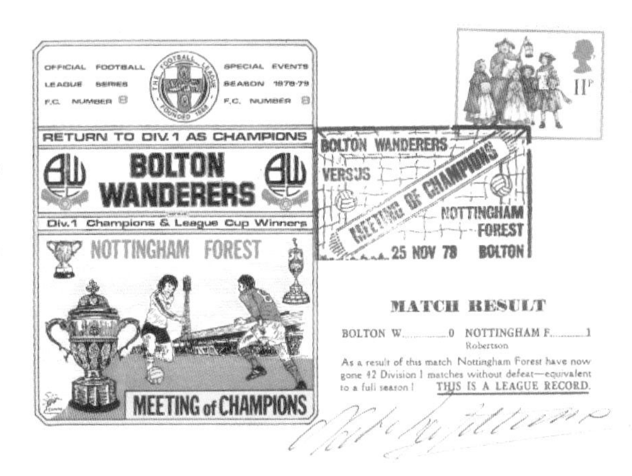

The best way to get over the loss was to set off on another unbeaten run. It wasn't quite as impressive, but Forest only lost three of the other thirty-nine games they played during the season. This started with a 3-1 League Cup quarter final win over Brighton & Hove Albion. Before the game Clough had been presented with a record ninth Manager of the Month award. John McGovern led by captain's example, scoring one and being the best player on the night. A 1-0 win at Birmingham, courtesy of Archie Gemmill's first goal of the season and a pair of draws over the Christmas period (0-0 at Manchester City and 1-1 versus Derby) left Forest well adrift of Liverpool before a weather enforced lay-off of fifteen days. Icy conditions caused the postponement of three games and then January was mostly taken up with cup ties. FA Cup wins at Aston Villa (2-0) and at home to York City (3-1, played with an orange ball on a snow covered pitch) sandwiched a League Cup semi-final first leg. Graham Taylor's Third Division Watford side had had a fairy tale ride to reach the last four, beating Newcastle and Manchester United along the way. The cup run had showcased some exciting young talent that Taylor was developing including the likes of future England international Luther Blissett, who had scored both goals in the Hornets' 2-1 win at Old Trafford.

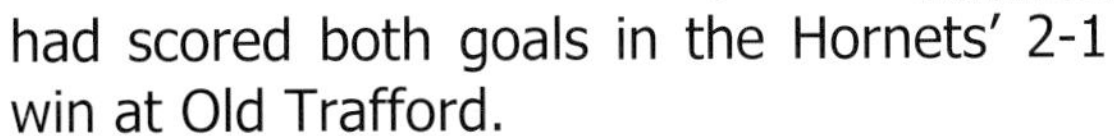

On an absolute quagmire of a pitch (even the Third Division side's players said it was one of the worst surfaces they'd had to play on) Forest went a goal down through that man Blissett who headed past Shilton in the ninth minute. Forest hit back right away with Ian Bowyer hitting the post before Garry Birtles fourteenth minute equalizer from twenty yards out. The visitors continued to give as good as they got as John Stirk should of scored right on half time and Brian Pollard forced a fine save from Shilton just after the re-start.

Forest took the lead against the run of play on fifty minutes though when Birtles' shot was deflected off Booth and past the helpless Steve Sherwood in the Watford goal. Watford weren't done, though, and Blissett hit the post with twelve minutes to go. The Reds heeded this wake-up call and within seconds Woodcock's (who had been a target for Graham Taylor back in the days when he'd managed Lincoln) corner fell to Robertson who scored to make it 3-1. The return leg two weeks later was an anti-climax as Forest shut down the home side on a frozen pitch and played out a 0-0 draw. Forest were back at Wembley for the third time in twelve months. The final was seven weeks away though and in-between there was the small matter of an FA Cup tie, a European quarter-final and five league games to negotiate. After winning the first of these games relatively easily, 3-1 at Middlesbrough, a piece of transfer history was made. Birmingham City, who had slumped to the foot of the table by Christmas, had let it be known that they needed to raise funds and were willing to sell their prize asset, striker Trevor Francis, in order to do so. Forest had been interested from the start but negotiations dragged on and on. The Plymouth born player had burst on to the scene when he scored fifteen goals in just twenty-one games at the age of sixteen. He signed professional forms a year later and had made his England debut in 1977. Though the British transfer record currently stood at £516,000 (the fee that West Bromwich Albion had paid Middlesbrough for David Mills), Birmingham had slapped a price tag of a whopping £1,000,000 on Francis. Coventry City had been interested but were put off by the price, as were Forest initially. Clough was unhappy about having to break the million barrier for a player – twice the current record. After weeks of talking, Birmingham's manager Jim Smith and Clough and Taylor were still £75,000 apart and Clough wouldn't budge. It was Peter Taylor who finally cracked and decided Forest should pay the asking price. He called Smith from home and simply said, 'You've got your million.' Then he called Clough at home and said, 'We've got Francis, I've paid their price.' Clough's reply was 'Good', then he put the phone down. After taxes the fee actually came to just off £1,150,000 a massive fee for a club the size of Nottingham Forest. In today's market it's the equivalent of about a £16,000,000 fee.

Further wranglings ensued over the contract between Forest and Francis, Clough wanted changes regarding Francis' agreement with American side Detroit Express and his obligation to play there in the summer. Forms were flying around all over the place when Clough put Francis in the third team at Grove Farm for a Saturday morning game as his Forest debut. The first £1,000,000 player was now playing in front of about twenty people. At half-time Clough arrived and insisted that Francis wear shinpads in the second half: 'We've paid a lot of money for these legs!' he explained. Due to the timing of the transfer Francis was not eligible to play for Forest in either the League or FA Cups that season and could only play in the European Cup if the Reds managed to reach the final. So he was on the sidelines when Arsenal visited Nottingham for the fifth round of the FA Cup on 26 February. Again Arsenal proved to be a 'bogey' side for Forest: despite having a host of chances the Reds couldn't score and were knocked out on their own ground. Frank Stapleton scored the only goal and now had four goals in five games against Forest, while Arsenal had had three wins in five matches since Forest's promotion. How Liverpool would have liked a record like that! The defeat was also the first home loss for forty-nine League and cup games stretching right back to the Cardiff game in Division Two towards the end of the promotion season, quite an achievement.

Trevor Francis finally made his debut, almost a month after signing, when Forest visited Ipswich. He had a quite game as Forest battled out a 1-1 draw, their twelfth in twenty-four League games. Mick Mills, who seemed to have a nightmare every time he played Forest since his 'has beens' remark, gave the ball away for the opening goal, which Birtles converted. Then in the fifty-third minute David Needham attempted to chest the ball back to Peter Shilton but Alan Brazil nipped in to steal the ball and score for Ipswich.

It had been over four months since the last round of the European Cup and now Forest faced Grasshoppers Zurich. Zurich had won the Swiss League for the seventeenth time in 1977-78 and, like Forest, had lost just three games on the way to the title. In the first round of the European Cup they had overwhelmed the Maltese side Valletta 8-0 and 5-3 and been paired against Real Madrid in the second round. A 2-1 loss in Spain was reversed with a 2-0 home win, with twenty-three year-old striker Claudio Sulser scoring twice. He now had a total of nine goals in the competition in just four games. Grasshoppers were again top of the Swiss League but were just coming out of a three month long winter break.

After just ten minutes Sulser made his presence felt at the City Ground. A long ball from the outside of Andre Meyer's right foot sent the striker away, he beat off first Lloyd and then Clark before poking a shot past Shilton for a shock 1-0 lead. Forest responded well, with John McGovern having a shot cleared off the line and then Tony Woodcock feeding Garry Birtles through the middle for the equalizer. Birtles was again involved when Forest took the lead in the second half. His trickery in the area lead to a handball and Robertson calmly sent the goalkeeper the wrong way and rolled the penalty into the opposite corner.

In the last half hour Zurich visibly tired as lack of match fitness because of the winter break, and the very heavy pitch, began to take their toll. Forest smelled blood and camped in the visitor's half. Birtles and Robertson both missed the target after good moves, and Martin O'Neill, in his first European game of the season, almost bundled one in. When it looked like Forest weren't going to add to their lead, they almost lost it. A similar long ball to the one that had brought the Grasshoppers goal again sent Sulser away but this time Shilton managed to get a hand to his shot for a vital save. After eighty-eight minutes what was almost 2-2 became a 3-1 Forest lead. Larry Lloyd had pushed forward and his right wing cross found Archie Gemmill ('It could have gone anywhere,' admits Lloyd) and the Scotsman stabbed it home for a two goal cushion. With just two minutes left Forest poured forward and O'Neill hit the bar from close with a header, Robertson had a shot deflected wide and Forest forced three quick corners in injury time. The last of these was met by Lloyd and his header bounced on the line and high into net. With two goals in the last two minutes, Forest now had a very healthy lead to take to Switzerland.

Trevor Francis took Martin O'Neill's place in the next two league games and he almost scored right from the kick off at Everton. As it was the returning Colin Barrett marked his comeback from several months out injured with a wonder goal to salvage Forest a point. The full-back lobbed the ball over a defender's head, ran around him and then unleashed a powerful volley into the net. The next game at Norwich saw Tony Woodcock return to goal scoring form as he notched a brace in a 2-1 win. These were his first League goals since Boxing Day.

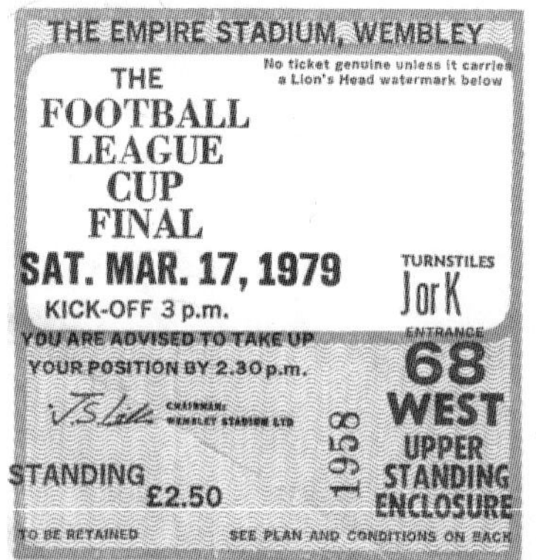

A heavy early-spring snowfall greeted Forest fans as they made ready for another trip to Wembley for the League Cup final against Southampton on 17 March. The Reds had been allocated 34,000 tickets (seats £5 to £10 and terrace tickets £2.50) but as fans made their way south they found the weather conditions to be more favourable and the game was not in danger of being cancelled. The official party had travelled down on the Friday, with Clough and Taylor using unusual methods of preparing the players for a major cup final. The night before the game the players were called to the hotel bar where the management had ordered around a dozen bottles of wine. They insisted that everyone sit down and have a drink together. Archie Gemmill, who

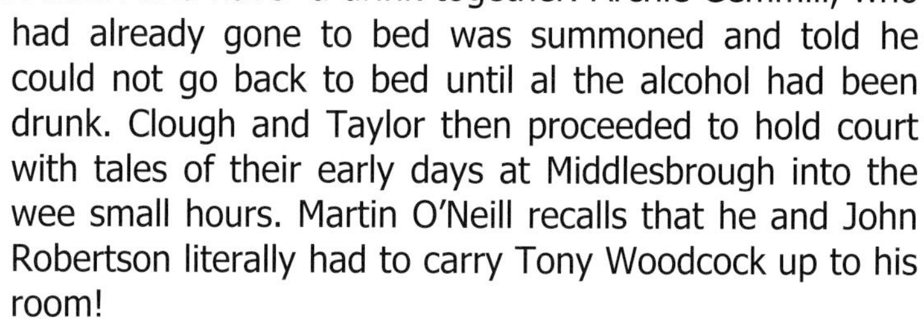

had already gone to bed was summoned and told he could not go back to bed until al the alcohol had been drunk. Clough and Taylor then proceeded to hold court with tales of their early days at Middlesbrough into the wee small hours. Martin O'Neill recalls that he and John Robertson literally had to carry Tony Woodcock up to his room!

Always full of surprises, the 'dynamic duo' produced another when Peter Taylor emerged from the tunnel, resplendent in his blue Forest blazer, to lead out the team. As they had been told they could not both walk out with the team, they had kept the decision quiet until the last minute to avoid any league intervention. Taylor said it was one of his proudest moments.

Southampton had qualified for the final by beating four First Division sides along the way. In the semi-final they edged Leeds, who Forest had beaten at the same stage the year before, 3-2 on aggregate. The Saints side included West Bridgford born Phil Boyer, Yugoslav full-back Ivan Golac, World Cup winner Alan Ball and ex-Forest winger Terry Curran, who had scored the winning goal in the semi-final. The Reds put in a subdued first half performance. Robertson was involved in most of Forest's attacks but couldn't carve out a clear cut chance and at the other end Curran seemed to be behind most of Southampton's good work. In the sixteenth minute Southampton took the lead. Full-back David Peach pushed forward, played the ball to Holmes and continued his run into the box. When the return pass came he found himself onside with just Shilton to beat, and his momentum took him around the

Forest keeper to roll the ball into an empty net. The game then stuttered to half-time without either team really getting into their stride.

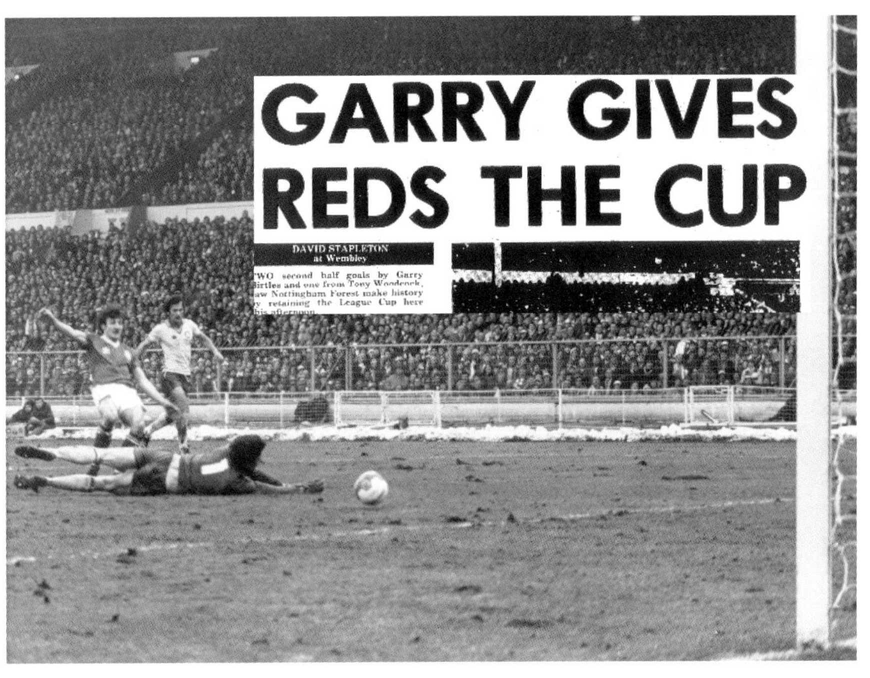

GARRY GIVES REDS THE CUP

DAVID STAPLETON
at Wembley

TWO second half goals by Garry Birtles and one from Tony Woodcock, saw Nottingham Forest make history by retaining the League Cup here this afternoon.

The second half was a different matter though. Right from the restart Forest laid siege to the Southampton goal that they were defending in front of the Forest fans as the game turned into the Garry Birtles show. A John Robertson cross was cut out by Chris Nichol but as he hesitated in his own area, Birtles darted in to take it off the defender's foot and then swivelled to deposit a shot high into the roof of the Southampton net. Forest were rampant now and twice Birtles was put through and scored only to have his efforts ruled out for offside. In both cases it was later shown that Chris Nichol was slow to come out and had actually kept the Forest forward onside. In the seventy-seventh minute there was no flag. Colin Barrett tackled Boyer and his quick pass to Woodcock was knocked to Birtles who took over and ran through the wide open defence and threaded it under Terry Genoe to put Forest ahead. If not for the over zealous linesman Birtles would have had a hat-trick in a Wembley final, or maybe even four goals. The game was put beyond reach after a short corner routine ended

with Archie Gemmill playing an inch perfect pass that Woodcock hooked over Genoe from a tight angle for 3-1 lead. Nick Holmes scored a late consolation but it didn't stop Forest from becoming the first team to retain the League Cup.

There was little time to celebrate, though, as the team flew out to Zurich for the second leg against Grasshoppers. The Swiss needed a 3-0, or better, win to take the tie and for thirty minutes Forest controlled them quite easily. Then an innocent challenge for a header by Viv Anderson was somehow adjudged to have been a foul and the Italian referee gave a penalty. Sulser sent Shilton the wrong way to make it a 2-4 aggregate. Forest had now conceded just two goals away from home and both had been dubious penalties. Before half-time Forest killed off any hopes of a comeback when Birtles' cross was bundled in from close range by O'Neill and the game ended 1-1. The other semi-finalists were Malmo, Cologne and Austria Vienna. Forest had five league games before the next stage of the European adventure.

Four of the aforementioned games were at the City Ground, and while the Reds still held on to an outside chance of catching Liverpool, they had to take advantage of these home fixtures. Clough found room to play Birtles, Francis and Woodcock as well as O'Neill and Robertson to give a five-pronged attack that was in stark contrast to the team that had struggled to score back in September. The two new arrivals had been obtained via the two extremes of the transfer spectrum - £1,000,000 for Francis, £2,000 for Birtles. The next two home games, against Coventry (3-0) and Chelsea (6-0) saw Birtles score twice and Woodcock and O'Neill get three each, but Francis failed to find the net. He opened his Forest account on 31 March with a last minute header that saved a point in a 1-1 draw with Bolton. Further comprehensive wins over Aston Villa (4-0) and Chelsea (3-1) saw Francis net in both. The Reds had picked up nine out of ten points in a two week span, scoring seventeen times and conceded just two. These games left Forest six points behind Liverpool with twelve games to go. They were in a confident mood as they prepared for their European Cup semi-final first leg with West German champions Cologne at the City Ground.

'On the Saturday before the Cologne game my brother was killed in a car crash' remembers John Robertson, 'and I remember being unsure if the game was going to be played [because of the weather] and whether I was going to play or not. I remember coming down to Nottingham on the Wednesday. It really poured and there was a wee bit of doubt about the game. The funeral was meant to be on the Thursday and if the game had been put back to the Thursday I wouldn't have been able to play. So, I was glad the game got played on the Wednesday night.' Viv Anderson did miss the game through suspension (Colin Barrett played at right-back), Trevor Francis was still cup-tied and David Needham continued in the place of Kenny Burns, though Burns had resumed training and was almost ready to be recalled.

This was Cologne's seventeenth European campaign; they had competed in Europe in every season throughout the 1970s and so were extremely experienced as a club. They had individual talent and know-how as well. Goalkeeper Harald Schumacher was on the verge of taking over from the legendary Sepp Maier in the West German national team (he would gain infamy in the 1982 World Cup when he knocked France's Patrick Battiston unconscious in the semi-final); centre-half Roland Gerber was a German B-international; full-backs Harald Konopka and Bernd Schuster were full internationals, as were Herbert Zimmermann and Herbert Neumann. The quality ran throughout the side with midfield general Heinz Flohe having over forty West German caps and Dieter Muller had been the top scorer with twenty-four goals in the 1977-78 season and, of course, he was another international. Muller's ammunition was supplied by two speedy wingers in the form of Belgian international Roger Van Gool (who would later play at Coventry) and ex-Japanese Player of the Year Yasuhiko Okudera. This would be Forest's most serious test since the Liverpool games.

Ian Bowyer, who started the game at left-back because Barrett was filling in for Anderson on the right, describes the first leg as 'Probably the most exciting game ever at the City Ground.' And he's right – it had everything. At kick off it was still light and the game started in slightly strange conditions. It had rained all day but the skies had cleared slightly for the start of the game. The pitch was an absolute mudbath before the start and it quickly got even worse as the game progressed, which did nothing for the nice clean all white shirts and shorts of the Cologne team. Only the areas around the four corners had any grass and the rest was pure mud, making it difficult to run never mind to play any decent football.

Despite the conditions Cologne started brightly. Van Gool proved to be a thorn in the Forest defence's side as he skipped inside past Colin Barrett and unleashed a shot that bounced just in front of Shilton, hit his right hand post, then bounced across the line and nestled inside the left hand post. The City Ground was silenced.

Worse was soon to come. A Forest attack was broken up by Neumann. He brought it out from the edge of his own area, released Van Gool, who had beaten the attempted offside trap and moved in on the Forest goal. He cleverly drew Shilton out then squared it for Muller to slide it into the empty net. Cologne were 2-0 up and Forest already seemed dead and buried.

Many teams might have folded under the avalanche but Forest buckled down and slowly hauled themselves back into contention. First Ian Bowyer had an eighteen yard shot that looped onto the bar and out, but on twenty-seven minutes the home fans did have something to cheer about. David Needham was supporting the attack and he headed back across the box to Garry Birtles who rose unchallenged at the penalty spot to head past the stationary Schumacher. Forest had a glimmer of hope, but even if they could equalize the

Germans had two precious away goals. 'We were taken aback a bit because they hit us pretty hard early on,' says David Needham. 'We made a couple of mistakes as a team and we were down. I was lucky enough to get myself up there and set up a goal so that was good.'

Cologne weren't content to hang on to their lead though. Konopka pushed forward and had a rising drive tipped over by Shilton then at the other end John McGovern had a shot pushed out for a corner. For a neutral viewer it was an absorbing end to end classic; for the Forest fans it was too nerve-racking to enjoy at the time. Woodcock was the next Forest player to go close. He turned, beat three Germans who ended up on their knees in the mud, and scampered into the area where his left foot shot sent the keeper the wrong way but hit Schumacher's foot and went wide (*pictured below*).

While Forest pushed for an equalizer the Germans inevitably found space at the other end. Van Gool got away again but his one on one chance beat Shilton but grazed the outside of the left hand post and the Reds survived to half time at just 2-1 down. This last chance by Van Gool had been chased down by Archie Gemmill and he suffered the consequences for his effort by rupturing his groin. This injury pretty much ended his season and his Forest career.

Clough had some stern talking to do at half-time and he rejigged the line-up: Ian Bowyer was pushed into midfield to replace Gemmill and Frank Clark came on to add some experience at left back. The moves immediately paid dividends in the second half. John Robertson flighted a chip on to Birtles' head, he knocked it down for Bowyer to run onto and the midfielder buried a right foot drive from sixteen yards. Somehow Forest were level. Like the Zurich game before, Forest sensed that the visitors were tiring on the muddy pitch and pressed forward in ever-increasing numbers. Also like the Zurich game, they were exposed at the back, but this time it was Roger Van Gool rather than Claudio Sulser providing the threat. John McGovern nipped in to capitalize on a German defensive mistake but his rising shot was pushed over by Schumacher. Then he played in Birtles on the right side of the German area. Birtles twisted and turned, one way then the other, before sending a right-foot cross to the far post. It looked like it was about to hit the German defender but out of nowhere Robertson appeared, parallel to the mud, to send his diving header into the net. Possibly the only goal he ever scored with his head. The City Ground faithful were in dreamland. Just an hour earlier they were dead and buried at 2-0, now they had a lead to take to Germany in a fortnight! Cologne had other ideas though. Van Gool beat both Barrett and Needham, pulled it back to Neumann but he side-footed over from inside

Okudera's goal sets Reds herculean task

NOTTM FOREST ... 3 F.C. COLOGNE ... 3

PETER SHILTON, perpetrating the worst mistake of his brilliant 19 months with Nottingham Forest, summed up a night of defensive mayhem at the City Ground last night that now leaves the Reds with a herculean task to lift

the box, it was a glorious chance that should have been taken. Maybe Forest should have learned from Liverpool's mistake in the first round, but they continued to push forward and again caught on the break. Van Gool's pass took out both Barrett and Bowyer, and Okudera, who had just come on to the pitch, cut back and sent a right foot shot that somehow snaked under Shilton. It was the first time he'd conceded three goals at home for Forest. The inevitable headline read FOREST SUNK BY JAP SUB. By all perceived common wisdom, Forest were finished. They would have to go to Cologne and win or get a high scoring draw (4-4 or better), to reach the final.

The let-down had to be quickly forgotten though as there were still important league games to be played. Wins away at Derby (which saw Kenny Burns return to the first team) and Birmingham were played either side of two frustrating home draws with Manchester United and Leeds. Forest really needed to be winning all of their home games to stand any chance of catching Liverpool. They were

FOREST
3
1FC COLOGNE
3
PHILIPS

89
SCORER
SUB.
14
14
EVERAR

now seven points behind the Merseysiders with a game in hand and a home game with them to come.

Before that was the small matter of a trip to West Germany. 'Everyone had written us off,' recalls Colin Barrett. 'My knee had gone again, so I was in hospital when they were in Cologne.' The bookies were giving odds of 4/1 against Forest, quite high for a one-off game and Peter Taylor for one took advantage of their 'generosity.' 'To be fair, Peter Taylor was insisting all along that we could win out there, he was in no doubt at all. He kept saying it, to the point that we believed him as well.' Tony Woodcock: 'I remember Cloughie just saying, "They'll come at us, so we'll absorb a bit of pressure it'll be 0-0 at half time. If we get a chance we might score or it'll be 0-0 at half time and in the second half we'll go out and after about twenty minutes we'll get a goal and we'll hang on to it and we'll win".' Tony Woodcock played for Cologne later in his career and heard the other side of the story after his move. 'We went over we didn't train' he says, 'We were in the hotel where I had stayed after I moved there so I got all the stories from the waiters. They'd been saying, "This side have got no chance at 3-3, they're not training, they're having a few beers every night and they're playing cards, they're going for a walk." So they all put money on Cologne. Cologne had also organized the tickets and the buses to go down to Munich for the final because they thought they were through with their star studded team!' If Forest had known that it would no doubt have been used in the team talk. As it was Taylor took the players out on the pitch for that before the match. 'Wait until eighty-nine minutes if we have to' he preached, 'We have to be patient.'

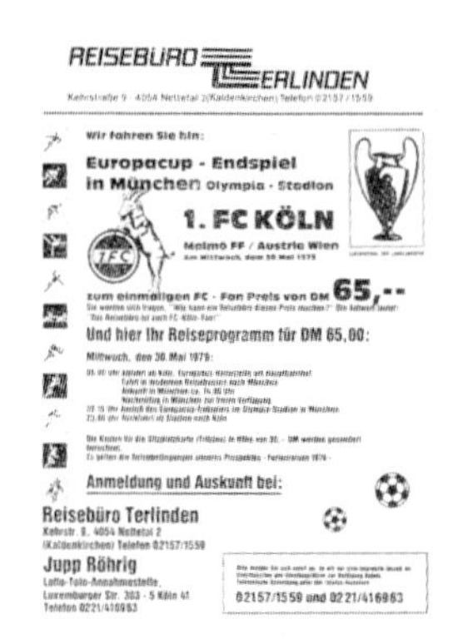

The Mungersdorf Stadium was a massive concrete bowl holding a capacity sixty thousand fans (six thousand of them from Nottingham), but with a running track around the pitch they didn't create the atmosphere that the home side would of liked. Cologne hadn't had a great build to the match and had been thrashed 5-2 at Bayern Munich the weekend before. The teams came out into a damp, cold, misty night with Forest in their all red strip. In lieu of any proper dug-outs, Clough and Taylor sat on a couple of garden chairs on the running track looking quietly confident. Barry Davies commentated for the BBC who were showing highlights later that night on their *Sportsnight* programme. Anderson and Burns back to bolster the defence from the first leg and Clark kept his place at left back to leave Bowyer in midfield. For Cologne, Strack replaced Gerber with the captain, Cullman, dropping to sweeper from the midfield role he played in the first game.

The home side were soon on the attack with Glowacz shooting over the bar from the edge of the area. Forest had a couple of half chances soon afterwards. Anderson got clear but then tripped and the ball trickled out for a goal kick; and then a Birtles cross from the left found O'Neill, but his volley under pressure flew wide.

Forest knew that a clean sheet was imperative and were content to let the Germans have possession in their own half. The Reds let them bring it to halfway where Woodcock, Birtles and O'Neill led the chase to force them back. Cologne's best chance fell to Muller, who got away from Lloyd in the area but shot across the goal from the corner of the six-yard box. The Romanian referee booked Konopka for trying to entice O'Neill to encroach at a free kick just outside the Forest area, and then booked O'Neill as well. The Irishman blocked it anyway. Before half-time Muller was replaced by Flohe. Muller had been saying in the press before the game that it was as good as won. 'He won't be sprouting off much longer!' promised Larry Lloyd, and as the German limped off it seemed that Lloyd had been true to his word.

The second half was tense up until the sixty minute mark. Then the Germans seemed to think they could end the tie with a goal and began pushing forward which fell right into the hands of Forest's counter-attacking plan. A Forest breakaway saw McGovern send Birtles clear midway in his own half. He beat two men with his pace, entered the Germans' area and tried to pull it back for Woodcock, but the pass was intercepted and play switched straight back to the Forest end where Flohe drove a chest high shot right at Shilton. The ebb and flow continued until Anderson won a tackle; the ball fell to Burns who played in Woodcock on the left. He won a corner. Robertson took his time, then swung the ball into the near post with his right foot, Birtles got a slight but important flick and Bowyer stooped to head the ball into the roof of the German net. Sixty four minutes gone and Forest fans were in dreamland singing 'We shall not be moved' and 'Are you watching Liverpool?' Now Cologne had to attack even more, a 1-1 draw would be enough to see them through. Barry Davies commented that 'You have to play to your instincts and Forest's instinct is to attack.' They didn't get a chance to though because the Germans' flooded forward but apart from a couple of scrambles, Shilton's only save of note was a thirty-five yard drive from Konopka in injury time. Time expired and Forest had done the impossible, they'd won 1-0 just as Clough had predicted to Tony Woodcock, and qualified for the European Cup final at the first attempt. Their opponents would be Malmo. 'The Cologne game was like the final really,' says Frank Clark. 'The final was almost an anti climax afterwards, because Cologne were the favourites and really no one had heard of Malmo.'

'My biggest reward for scoring was when we got back to East Midlands Airport,' says Ian Bowyer. 'I was in this big queue to pay at the car park and Viv Anderson was shouting, "Coming through!" and moved everyone out of the way and I got to the front of the queue.'

'What made that special' says Brian Clough, 'apart from the fact we won and apart from the fact

that it was the Germans, which obviously that made it that much sweeter, was that I always recall that I was regarded as the awkward one giving interviews. What a load of rubbish, nobody did more interviews in the whole lifetime of football than me! After the home game against Cologne I was caught coming out of the dressing room into the car park where the players used to park and Gary Newbon had grabbed me literally as I opened the door and he said something and I snapped at him as usual and said, "Anyone that thinks this tie is over must be an idiot" and that's all I said and it proved right. The Germans were wary of us and they came up with the absolute brilliant excuse after the match, after we'd beaten them: they came to me, several of them and said, "It would have been better if we'd have been losing 1-0. It would have given us a more incentive." I said 'What a load of rubbish. You didn't score 'cos you couldn't. Simple as that!"

The whole of Nottingham was caught up in European Cup final fever even though Forest still had an outside chance of the league title and Liverpool were the next visitors to the City Ground to start a sequence of three

games in five days. Forest would have to win them all to have any chance of making up the lost ground. It wasn't to be. Liverpool did what Forest had achieved in earlier games at Liverpool and frustrated the home side for a 0-0 draw. When the Reds then lost 1-0 at Wolves two days later the title was conceded. But it was hard not to have one eye on the final in Munich at the end of May.

For the last two home games of the season the capacity of the ground was almost halved as demolition of the old East Stand was commenced. The success of the last two years had left money available to redevelop that side of the ground and plans had been drawn up to build a two tier eight thousand seater stand incorporating thirty-six executive boxes. Building work would take around forty weeks to complete and so was started before the season ended.

There was still a chance to finish as runners-up and the players had the importance of finishing as high in the league as possible drummed into them – there was to be no coasting before the big game at the end of May. An away draw at Norwich and wins over Manchester City and Leeds meant Forest could grab second place if they could beat the current second placed team, West Bromwich Albion, at the Hawthorns on the last day of the season. Trevor Francis scored the only goal in a 1-0 win and Forest leapfrogged the Baggies to get a little revenge for the FA Cup loss an year earlier. It was the culmination of seven league games in just twenty-one days and again Forest had only lost three league games all season, while the champions, Liverpool, had lost four.

First Division, Final Table 1978-79

	Pld	Pts	GD
Liverpool	42	68	+69
FOREST	**42**	**60**	**+35**
West Bromwich Albion	42	59	+37
Everton	42	51	+12
Leeds United	42	50	+18
Ipswich Town	42	49	+14
Arsenal	42	48	+13
Aston Villa	42	46	+10
Manchester United	42	45	-3
Coventry City	42	44	-10
Tottenham Hotspur	42	41	-13
Middlesbrough	42	40	+7
Bristol City	42	40	-4
Southampton	42	40	-6
Manchester City	42	39	+2
Norwich City	42	37	+2
Bolton Wanderers	42	35	-21
Wolverhampton Wanderers	42	34	-24
Derby County	42	31	-27
Queens Park Rangers	42	25	-28
Birmingham City	42	22	-27
Chelsea	42	20	-48

Just before flying out to Germany, Forest played Mansfield in the County Cup Final. The main significance of the game was the chance to give Archie Gemmill a run out for the first time since his injury against Cologne and he came on for the last twenty minutes. Martin O'Neill and Frank Clark were also carrying injuries when the squad, minus Brian Clough flew out to Munich. The players trained for a day or two and then Clough arrived. He had to make some important team selection decisions. Four players were battling for just two places – one in midfield and one at left back. 'There was Trevor, Martin, Archie and myself,' recalls Frank Clark. 'Obviously if Archie had played in the team, Ian Bowyer would drop in at left back. Myself, Archie and Martin had all been injured so he decided to go for Trevor leaving the three of us for the one spot. He could have played either one of us and moved it around a bit and fortunately enough he picked me. He asked us all face to face, on the morning, "Were we fit?" and of course we all said 'Yes'. I think he thought he could trust me more than the other two, I wasn't 100 per cent fit I was 99 per cent. I'd strained my groin at Leeds towards the end of the season and we all were probably about the same to be fair. So Archie and Martin were unfortunately on the bench and not very happy at all, Archie was gutted.' In fact Gemmill was so upset he launched a verbal attack on Clough and Taylor. 'It was a hammer blow to me,' says Gemmill. 'I 'd been promised by the management team that if I proved my fitness I was playing. So when I was dropped I said what I thought about that and the verbal attack was seen by them as overstepping the mark and I think that had a lot to do with me leaving the following summer.'

'Being unable to play in the quarter-final of the European Cup and unable to play in the semi-final, I was obviously desperate that they could progress to the final to give me a possibility of making my debut in the final' says Trevor Francis, 'I was hoping that I would play, and there was plenty of positive speculation prior to the build up to the game in Munich that I would make my debut. I remember rooming with John McGovern, who was obviously a very influential member of the team as the captain, and I remember on the day before the game asking John if he had any idea of what the team would be. He didn't, of course. Cloughie kept it very, very close to his chest and it was only Wednesday morning that we went down to the stadium to have a little look at the surroundings have a look at the pitch and that's when he sat us down on the side of the pitch and it was about half ten, eleven o'clock and announced the team and that's the first I knew that I'd be playing. He went through the eleven players who would be starting and obviously it was great joy for the eleven. I think that for most of the eleven they were reasonably sort of confident that they would be starting. But there were a couple of outstanding players who weren't in the starting line-up that had contributed you know so much to get the team to the final. That was Archie Gemmill and Martin O'Neill.'

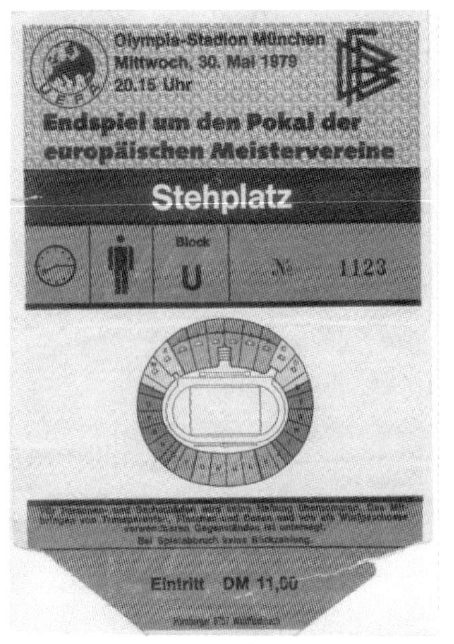

Before the game Birtles and, surprisingly, Kenny Burns were two of the most nervous players. Birtles hadn't shaved for a few days and, as the team waited for the bus at the hotel Clough saw him looking tense and made him go and shave. Clough provided the razor and Chris Woods some aftershave. It was purely to take Birtles' mind off the game for a few minutes. Tony Woodcock remembers Clough saying to Birtles, 'Get it done or you're not playing' and that when Birtles returned 'He was all cut up, all paper all over his face!' Maybe giving a nervous man a razor wasn't that good an idea! The journey to the stadium was a subdued one. 'I can remember is it was pretty quiet on the bus' says Woodcock, 'I can remember Clough coming down the bus and saying, "Anyone want a beer? Larry do you want a beer?" and then one of the fans walked into a lamppost while having a look in the bus and suddenly *boom* that just broke the ice.'

And so the game had finally arrived. Just two years after waiting for a Bolton Wanderers result to see if they had got out of the Second Division, Forest were in the European Cup Final. It was, and still is, almost unbelievable. Malmo had got through as the surprise package of the competition and most people knew very little about them. The English press were keen to portray them as the equivalent of a Second Division side and Brian Clough had his work cut out to impress upon everyone that they had reached the final of the European Cup and couldn't be that bad! Forest had taken over twenty-five thousand fans to Germany, at the time it was the biggest ever following for an English team abroad. Malmo had a much smaller following which contributed to the crowd being only fifty-eight thousand in the eighty thousand capacity Olympic Stadium. Radio Nottingham's Dennis McCarthy broadcast his afternoon show live from the centre of Munich and millions tuned in to watch the showpiece event on TV.

As the teams came out Clough had a quick word with Malmo's English coach, Bobby Houghton – 'I'll tell you the key to the game' he said, 'after it's over!' Forest wore the all red colours that had been a good omen for them in Cologne while Malmo wore sky-blue shirts and white shorts. The biggest game in Forest's long history was now underway. 'The gaffer always said that your first pass, kick, header, tackle sets your standard of play for the game,' says Kenny Burns. 'If the first pass was sloppy, your play would be sloppy.' Burns first touch was a nervous looking back header to Peter Shilton that landed on the foot of Tore Cervin

'There was no guarantee that I would play in the final. I was very realistic because the team had done so well with the players that got them to the final. I fully realised that it would be tough to take somebody out of the team to bring me in.' – Trevor Francis.

but luckily for Forest his touch let him down and Shilton collected it. 'I had a nightmare' admits Burns, 'Larry had a great game, covered for me and that's what he's there for. To help me out and vice versa.' Burns didn't have too much to do throughout the game though.

The Swedes had lost a couple of players to injury and had limited attacking options. For most of the game they were happy just to get men behind the ball and stifle the Forest threat. These tactics worked well for forty-four minutes. John McGovern deflected a Swedish pass to Ian Bowyer, he switched the play wide to John Robertson, who dropped his shoulder and left two defenders in his wake as he made for the by-line. Robertson's cross bypassed six defenders and the 'keeper but found Trevor Francis sprinting in at he back post. Francis headed it high into the net: 1-0!

'I played well in the first half' recalls Ian Bowyer, 'We were disappointed in ourselves that we didn't win with more style and it was something of an anti-climax. Now when they show the goal on TV they don't show the ball from me going to Robbo!' John Robertson: 'I remember Barry

Davies saying, when I saw it back on television, he wanted me to do that all night. Well that's all well and good but people don't just allow you to do that. They wanted to show me inside, they weren't idiots. The goal came from the first time we got a good switch of play. It was a great ball from Ian Bowyer that gave me the time to actually get on a run.'

'I remember the goal very well' says Trevor Francis. 'It wasn't my favourite position playing on the right hand side of midfield. But I was learning the position and one of the things that was always instilled into me was that when the ball was on the left hand side, especially at the feet of John Robertson, it was my responsibility to try and get at that back post. When the ball was delivered out to John I was probably still forty yards from goal so I had a lot of work, a lot of ground to make up recognizing that there was a good chance that John, as he's done so regularly over the years, would go past his man, and I timed my run almost to perfection. The ball just slightly went behind me and I had to head it back but managed to do it successfully and it was a wonderful moment. It was close to half time and just gave us that fillip that was needed going into the interval because we had pressed and pressed but didn't really sort of look like getting the breakthrough so it came at a very appropriate time.'

'The final against Malmo went nearly unheralded in the sense that it was "Malmo" and "Nottingham Forest"' says Clough. 'I've got a picture in my study now to this day of when we scored. They'd got nine back in the penalty area. Now to score from a cross with nine opposition in the penalty area it's got to be a good goal for a start. It was the feet of a genius called John Robertson and somebody's head called Trevor Francis – who they said I'd paid too much money for. He won the European Cup Final.'

The second half was much like the first. Malmo massed people behind the ball and showed little adventure going forward. It wasn't because they didn't want to attack and try to get an equalizer, they just couldn't. They did have a number of free-kicks around the Forest area but failed to hit the target on each occasion. The best chance came at the other end as Francis used his electric pace to outrun several markers and pull the ball back for John Robertson. Robertson hit it well but the ball came back from the foot of the post. 'If John had scored then obviously it would have been a more than comfortable sort of end to the game for us,' says Francis.

'Yes, I should have scored,' admits Robertson. 'I remember Trevor Francis had gone down and pulled a great ball back I was coming onto it and had a clear sight of the goal. Maybe I didn't catch it right but I still should have scored.' It was only the second time that Robertson had really found any space – the first time had been for the goal. In one spell during the second half he was being covered by three men and was fouled four or five times in a two minute passage of play. The Swedes weren't being deliberately cynical, they just couldn't cope with Robertson's wing play. Garry Birtles, the top scorer for Forest in Europe, found chances hard to come by in the final. 'They worked hard, got ten men behind the ball' he says 'I got a half-chance and it landed on the roof of the net and Robbo's shot hit the post and I thought I was going to get the rebound but didn't.'

'I thought they were a very ordinary side' says Larry Lloyd, 'I remember thinking at the time 'how the hell did they get to the final?' They didn't cause us an ounce of problem at the back. In fact it was one of our easiest games through Europe. Our problem was breaking them down 'cos Bobby Houghton was the manager, wasn't he, and he was a good tactician and he had them solid at the back. They had numbers and we found it difficult to break them down.'

'I think that if I was watching the game as a neutral rather than being involved in it as a Nottingham Forest player I think I would have been very disappointed with the game' says Trevor Francis. 'Malmo regularly employed the offside trap and it worked very effectively and we found it very difficult to impose ourselves on the opposition. We were always the better side but we didn't play as we would have liked but when you're in a game of that magnitude obviously the most important factor is not trying to please the world and giving them a game to remember. Obviously if you can do that then great, but the most important factor is to get the game won and win the European Cup. We did it not as we would have liked but it was still a comfortable 1-0 victory if there's such a thing as a comfortable 1-0 victory.' Francis was named as the game's Man of the Match and gained fame on an international scale.

At the final whistle the celebration we somewhat muted for a team winning the European Cup. John McGovern collected the oversized trophy and the team did its lap of honour, as did Malmo to warm applause – reaching the final had been the best they could hope for. 'It was a bit of an anti-climax' says Viv Anderson, 'The game was not the most enjoyable or the most spectacular game for the supporters because it was 1-0 and they were very defensive I thought at the time and all the emphasis was on us to break them down and we plugged away. I always remember Frank Clark on the bus saying 'it doesn't get any better than this'. You don't really appreciate it at the time when you are only nineteen or twenty. Frank was right at the time. You should savour every minute of it because it doesn't come around that often.'

'After the game we were sitting in the changing rooms' remembers Tony Woodcock; 'we weren't sort of jumping around or anything and Peter Taylor came in and said, "Lads you've won! It's been a fantastic tournament." Because we were all a bit disappointed that we hadn't done it in style. You know we won the European Cup but we didn't win 3-0 and we didn't do it in style with fantastic football. The lads doubted it a bit until he said, "Come on, let go and enjoy it now".'

'We were all a bit deflated in the dressing room at the end' adds Frank Clark, 'and Brian said, "Forget about the performance, nobody will remember that, all you remember is the European Cup," which was absolutely right.' Trevor Francis: 'I can remember at the end of the game there weren't the scenes of jubilation that I would have expected from the management team. It was a very subdued Clough and Taylor. Obviously inwardly they were quite thrilled at winning a European Cup but I think they believed in playing the game in the right way and they put a great emphasis on trying to pass the ball well and creating opportunities and they were slightly disappointed that their team were unable to do that. So I think there was an element of disappointment surrounding the whole evening but inwardly obviously they were delighted that they'd succeeded in bringing the European Cup to Nottingham.'

Because the German authorities had put a ban on night flights from Munich there was a split in the group to make alternative hotel arrangements. The management and directors went to Augsburg outside Munich to stay overnight before the flight home the next morning and the players stayed in the city. As Peter Taylor recounted, 'I celebrated with an hour on a bus, I didn't even have a drink.'

'After the game, the wives had come across for the game, and were staying at a different hotel' recalls Frank Clark, 'My wife hadn't come because

Above: The victorious team. Back row (left to right): Viv Anderson, Peter Shilton, Chris Woods, John McGovern, Ian Bowyer, David Needham , Trevor Francis, Frank Clark, Jimmy Gordon. Front row (left to right): Larry Lloyd, John Robertson, Tony Woodcock, Kenny Burns, Garry Birtles.

Left: Ian Bowyer and Kenny Burns on the lap of honour.

she'd had a baby about five months before. It was so typical of Clough and Taylor, they'd never organized any celebrations, they were never into that for anything. The lads just went off with their wives and did their own thing, so there was me, Archie [his wife didn't go either], Chris Woods, who hasn't ever bought me drink in his life, and Tony Waddington, the ex-Stoke manager. Brian had invited Tony as his guest to come to the game. So that's how I celebrated winning the European Cup - having dinner with Archie, who was absolutely as miserable as hell, Woodsy who never bought a drink ever and Tony Warrington who was drunk. So I had a wonderful evening!' History shows that the European Cup final was Clark's last game as a player. He was thirty-six the next September and after coming to Forest when well into his thirties, he'd won more in two years than the rest of his career combined. 'I'd love to be able to say that I'd always planned to go out at the top but it was nothing like that at all' he says, 'I still had a year to run on my contract and I was quite happy, when I say I was quite happy, I knew my body was telling me that the end was coming because I had quite a few injuries that season, but I was quite happy playing in the reserves. Then right out of the blue this offer came from Ken Martin, who I hardly knew, saying did I fancy going to be the assistant manager at Sunderland? I thought about it and for once in my life took the brave decision.'

The team were greeted by fans at East Midlands Airport and then at the Notts County Council buildings by Trent Bridge. A second civic reception was arranged at the Council House and an open top bus tour took the players from one to the other. An estimated two hundred thousand people lined the route and packed the Old Market Square to see the European Cup paraded through the streets of Nottingham. Who would have thought it?

Evening Post
EUROPEAN CUP SPECIAL
May 31, 1979
FOREST MALMO
Salute Forest! New Kings of Europe
FOREST....1
MALMO...0

EURO CUP SPECIAL EURO CUP SPECIAL EURO CUP SPECIAL
The goal that gave Forest Euro-Cup
Pictures from Munich by TREVOR BARTLETT

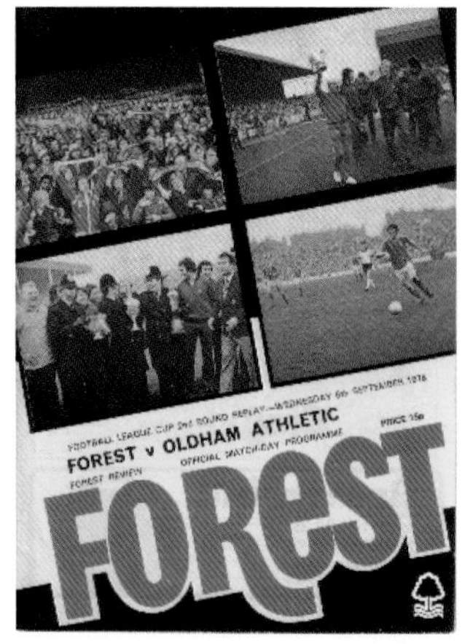

July 1978

25	Red Star Belgrade, Serbia	A	2-3	PSF
27	Dinamo Zagreb, Croatia	A	1-1	PSF
30	NK Osijek, Croatia	A	1-1	PSF

August

2	AEK Athens, Greece	A	1-1	PSF
12	Ipswich Town	N	5-0	ChSh *
14	Celta Vigo, Spain	A	1-1	PSF
16	Porto, Portugal (in Spain)	A	0-1	PSF
19	Tottenham Hotspur	H	1-1	
22	Coventry City	A	0-0	
26	Queens Park Rangers	A	0-0	
29	Oldham Athletic	A	0-0	LC2

September

2	West Bromwich Albion	H	0-0	
4	Mansfield Town	A	6-1	F*2
6	Oldham Athletic	H	4-2	LC2R
9	Arsenal	H	2-1	
13	Liverpool	H	2-0	EC1-1
16	Manchester United	A	1-1	
19	Mansfield Town	H	4-0	CCF*3
23	Middlesbrough	H	2-2	
27	Liverpool	A	0-0	EC1-2
30	Aston Villa	A	2-1	

October

4	Oxford United	A	5-0	LC3
7	Wolverhampton Wanderers	H	3-1	
14	Bristol City	A	3-1	
18	AEK Athens, Greece	A	2-1	EC2-1
21	Ipswich Town	H	1-0	
28	Southampton	A	0-0	

November

1	AEK Athens, Greece	H	5-1	EC2-2
4	Everton	H	0-0	
7	Everton	A	3-2	LC4
11	Tottenham Hotspur	A	3-1	
18	Queens Park Rangers	H	0-0	
25	Bolton Wanderers	A	1-0	

December

5	Dinamo Zagreb, Croatia	H	2-0	F
9	Liverpool	A	0-2	
13	Brighton & Hove Albion	H	3-1	LC5
16	Birmingham City	H	1-0	
23	Manchester City	A	0-0	
26	Derby County	H	1-1	

January 1979

10	Aston Villa	A	2-0	FAC3
13	Arsenal	A	1-2	
17	Watford	H	3-1	LCSF-1
27	York City	H	3-1	FAC4
30	Watford	A	0-0	LCSF-2

February

3	Middlesbrough	A	3-1	
19	Exeter City	A	5-0	F*4
21	West Bromwich Albion	A	0-0	F*5
24	Bristol City	H	2-0	
26	Arsenal	H	0-1	FAC5

March

3	Ipswich Town	A	1-1	
7	Grasshoppers Zurich, Swit.	H	4-1	EC3-1
10	Everton	A	1-1	
14	Norwich City	H	2-1	
17	Southampton	N	3-2	LCF*6
21	Grasshoppers Zurich, Swit.	A	1-1	EC3-2
24	Coventry City	H	3-0	
28	Chelsea	H	6-0	
31	Bolton Wanderers	H	1-1	

April

4	Aston Villa	H	4-0	
7	Chelsea	A	3-1	
11	Cologne, West Germany	H	3-3	ECSF-1
14	Derby County	A	2-1	
16	Leeds United	H	0-0	
18	Manchester United	H	1-1	
21	Birmingham City	A	2-0	
25	Cologne, West Germany	A	1-0	ECSF-2
28	Liverpool	H	0-0	
30	Wolverhampton Wanderers	A	0-1	

May

2	Southampton	H	1-0	
5	Norwich City	A	1-1	
9	Manchester City	H	3-1	
11	Southampton	A	4-0	F*7
15	Leeds United	A	2-1	
18	West Bromwich Albion	A	1-0	
23	Mansfield Town	H	3-1	CCF*8
30	Malmo, Sweden	N	1-0	ECF*9

	Pld	W	D	L	F	A	PTS	GD
Home	33	21	11	1	70	22	53	+48
Away	43	21	17	5	71	31	59	+40
League	42	21	18	3	61	26	60	+35
League Cup	8	6	2	0	21	8	14	+13
FA Cup	3	2	0	1	5	2	4	+3
European Cup	9	6	3	0	19	7	15	+12
Charity Shield	1	1	0	0	5	0	2	+5
County Cup	2	2	0	0	7	1	4	+6
Friendlies	11	4	5	2	23	9	13	+14
Total	**76**	**42**	**28**	**6**	**141**	**53**	**112**	**+88**

* = at Wembley/ *2 = Sandy Pate testimonial / *3 = for 1977-78 / *4 = Nick Jennings testimonial / *5 = Trevor Stokes testimonial / *6 = at Wembley / *7= Lawrie McMenemy testimonial / *8 = for 1978-79 / *9 = at Olympic Stadium, Munich, West Germany

Back row (left to right): Burns, Bowyer, Anderson, Barrett, Clark.
Middle Row (l to r): Gordon, Needham, O'Hare, Woods, Shilton, O'Neill, Lloyd, Clough.
Front row (left to right): Woodcock, McGovern, Robertson, Gemmill.

1978-79 Player Statistics

	Lge	FAC	LCup	ChSh	EC	CC	F	Totals
John Robertson	42-9	3	8-4	1-1	9-2	2-2	10(1)	75(1)-18
Peter Shilton	42	3	8	1	9	1	11	75
Viv Anderson	40-1	3	7-2	1	8	2	11-1	72-4
Tony Woodcock	36-10	3-1	8-3	1	9-1	1	11-3	69-18
John McGovern	36	3-1	7-2	1	8-1	2-1	11	68-5
Larry Lloyd	36	3-1	6-1	1-1	9-1	1-1	9	65-5
Garry Birtles	35-14	3	7-6	0	9-6	1	3-4	58-30
Martin O'Neill	28-10	3-1	6-1	1-2	4-1	0	10-1	52-16
Archie Gemmill	24-1	3	7	1	7-1	(1)	9	51(1)-2
Kenny Burns	25	1	5-1	1	5	2	9	48-1
Ian Bowyer	26(3)-4	1	5	0	7-2	1	3(5)-4	43(8)-10
David Needham	23(3)-2	2-1	6-1	(1)	4-1	1	4(4)-1	40(8)-6
Frank Clark	20	2	3	0	6	1	5	36
Colin Barrett	11-1	0	3	1	3-1	(1)-1	5(2)	23(3)-3
Trevor Francis	19(1)-6	0	0	0	1-1	1-1	1(1)	22(2)-8
John O'Hare	9(3)	0	(1)	0	1	2	1	13(4)
Steve Elliott	4	0	2	0	0	1	2(3)	9(3)
Peter Withe	1	0	0	1-1	0	0	6-2	8-3
Gary Mills	4-1	0	(1)	0	(1)	1	(1)-1	5(3)-2
Chris Woods	0	0	0	0	0	1	(1)	1(1)
Stephen Burke	0	0	0	0	0	1-1	0	1-1
Bryn Gunn	1	0	0	0	0	0	0	1

The 1979 - 80 Season

For the first time in a couple of years, the summer brought a number of significant changes to the Forest Squad. A total of six players were on the move, three on the way out and three coming in. Peter Taylor had taken the success of overseas players coming into the English game as his template and had scoured the Continent in search of new talent. Dutchman Rudi Geels and West German international Rainer Bonhof were just two players who had been scouted, but eventually Taylor turned his attention back to the domestic scene. The retirement of Frank Clark, and the continuing injury problems for Colin Barrett, meant signing a left-back was a priority. Ian Bowyer had filled in well in that position when required, but he was more valuable as a midfielder. So it was Frank Gray, Leeds United's Scottish international, that Taylor approached. A fee of £500,000 was agreed and Taylor made his move. 'I went to Peter's house actually,' says Gray. 'We had a chat and at that time Brian Clough was on holiday in Majorca so I agreed things with Peter and it just happened very quickly. One meeting was all it took. I vaguely knew John McGovern and John O'Hare already from Leeds and I knew John Robertson and Kenny Burns from playing for Scotland so it was quite easy fitting in.'

Colin Barrett battled against his persistent injuries, but the 1979-80 season was where he finally had to call it a day. 'I'd worked really hard to build the leg up,' he says, 'But it would just give way if I twisted. The surgeon had a look at it. They'd had a look at it after Cologne [the previous April] and they said have a rest and come back next season. I worked really hard through pre-season and I worked really hard throughout the year but I didn't play a league game that year. Then at the end of my contract Cloughy said, "We're going to release you." I had a three year contract and that was the final year. So that was the end of my career at Forest. When you look at what players are doing now and how they are getting back, they seem to be getting back quicker [from injury] and the technology is getting better, the rehabilitation is quicker. With cartilage operations in my day they did a massive cut in your leg and take your cartilage out. Now it's all this keyhole surgery and you're in and out in one day. The work rate you have to do now whilst you are injured is much higher. In my day they said, "You're injured have a rest."'

The other major change came in midfield. Ever since his outburst at being dropped from the European Cup Final side, Archie Gemmill had thought his days at Forest might be numbered, and he was proved right. 'They showed me who was the boss,' says Gemmill. 'Peter Taylor said, "Can I see you in the office – Birmingham want you and I want you to go. You're finished here."' So Gemmill moved to the West Midlands club for £150,000 and was replaced by another Scottish international – Manchester City's Asa Hartford. Hartford came in for £500,000 and was expected to be Forest's playmaking midfielder.

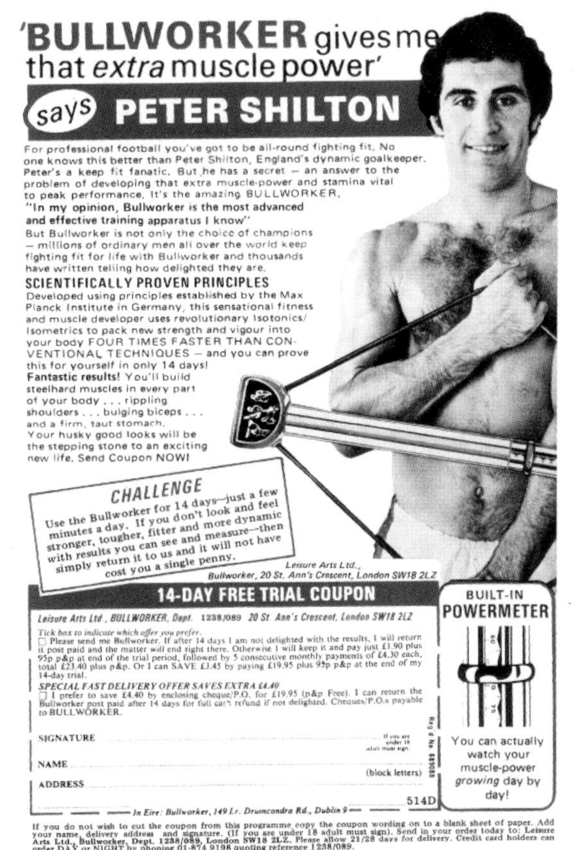

The third swap came in the back-up keeper's position. Chris Woods' contract expired and as he saw that there was no chance of getting in the team while Peter Shilton was around, he asked for a transfer. Queen's Park Rangers soon snapped him up for £250,000 and he went on to become an England international and have a long career in the top flight. To replace Woods Jim Montgomery was drafted in from Birmingham. Montgomery was realistic about his chances to play, but at the age of thirty-six (he'd even played in the same Sunderland team as Clough many years earlier) the prospect of even just being on the bench for games in the European Cup seemed attractive.

The only other playing change for the pre-season schedule was the absence of Trevor Francis who was still playing in North America as part of his summer contract with the Detroit Express.

Forest's summertime fixture list included trips to Denmark, West Germany, Spain and France against some top quality opposition. The opening game turned out to be an easy 5-1 win, but the interesting point is that for the second half Forest actually faced Peter Shilton. After racing to a 4-0 half-time lead it was agreed to let Shilton switch sides to get some work in the second period. He was kept busy and only conceded a penalty to John Robertson after seventy-seven minutes.

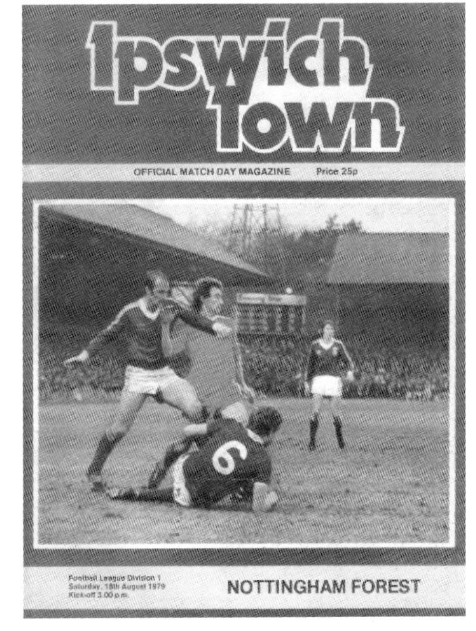

Frank Gray made his debut in the next game at Bayern Munich, and Asa Hartford again played in midfield. The Germans proved too strong though and having been training for longer due to the early start of their domestic league they out-ran Forest in a 5-0 win.

As European champions Forest were not short on offers to play around Europe and they next took part in a prestigious Spanish tournament. In the semi-final they beat Botafogo from Brazil 2-1. In an exciting game Peter Shilton had to be at his best before Forest took the lead after fifty minutes. The South Americans grabbed an equalizer after eighty-five minutes before Tony Woodcock gave the Reds a last gasp win. In the final Forest faced an entirely different proposition with a match against the solid Dynamo Bucharest team. Forest again won 2-1 to clinch the tournament. John Robertson scored with a rare header and then a penalty. A 1-0 over French Second Division side Montpelier completed the pre-season tour.

As with the previous season's Charity Shield game, it was Ipswich Town who provided the first domestic game of the new season. This time it was a much closer affair in a league game at Portman Road, and despite being under pressure for long periods of the game the Reds carved out a 1-0 win thanks to a Woodcock goal.

The midweek home opener against Stoke City showcased the new Executive Stand, the lower tier of which was already open and in use. A relatively small crowd of 26,147 witnessed City put up a spirited defence for eighty-two minutes before Martin O'Neill hammered in the only goal of the game. When Coventry City visited the City Ground a few days later they provided a more attacking threat but they failed to match Forest punch-for-punch. The Reds exploded for a 4-1 win, with John McGovern grabbing a couple of the goals. Though Forest had now won their first three games of the season, the management were unhappy with the way that the team were playing and hours before the first leg of a League Cup game at Blackburn they shocked the football world by selling Asa Hartford to Everton after just three competitive games. Ian Bowyer took his place but the Blackburn game produced only a 1-1 draw.

The next game was Forest's first real test of the fledgling season – a visit to West Bromwich Albion, whom they battled for the runners-up place last year. Things looked ominous when Gary Owen scored for Albion after only seventy seconds but Forest soon took control and ran out 5-1 winners. Ron Atkinson, the Albion manager admitted afterwards that it could easily have been seven or eight – especially as a Kenny Burns shot that flew into the top corner from thirty yards on the stroke of half-time was ruled out as the referee had blown his whistle while the ball was in the air! Garry Birtles helped himself to his first hat-trick and Frank Gray added his first goal for the club. Forest led the First Division and they still had Trevor Francis to come back.

First Division Table (Top five only)

	Pld	Pts	GD
FOREST	**4**	**8**	**+9**
Norwich City	4	6	+5
Manchester United	4	6	+3
Middlesbrough	4	5	+4
Crystal Palace	4	5	+4

(*after games of 1 September 1979*)

The return leg of the League Cup tie with Blackburn Rovers saw Duncan McKenzie return to the City Ground and the former Reds hero was given a warm reception. Rovers managed to keep the game close and Forest were leading only 2-1 after an hour. They stepped things up late in though and rattled in four late goals for a comprehensive 6-1 win.

The following two league games were something of a let down. A 0-0 draw at home to Leeds saw Forest well on top but unable to beat David Harvey (whom Clough had tried to sell during his brief spell as Leeds manager) and then a 3-1 loss at Norwich saw Forest out-played. Hardly the best warm-up for the opening game in their defence of the European Cup.

The first round European Cup opponents were Oesters Vaxjo, the inheritors of Malmo's Swedish league crown. A small crowd of twenty-two thousand turned out for the game which Forest won comfortably. Without ever really getting into top gear the Reds controlled the first half but the closest they came to scoring was in the thirty-fifth minute when Kenny Burns hit the post. Ian Bowyer then stepped forward to impose Forest's superiority with goals after sixty-two and seventy-five minutes. The game ended 2-0 and was expected to be enough for the second leg in a fortnight.

With one cup campaign underway the task of winning the League Cup for a record third consecutive time was begun. A potentially tricky tie at Middlesbrough saw the Reds under pressure for the first twenty-five minutes before eighteen year old Gary Mills broke forward and produced the opening goal for Tony Woodcock. Forest were then content to play conservatively and hit the home side on the break, and though a Larry Lloyd back pass eventually let David Armstrong score after fifty-two minutes but two more goals by Woodcock in a six minute span iced a fine 3-1 win. This fine form was carried over into Liverpool's visit to the City Ground on 29 September which Forest won 1-0. This was the Reds first league victory over Liverpool since their return to the First Division two years earlier. Garry Birtles scored the winning goal after some fine work by Martin O'Neill.

Left: Ian Bowyer correctly predicts where John Robertson's penalty is going in the cup-tie against Blackburn at the City Ground.

Below left: Viv Anderson and Larry Lloyd battle in through the rain against Oesters Vaxjo in the European Cup.

Below: Peter Shilton and Viv Anderson look at each other after conceding a goal at Norwich.

Though Forest travelled to Sweden for the second leg against Oesters in a confident mood, they did have to be on their guard. The afternoon before Forest's game had seen Liverpool crash out of the competition with a shock 3-0 loss to Dinamo Tbilisi. This warning held some weight and after fifty-three

minutes Oesters led 1-0 after a Viv Anderson mistake had allowed Evesson to cross for Nordgren to score. The aggregate score was now just 2-1 and good work by Gary Mills was required to supply a cross for Tony Woodcock to calm the nerves with a headed goal to end the scoring. Forest were still unbeaten in their eleven European Cup matches to date.

Trevor Francis was now back in the country and ready to play in the home league game against Wolverhampton Wanderers. 'Unfortunately I was hampered towards the end of my time over in Detroit,' says Francis, 'I had a groin problem and as a result of it it forced me to miss the first few games back in Nottingham. That was disappointing because having joined the club half way through the last season it would have been nice if I could have had a full pre-season and then started the season with the team but I wasn't able to do that. I played it very hard in Detroit and whilst it wasn't of the standard that we'd come to expect in England, as the big star in the team I had to perform at the highest level every time I played. When I first started in Detroit I think the first crowd was about nine thousand and then we got to the play-offs and we were up to thirty thousand. So it was certainly gathering momentum. I really enjoyed my time there. It was a great place to play and a great place to live.'

Francis marked his return in fine style with a goal in the opening seconds as Forest won 3-1. A draw at Stoke and a loss at Manchester City was swiftly forgotten after a 5-2 thumping of Bolton stretched the Reds' unbeaten home record to fifty games.

Another low key European Cup encounter with Romania's Arges Pitesti again failed to catch the public's imagination and fewer than twenty-five thousand attended the home leg on 24 October. Woodcock and Birtles scored the goals in a 2-0 win against the over-physical Romanians, who had Mihai Zanfir sent off for two yellow cards. Though it was another healthy first leg lead it was noted that Pitesti had come from behind to beat AEK Athens in the first round – they had lost the away leg 2-0 but won 3-0 at home to set up the Forest clash.

Forest's away form continued to be a problem and a loss at Spurs and a League Cup draw at Bristol City were seen as even more disappointing after a good 2-0 home win over

Ipswich. These poor away displays gave Reds fans a modicum of trepidation about the trip to Romania for the next European Cup game. 'There was more talk about Dracula because Vlad the Impaler was from that area,' says John McGovern. 'We had to eat what was given to us and red cabbage and garlic sausage was the staple diet. We didn't take our own food in those days, we just had to put up with it.'

'The food was terrible,' agrees Garry Birtles. 'You had to book a phone call hours before you made it, it was like a Third World country.' Larry Lloyd was equally unhappy on the trip, 'I thought it was the end of the world! The food was awful. Its the worst place I've ever been to.' The game was given an afternoon kick-off time because the ageing stadium didn't have any floodlights. The ground starting filling up at lunchtime and the atmosphere gradually built up until kick off. The hostile home crowd was quietened after just five minutes though. A John Robertson corner was chested down by Larry Lloyd and Ian Bowyer pounced to extend the overall lead to 3-0. Then a flowing move ended with a Tony Woodcock cross for Garry Birtles to score. Pitesti's only reply was a harsh penalty on the hour that left the final aggregate score as 4-1. If only this form could be transferred to away games in the league.

The next fourteen days proved to be the low point of the season. A League Cup win over Bristol City (3-0) was the lone highlight of the fortnight which included devastating 4-1 losses at both Southampton and Derby. These were the biggest losses for many years and the Derby one was even more appalling as the Rams were struggling at the foot of the table. Amidst this carnage the long running unbeaten home streak came to an end with a shock 1-0 defeat to lowly Brighton & Hove Albion in which John Robertson missed a penalty. If all of this wasn't bad enough it was then revealed that Tony Woodcock had been sold. 'I knew Cologne had been interested and they'd conducted themselves very well,' recalls Woodcock. 'I went to see the [Forest] management and told them what I wanted to earn and they just laughed and said "No." So I agreed all the terms with Cologne and then Clough took me out to lunch and said "Whatever you want you can have it, lets get that contract signed." But it was too late, if he'd said that a few weeks earlier I probably would have stayed, who knows?' Woodcock moved for a discounted price of £650,000 (UEFA had a ceiling on European transfer fees) and he soon became a star in West Germany. 'It went from having to ask Clough if I could do an interview to getting there and having all the German press at the airport and seven thousand people turning up at training to see me' says Woodcock. The last few weeks had been the most difficult in quite a while and the team were taken away for a break in Egypt at the end of November. While there they played a friendly against a Cairo Select XI. 'As European champions we were offered a lot of money to go and play,' explains Garry Birtles. 'I played so many games that year I wondered why I had blood blisters at the end of the season! The Egypt trip was nice and we were at a hotel overlooking the Nile and we saw the pyramids and things like that.'

John Robertson in action against Arges.

Ian Bowyer scores in Romania.

Forest's inconsistent form continued to be a problem after the return home. Arsenal came to the City Ground and held on for a 1-1 draw as Frank Stapleton scored against Forest again. Garry Birtles equalized for Forest late in the game. Another draw, this time at Second Division side West Ham United, in the League Cup, was a hard fought affair with Trevor Brooking pulling the strings for the team in front of a highly charged crowd. Another trip to London was less profitable as the Reds lost 1-0 at Terry Venables' newly promoted Crystal Palace. The League Cup replay with West Ham was another hard slog of a game. Played in pouring rain, the visitors matched Forest and took the game into extra time. The Reds eventually broke the visitors' resistance in the extra session as John O'Hare, in his best game of the season, opened the scoring with further goals being added by Birtles and O'Neill.

The loss of Archie Gemmill, and then Asa Hartford, had still not been fully addressed and it was no secret that Peter Taylor was still looking to add to the Forest squad. With the departure of Tony Woodcock he had the need for another goal scorer as well as a midfielder. At one point it looked as though he might bring young striker Peter Ward to Nottingham from Brighton, then Forest almost swapped Martin O'Neill for Coventry's Mick Ferguson but both deals fell through. When Taylor did finally sign a new player it was a complete surprise – Queen's Park Rangers' Stan Bowles.

Bowles had a reputation of a gambler and a drinker and seemed an unlikely candidate to fit in with Clough and Taylor's disciplined football philosophy. But then again, so had Kenny Burns and Larry Lloyd and they had done superbly well at Forest. It was well known that Bowles was no longer the player that had terrorized opposition defences in the mid-70s, but he still had a high degree of skill even if some of his pace had gone. Rangers had been relegated to the Second Division and new manager Tommy Docherty had all but replaced Bowles with Tony Currie. 'I knew that under the manager's discipline Stan wouldn't be a problem,' says John McGovern. 'He settled in after about ten seconds, he was a bubbly character and he did everything with enthusiasm.' Bowles was given an attacking midfield role by Clough and he made his debut in a friendly in Cologne which had been arranged as part of the Tony Woodcock transfer deal. Lloyd scored for Forest and Woodcock scored his first goal for Cologne.

First Division Table, Top 10

	Pld	Pts	GD
Liverpool	19	28	+29
Manchester United	20	28	+16
Arsenal	20	23	+10
Crystal Palace	20	23	+5
Norwich City	20	22	+4
Wolverhampton Wanderers	19	22	0
Southampton	20	21	+5
Aston Villa	19	21	+1
Tottenham Hotspur	20	21	-4
FOREST	**19**	**20**	**+4**

(*before games of 22 December 1979*)

Bowles' league debut came the following Saturday at Old Trafford. United had moved up the table and were currently joint top with Liverpool, with Forest lagging eight points behind. The whole division was very close and just six points separated the third and nineteenth placed teams. If Forest could get their away form to something approaching respectability they could be back in the hunt in a hurry. It wasn't to be against Manchester United though. By half-time United led 3-0 and despite having a good second half the Reds couldn't get back into it and there was no further scoring. Forest's away record in the league was now almost the worst in the division: Pld11 W2 D2 L7 F11 A20 Pts6. Luckily the excellent home form (only one loss in ten home games) was keeping the Reds in a mid-table position.

Bowles had his biggest effect for Forest in the next two games. He scored the winner at home against Aston Villa (won 2-1) and he scored again in a rare 3-0 win at Coventry three days later. These were the only goals he scored during his time at Forest. Normal service was resumed on New Year's Day at Everton as the Reds slipped to a 1-0 defeat.

So the trip to Leeds for the third round of the FA Cup didn't fill the Forest faithful with too much confidence. It was another example of Forest's Jekyl and Hyde character though because Forest ran out easy 4-1 winners at Elland Road. It was an especially sweet return for Frank Gray, his first in a Forest shirt. 'I got a fairly good reception,' says Gray, 'but I don't think they were too keen on me after the first minute.' That's because Gray gave Forest the lead in the first seconds of the game. 'I was a little bit apprehensive,' he says, 'because I'd been at Leeds for a long time. It was my first trip back and we got a free-kick twenty yards out in the first minute and luckily enough I managed to put it in the corner.' Birtles, Bowyer and Robertson also scored in the 4-1 win.

After another home win (3-1 over West Bromwich Albion), Forest again visited Elland Road, this time in the league. In the gap between the two visits to Leeds, Forest had brought in Charlie George from Southampton on a months loan. He, like Bowles, was seen as something of a maverick character and the sight of the two of them in the same Forest line up went against all that the public at large thought of Brian Clough's team selection policies. But of course Clough was nothing if not unconventional. After the Reds went 2-1 ahead at Elland Road it was George and Bowles who helped kill the game off by keeping the ball from the home side for long periods of the second half. The win pushed Forest back towards a more respectable league position, which was important because only one of the next six games was for league points. The next two games were real key match ups as Forest faced Liverpool at the City Ground in the League Cup semi-final *and* the fifth round of the FA Cup.

The League Cup clash saw Liverpool spurn chance after chance as Forest struggled to get into the game. Graeme Souness hit the post, Shilton made two breathtaking saves from Kenny Dalglish (who stretched his personal scoreless streak against the Reds to nine games) and Jimmy Case shot over the bar when he looked like scoring. Forest got back into the game after the break with Trevor Francis going close, but just when it looked like being a goalless draw, Forest were awarded a very late penalty which John Robertson converted. The relief at getting the goal was tempered a little by

the thought of having to defend the lead at Anfield which, bearing in mind the current away form, would be a massive task to undertake. The FA Cup game showed how difficult the Reds' task would be as Liverpool carved out a 2-0 win. Dalglish finally beat Shilton in the first half and after Dave Needham handled the ball, Terry McDermott scored a penalty to seal the visitors triumph. Forest now had three weeks to prepare for the trip to Anfield.

In the mean time there was a pair of attractive games against Spanish giants Barcelona in the UEFA Super Cup, played between the winners of the European Cup and the European Cup Winners' Cup. Forest hosted the first leg and the Spaniards, managed by Brazilian great Carlos Alberto and featuring Danish star Allan Simonsen, played a containing game to keep the score down. Even when the Reds took a ninth minute lead from a Charlie George header Barcelona were happy to keep players behind the ball. The return leg was in the heaving cauldron of the Nou Camp, which had ninety thousand crammed inside expecting the home team to overrun Forest and take the trophy. Unlike the first leg Barcelona attacked in waves and they got a penalty, after a Frank Gray foul, on the thirty-minute mark. Forest nerves were settled before half-time as Kenny Burns regained the overall lead for the Reds. Kenny Burns recollection of the goal is typically to the point: 'When we went to that wonderful stadium we walked down the tunnel and they'd got a chapel in there and their players were all going in there and crossing themselves. They scored first and then we got a corner. Larry

[Lloyd] went to the near post, got a flick on and I came in the middle and scored the goal. That shut them up!'

Early in the second half John Robertson had a great chance to put the tie beyond reach but he missed from the penalty spot after Bowles had been tripped. There was no further scoring and Forest added another cup to the trophy cabinet. It was the first (and last) medal that Stan Bowles ever won.

Above: Kenny Burns shuts them up in Barcelona!
Below left: The Super Cup winners. Back row, left to right: O'Neill, Lloyd, Anderson, Bowles (closely inspecting his first medal), George, Needham, Shilton. Front row, left to right: Gray, McGovern, Burns, Birtles, Robertson.

Having won in the FA Cup at the City Ground, Liverpool had high hopes of overcoming the 1-0 first leg deficit. Against the odds Forest put up one of their best away performances of the season despite the absence of Francis, Bowles and George. Martin O'Neill was pushed into an out-and-out attacking role alongside Garry Birtles and young Gary Mills came in on the right side of the midfield. It was O'Neill's attacking endeavour that put him through on goal forcing Ray Clemence to bring him down for a penalty. Robertson made no mistake this time and gave Forest the vital away goal and a 2-0 aggregate lead. Liverpool were visibly deflated and Gary Mills had a great chance to score again before Liverpool substitute David Fairclough pulled back a consolation goal in the dying seconds. It was too little too late and Forest were going back to Wembley for an unprecedented third straight League Cup Final.

Right: Yet another victorious team group, this time after the League Cup semi-final win at Anfield. Back row, left to right: Gray, O'Neill, Burns, Lloyd, Mills, Robertson, Birtles, Anderson, Bowyer, Needham. Front row, left to right: McGovern, Taylor, Clough, Shilton.

Just a week later Forest were back at Anfield for the fourth Liverpool-Forest match of the last four weeks. Again Forest frustrated Liverpool, for eighty minutes at least. Eventually the home side took the points with two late strikes. It was the same old story in the league – lose away, win at home. A 4-0 thrashing of Manchester City at the City Ground (with a hat-trick from Trevor Francis) was followed by a 1-0 loss at Bolton. Not exactly ideal preparation for the quarter-final of the European Cup.

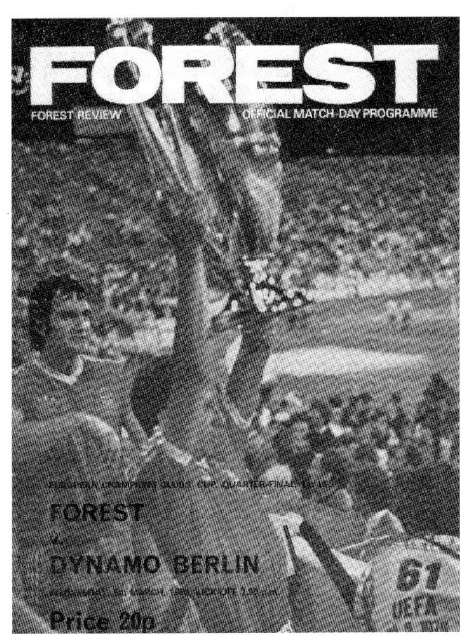

Dynamo Berlin, the East German champions, were the opponents in the last eight. Dynamo had won their domestic league, losing just one of their twenty-six league games on the way to the title. Their side, which made up over half of the East German national team, included six foot six goalkeeper Bobo Rudwaleit, prolific centre-forward Hans-Jurgen Reidiger and hard-working captain Frank Terletzki. They'd reached the last eight by winning both home games and drawing both away ones against the champions of Poland and Switzerland. Forest entered the

game with a full strength side with the exception of the suspended Viv Anderson. Bryn Gunn took the right-back berth. Berlin put in a classic European away performance: they defended in numbers and attacked on the break. They also took a chance when it came their way. For the first hour Forest had hardly been troubled at the back but had also been unable to break down the stubborn East German defence. On the sixty-three minute mark Forest were attacking in numbers when Stan Bowles gave the ball away on the edge of Berlin's penalty area. A long pass to the German's left-wing suddenly spelled danger for Forest. A quick switch of play to the right side left Frank Gray exposed and Reidiger cut inside him and scored. Things could have been even worse, but Peter Shilton pulled off a great save in the last moments of the game to keep the Reds in the tie.

Forest didn't have time to dwell on the disappointment as a league game at home to Tottenham and the League Cup Final at Wembley were the next two games. The Spurs game saw a backlash to the European defeat and Forest won convincingly with goals from Burns (two) and Francis (two).

Wembley had become Forest's second home during the past three years, and the League Cup Final was in danger of being taken for granted. This third final in three years brought them up against Midland rivals Wolverhampton Wanderers. Wolves had been promoted with Forest back in 1977, but since then had hovered just above the relegation places for two years. At this point in the 1979-80 season they were holding a respectable mid-table position just below Forest. Manager John Barnwell (an ex-Forest player) had reshaped the side bringing in ex-Liverpool captain Emlyn Hughes and striker Andy Gray from Aston Villa for a new record transfer fee of £1.5 million. Their road to Wembley had been a tricky one with three replays required, including two against Grimsby Town, and a close encounter with Third Division Swindon Town in the semi-final. Wolves finally edged through 4-3 on aggregate after losing the opening leg 2-1. Forest had required a couple of replays on the way but some of their best form of the season had come in this competition – most notably the semi-final against Liverpool. Overall Forest had scored nineteen goals in nine League Cup games.

As usual, Wembley was at its capacity of one hundred thousand for the game, and as usual the Clough and Taylor partnership were more than happy to spring a surprise. Clough had led the team out in the 1978 final against Liverpool. Taylor had led them out the previous year against Southampton. This time they gave the honour to trainer Jimmy Gordon. Gordon was only told of their decision just before kick-off and didn't have time to change out of his tracksuit. The team he led out was at full strength apart from the suspended Larry Lloyd who was replaced by David Needham.

Forest set out their stall to attack right from the off and for over an hour they probed the Wolves defence without any luck. Wolves 'keeper Paul Bradshaw as surviving on an equal measure of luck and ability, but Forest just couldn't score. Then after sixty-seven minutes, Wolves' Peter Daniel hit a long hopeful ball towards the Forest area. There seemed to be no danger as David Needham recalls: 'Everyone remembers this of course! It was the second League Cup Final that I'd played in. I was up against Andy Gray and I was having a really, really good game. I was really enjoying it and on top of my game. They hadn't caused us any problems and Andy hadn't had a kick. Then they threw this long ball right into the edge of the box and on a normal day I suppose I would have headed it back to the halfway line and be done with it, but I went to chest it down to Peter Shilton in goal. Unbeknown to me, and very unusually for Peter, he'd come for the same ball. Now there's a disagreement, I always say he didn't shout, he always says he shouted and because of the crowd I didn't hear him. We have that little argument every now and again. But as far as I was concerned I heard no shout and I thought it was going back into his arms. But we collided on the edge of the box.' With Shilton and Needham on the floor the ball rolled towards the unguarded net and Andy Gray had the easy task of knocking it over the line. He then celebrated like he'd just scored the best goal ever. Maybe it was just the thrill of scoring against the two time holders at Wembley. For the rest of the game Forest camped in the Wolves half but it was not to be. The twenty-five game unbeaten run in the League Cup was over.

'It was just one of those games,' says Frank Gray. 'They got a lucky break for their goal, it was probably the easiest goal Andy Gray ever scored, and it was just one of those games where we weren't going to score a goal. It was a big disappointment.' John McGovern: 'One fluke goal won it and we were bitterly disappointed. We wanted to win it three times in a row and keep the trophy.'

Yet again Forest had no time to sulk as the following Wednesday they had to retrieve a one goal deficit in East Germany to keep hold of the European Cup. European success was becoming even more important because with the League Cup loss and the mid-table league position Forest would not qualify for any European competitions unless they did so as holders of the European Cup.

Travelling to East Berlin was not an easy situation for a western team to find itself in. The players were a little shocked to see guards at the airport with machine guns on full view and John Robertson was detained for questioning for about half an hour at Customs. Then the club secretary, Ken Smales, had to explain why the official travel arrangements listed one more member of the party than was actually present – this was due to Kenny Burns being suspended and not making the trip. Eventually the team got through the red tape and to the hotel. The first day in Berlin was taken up with some light training and a sightseeing tour of all the famous landmarks. The Wall, Checkpoint Charlie and the Brandenburg gate were all visited. John O'Hare also recalls that the players had the chance to go shopping but that it was a 'really sombre place'.

On the morning of the game the squad visited the ground for a training session. 'It was absolutely freezing. We are talking *cold*,' says Larry Lloyd. 'I remember the morning of the match we went down to get our training kit and Jimmy Gordon gave us the socks, the shorts and the shirt but no jumpers, no tracksuits or anything. We were all complaining and Cloughie walked in and says "What?! Do you think you'll be wearing a tracksuit tonight? Go out and get used to it." The people watching us thought that we were mad.'

'It was a bitterly cold night,' says Francis. 'One of the coldest nights I've ever experienced playing football.'

John McGovern agrees, adding 'It was the coldest night I ever played a game on.'

'Trevor Francis was electric that night.
He scored a couple of goals and played very well. It was probably one of our best performances that year.'
- Frank Gray.

Like the Cologne game twelve months earlier, everyone outside the club had Forest written off. The defeat at Wembley only increased the number of doomsayers. Trevor Francis had come in for particular criticism from the management after the Wembley loss. 'Literally an hour before the kick-off Brian Clough pulled me to one side,' says Francis, 'he said, "Where do you want to play?" I said "Well I want to play up front, up the middle." I'd played wide at Wembley against Wolves. He said, "Well start up front, and make sure you stay there!" I think he'd made his mind up already and I don't think he needed confirmation from me because he knew what my favourite position was. I think that Peter [Taylor] quite liked John [Robertson] on one side with his cleverness and his trickery and myself on the other side giving a totally different option with my pace on the other side. But Cloughie wanted me to play up the middle.'

Forest fans behind the Berlin Wall.

It was another classic case of the Forest camp being confident, seemingly against all the odds. 'I think the whole thing about Taylor and Cloughie was that they were unconventional,' explains David Needham, 'more like Morecombe and Wise than football managers. Peter was always winding people up, keeping them on their toes with funny stories, but there was always a serious sort of meaning to what he was saying.' John O'Hare adds that 'There was never any trepidation and that came from Clough and Taylor, they gave you a massive amount of confidence to go and win any game.'

Dynamo had had slightly better preparation for the game – they won a league game the previous weekend 10-0! The Jahn Sportpark was filled to its thirty thousand capacity but Dynamo had received applications for 150,000 tickets. The Forest side was very similar to the League Cup Final, David Needham kept his place because of Burns suspension and Larry Lloyd returned to partner him at the centre of the defence. The teams left the dressing room for an extra long walk to the pitch (about a quarter of a mile) in freezing conditions. Forest's non-playing staff were also exposed to the elements, their was no cover for the team bench, just a row of seats on the running track that circled the pitch. Peter Taylor was wrapped in a winter coat and wore his trademark flat-cap and Brian Clough was wrapped in a heavy blanket. The subs were huddled together alongside, shivering in the extreme cold. With the player's breath making clouds before their faces Forest kicked-off, knowing that at least two goals would be needed to get through and a draw or loss would see them tumble out of Europe.

Viv Anderson and Frank Gray were both eager to push forward from their full-back positions on either flank, but the Germans were again employing a very disciplined, tight-marking system. An Ian Bowyer shot that deflected for a corner was the closest that either side came in the opening fifteen minutes. Moments later Bowyer was fouled just inside the Dynamo half. David Needham pushed forward for the free kick which was going to be taken by Larry Lloyd. Lloyd hit it long towards his defensive partner. Needham got between two defenders at the Dynamo penalty spot and flicked the ball back with his head. Trevor Francis showed his lightning quick pace to get a step ahead of Ullrich and poke it past the goalie from six yards. The tie was all equal again after just seventeen minutes. Forest were visibly growing in confidence now. Garry Birtles got a chance to turn and moved away from his marker. His low shot from thirty yards whizzed just wide of the left hand post with the keeper well beaten. Berlin realized that they couldn't be content to just sit back this time, and they too started to push forward, making for a fairly open game. A Berlin free-kick just outside the Forest box caused an anxious moment when it was passed inside, and the quick shot that came in looked to be past Shilton, but he dived full length and pushed it out for a corner.

The game was flowing from end to end now. A long pass by Needham sent Francis away down the right and he crossed to Birtles, whose low, stopping header almost caught out Rudwaleit at his near post. Terletski was proving to be a constant threat with his probing down the left wing and a Reidiger header from a corner looped over Shilton but luckily drifted wide of the far post. Terletski then set off on a quick break but shot high at the end of it.

With ten minutes to go until half-time Forest struck again. A great move involving Anderson, McGovern and O'Neill working some close passing triangles produced the opening. An incisive ball to Trevor Francis with his back to goal didn't seem immediately dangerous but all in one motion he managed to turn his marker and shoot high under the bar for his second goal. Forest now led 2-0 on the night and 2-1 overall. Even if Dynamo pulled one back the Reds would go through on away goals. 'The second goal was as good as Maradona or anyone,' says John McGovern, 'that showed why we paid a million pounds for him.'

Peter Taylor had commented after the Wolves game that Frank Gray had been the best player at Wembley and he continued that form here, putting in one of his best performances in a red shirt. He was crucially involved in the move that led to Forest's third goal. John McGovern broke up an attack on edge of his own box and sent Gray away down the centre of the pitch. He played in Birtles, who fed Robertson out on the right wing for a change. As he went to beat the defender he was brought down for a penalty. He picked himself up, scored the spot kick and Forest were in dreamland. Three-nil up at half-time.

Dynamo came out with renewed vigour in the second half and Forest had to defend well throughout the whole team. Unfortunately it was Robertson, working back well to help Frank Gray at left-back, who gave away a penalty early in the second period. Shilton got a hand to the kick and almost saved it, but it was too powerful and Forest were left with forty minutes of defending to do. Berlin did have their moments. At one point Anderson seemed to have been pulled down but instead Berlin were given a free-kick on their left-wing. It was sent over to the far post but the incoming header hit the underside of the bar and was scrambled away. Their only other real chance came with ten minutes left when Netz volleyed wide from eight yards when he should really have scored. It really had been the proverbial 'game of two halves.' For the first forty-five minutes Forest had showed all of their flair, pace and attacking prowess; then for the second forty-five they displayed a stubborn resilience to close out the victory. In doing so they became the first club in the history of the European Cup to lose a first leg at home and still progress to the next round. On their return to East Midlands Airport at 1 a.m. there were several hundred fans waiting to welcome them home in the cold, but compared to Berlin the Nottinghamshire night was positively balmy.

32 Evening Post, Thursday, March 20, 1980

ro Cup special ★ Euro Cup

TWO OF THE BEST FOR TREV!

DYNAMO BERLIN . . . 1, NOTTINGHAM FOREST . . . 3
(Forest won 3-2 on aggregate)

SEASONED Scot John O'Hare should have been given a mc attentive hearing before Nottingham Forest's brilliant Europe Cup fightback in East Berlin last night ended in their progressi to the semi-finals.

O'Hare, who knows Brian Clough and Peter Taylor as well as any pla in the game, said as the champions went into the second leg 0-1 down faced what some considered a virtually impossible task: "The managem are never more dangerous than when they have been written off."

Late March and early April saw the Reds avenge a couple of defeats from earlier in the season as they topped Southampton and Manchester United at home, both by 2-0 scores. The away form continued to suffer though, a 3-2 loss at Aston Villa and a 1-0 loss at Brighton prevented Forest from moving very far up the table. Europe was providing a nice distraction from the infuriating league performances and now the Reds were faced with the exciting prospect of a semi-final challenge against three-time European champions Ajax.

Ajax were probably the most famous name that Forest had to face on their European travels. The Dutch side had won three consecutive European Cups in the early 1970s but that team had now largely been broken up. Their sweeper, Rudi Kroll was the sole surviving member of those glory years, but he had a strong, new supporting cast around him. Goalkeeper Piet Schrijvers had kept goal for Holland in some 1978 World Cup games, attacking midfielder Soren Lerby was their star import from Denmark and Frank Arneson was the Dutch Player of the Year. En route to the semi-final Ajax had already rattled in an astonishing thirty goals, nine of which had been scored by Lerby. In the first round they easily disposed of Finnish champions Helsinki JK 8-1 at home and 8-1 away. A crushing 10-0 home win over Omonia Nicosia in the second round allowed Ajax to field a weakened team in the return and they lost 4-0. The quarter-finals had seen a relatively easy 4-0 aggregate win over Strasbourg.

Forest were the first side they'd come up against that actually came out and attacked them. The Reds pushed forward throughout the game, sometimes they had nine men in and around the Ajax penalty area. It took the Reds until the thirty-third minute to open the scoring. First a short corner allowed Robertson to fire in a cross shot that beat the keeper but whistled wide. Soon after another corner was whipped into the near post where Lloyd was being man-marked by Lerby. The ball eluded them both and almost went straight in but the combination of the defender standing by the post and a sprawling Schrijvers diverted it out to a grateful Trevor Francis who volleyed the rebound in from five yards out. Forest had to wait until the sixty minute mark to increase their lead. Stan Bowles and Garry Birtles worked an opening for Francis who managed to lob the ball from an acute angle, across the penalty are, past the keeper and into the six-yard box. The ball bounced awkwardly in front of the defender Zwamborn, who panicked and handled the ball while trying to get in under control – penalty. Robertson made no mistake from the spot. Within seconds it was almost 3-0 when Francis had a shot saved from ten yards, but 2-0 was a decent score to take to Amsterdam.

The only league game between the Ajax matches was the local derby at home to struggling Derby County. Frank Gray's free-kick was the only goal of the game, one which went a little way to wiping out the memories of the 4-1 defeat at the Baseball Ground and was just about the final nail in the coffin which condemned Derby to the Second Division.

As was becoming usual before the big European Cup games, Forest spent the two days leading up to the Ajax match doing just a little bit of light training and plenty of relaxing. On the night before the game Clough and Taylor took the squad on a walking tour of Amsterdam, including the famous red-light district. The methods used to team-bond and relax the players reached new heights of strangeness when Peter Taylor spent a few minutes bartering at the door of a strip joint while trying to get a discount for a group booking! He never intended to take the players in but the sight of him haggling with the doorman gave everyone a good laugh and they all went to a standard bar for a couple of drinks afterwards.

Ajax had an even more impressive home European record than Liverpool – just a single loss in forty-six home games. Because of the demand for tickets the home side had changed the venue from their own twenty-five thousand capacity ground to Amsterdam's sixty-five thousand capacity Olympic Stadium. The larger venue still sold out very quickly, including a strong following of eight thousand Forest fans. The

game kicked-off in a near hysterical atmosphere as Ajax fans tried to will their team into the European Cup Final for the first time in seven years. Forest fielded a full-strength team and they needed to. Ajax pushed forward with attack after attack, while Forest needed all of their counter-attacking skills to be in top gear. Peter Shilton also needed to be in top form, and he was. Two of the scariest moments for Forest fans came when Ajax had a couple of free-kicks on the edge of the area. A great save from one by Bonsinnk in the first half was bettered by one from a Soren Lerby shot in the second half that deflected off the Forest defensive wall.

Forest desperately wanted an away goal, which would have killed the tie dead. Their best chance came early in the second half when a Frank Gray cross was headed wide by Trevor Francis from five yards. Francis also had defensive duties to stick to as well. 'I was given a job to do by the manager,' he says, 'Whenever we didn't have possession of the ball it was my responsibility to be the first one to go in and close down as quickly as possible on Ruud Kroll. He was one of the world's outstanding defenders at the time and a fantastic passer of the ball. I mean Franz Beckenbauer was regarded as probably one of the greatest sweepers there's ever been but I think Ruud Kroll was certainly up there with him.'

After sixty-six minutes, the Ajax pressure finally paid dividends when a left-wing corner from Jensen was headed home by Lerby at the far post. Ajax rushed back to the centre circle to get the game restarted but that was the closest they came to salvaging the tie. Forest lost the game 1-0 but qualified for the final 2-1.

The Reds did finally manage to put some consistent league form together after the Ajax game as they went on a run of three wins and two draws. These games included the many games in hand that they had left to catch up on. A draw at Middlesbrough and a 2-0 home victory over Norwich helped the league position look even better and then Crystal Palace visited the City Ground on 3 May 1980. Under Terry Venables, Palace had played some attractive, attacking football during the season, with the tricky Vince Hilare on the wing and Gerry Francis play-making from the midfield. This easy-on-the-eye style had also translated into league points early in the year but by May they had slipped to eleventh place after drawing sixteen of their forty-one league matches. Before the game Larry Lloyd was presented with his Supporter's Club Player of the Year award. The Reds were in the mood to attack and they proceeded to take Palace apart. Lloyd added to his enjoyment of the afternoon by scoring a goal to go with a John Robertson and two Trevor Francis strikes that left Forest 4-0 ahead going into the last twenty minutes with the probability of more goals to come, especially with Francis chasing a hat-trick.

As predicted, Forest attacked again. Trevor Francis sprinted towards the Palace goal at the Bridgford End, with no defenders near him, and he just fell to the ground clutching his ankle. After receiving treatment on the pitch for several minutes he was placed on a trolley and wheeled around the edge of the pitch and back to the dressing room to a standing ovation. It couldn't be that serious could it? No one had been near him when he fell. 'I got a couple of goals and we were 4-0 up and I had so much to look forward to,' recalls Francis. 'The European Championships with England were that summer plus the European Cup Final for Forest. I was carted off to hospital where it was diagnosed that I would be out for seven or eight months with a ruptured Achilles tendon. I knew more or less how bad it was when I was in the ambulance, but it was confirmed when I got to the hospital. It was a desperately disappointing moment for me. The previous season, first chance I had to play [in the European Cup] was in the final and I felt as if I was it wasn't justified. Whilst I was very

happy to play in the Final I felt that in the second year I'd certainly played my part in helping them get there and I thoroughly deserved to be in the Final.'

With Francis out for the season it left Forest with a big problem. The transfer deadline had long since passed so there was no chance of bringing someone else in, and Garry Birtles was now the only recognized striker in the squad. With the team in a state of shock they limped through the last three league games with Arsenal (0-0), Everton (1-0) and at Wolves (1-3). The Reds were extremely disappointed to finish fifth in the table. Two seasons earlier they would have jumped at the chance to do so. The inconsistent mid-season form had definitely cost them the chance of a championship challenge, especially as Liverpool won the title with only sixty points, eight less than 1978-79. The Mersysiders had lost seven league games during the season, while Forest had lost only six in the two previous seasons combined!

First Division Table, Top 7

	Pld	Pts	GD
Liverpool	40	58	+49
Manchester United	41	58	+22
Ipswich Town	41	53	+30
Arsenal	38	47	+19
Wolverhampton Wanderers	39	44	+10
Aston Villa	40	44	+3
FOREST	**37**	**41**	**+15**

(*before games of 30 April 1980*)

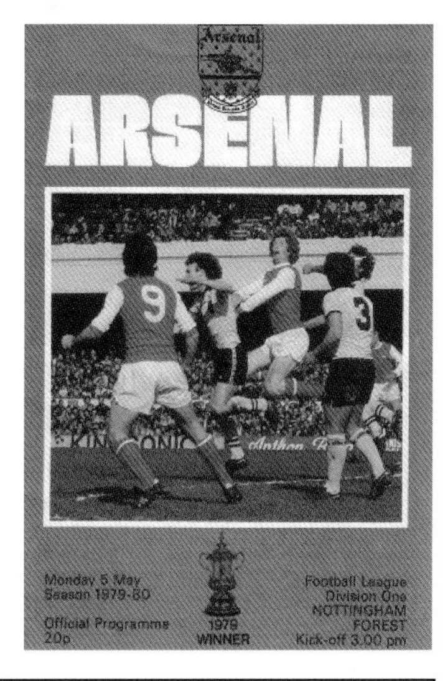

Forest had a record of W10 D5 L2 at the start and end of the year, but the middle section had been only average with W10 D3 L12. The Reds had lost ten games by a score of 1-0 that season, and it showed how close the line was between being a very good side and being an excellent one. If they had managed one goal in each of those ten losses (or kept a few more clean sheets – as they had done in 1977-78), they would have won the league title again and forced a replay in the League Cup Final. Ten more goals might have meant a treble.

First Division, Final Table 1979-80

	Pld	Pts	GD
Liverpool	42	60	+51
Manchester United	42	58	+30
Ipswich Town	42	53	+29
Arsenal	42	52	+16
FOREST	**42**	**48**	**+20**
Wolverhampton Wanderers	42	47	+11
Aston Villa	42	46	+1
Southampton	42	45	+12
Middlesbrough	42	44	+6
West Bromwich Albion	42	41	+4
Leeds United	42	40	-4
Norwich City	42	40	-8
Crystal Palace	42	40	-9
Tottenham Hotspur	42	40	-10
Coventry City	42	39	-10
Brighton & Hove Albion	42	37	-10
Manchester City	42	37	-23
Stoke City	42	36	-14
Everton	42	35	-8
Bristol City	42	31	-29
Derby County	42	30	-20
Bolton Wanderers	42	25	-35

ADVANCE WORKWEAR SERVICE
PLESSEY
DERBYSHIRE
Radio Rentals

All thoughts now turned to the European Cup Final against Hamburg in Madrid. John Robertson was granted a testimonial game for which Stan Bowles was dropped. He felt it unfair and walked out on Forest, passing up the chance to play in the biggest game of his career in Madrid. There was a twelve day break between the testimonial and the Final and the Reds headed off for a break in Majorca before moving to the mountains outside Madrid for some more serious preparations.

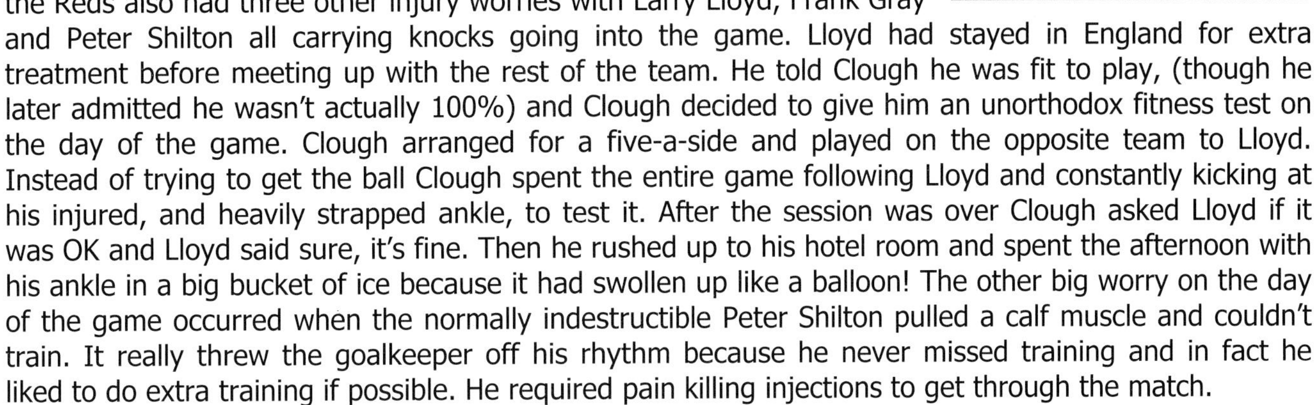

Winning the European Cup was now the only way Forest would qualify for Europe the next season, so it took on even more importance if that was possible. The squad had plenty of time to think about that in the days leading up to the game. 'The Germans only had a week between their last league game and the final,' explains John McGovern. 'We went to Majorca to get away from the publicity and to train and relax where it was nice and warm. We just did enough training to keep ticking over. We ended up training in the middle of a dual carriageway because we couldn't find any grass anywhere and we didn't want to travel far from the retreat!

With Francis injured and Bowles missing Forest were already down to the bare bones of their small squad. It was kept quiet at the time but the Reds also had three other injury worries with Larry Lloyd, Frank Gray and Peter Shilton all carrying knocks going into the game. Lloyd had stayed in England for extra treatment before meeting up with the rest of the team. He told Clough he was fit to play, (though he later admitted he wasn't actually 100%) and Clough decided to give him an unorthodox fitness test on the day of the game. Clough arranged for a five-a-side and played on the opposite team to Lloyd. Instead of trying to get the ball Clough spent the entire game following Lloyd and constantly kicking at his injured, and heavily strapped ankle, to test it. After the session was over Clough asked Lloyd if it was OK and Lloyd said sure, it's fine. Then he rushed up to his hotel room and spent the afternoon with his ankle in a big bucket of ice because it had swollen up like a balloon! The other big worry on the day of the game occurred when the normally indestructible Peter Shilton pulled a calf muscle and couldn't train. It really threw the goalkeeper off his rhythm because he never missed training and in fact he liked to do extra training if possible. He required pain killing injections to get through the match.

It was fitting that the twenty-fifth European Cup Final was taking place in Real Madrid's magnificent Estadio Santiago Bernabeu, after all the Spanish side had won the Cup for the first five years it was played for. Gary Mills was picked to replace Trevor Francis and play up front alongside Garry Birtles in the usual 4-4-2 formation. The sparse nature of the squad was highlighted with Forest having only four substitutes instead of the allowed five – Jim Montgomery, John O'Hare, David Needham and Bryn Gunn.

Hamburg, playing in all white to contrast with Forest's all red strip, were the red hot favourites. They were filled with German international players like Manny Kaltz, Horst Hrubesch and Felix Magath plus the Yugoslav Ian Buljan and England's Kevin Keegan. 'In the tunnel before the game, we were very cold towards Keegan,' says Ian Bowyer. 'If we'd said "Hello" he might have relaxed, so we wanted to keep him on edge.' Forest kicked-off but were soon under pressure themselves. Using the lessons learned at Cologne and Liverpool, everyone patiently got behind the ball and allowed Hamburg to keep possession in their own half. But when they came forward the Forest players worked in packs to chase the ball down and disrupt the German's approach play. On the other hand, Hamburg pushed forward as much as possible and tried to disrupt Forest's passing as soon as the full-backs had possession with three or four Hamburg players deep in the Forest half. Even at this early stage the midfield's were working hard and doing a lot of running on both sides.

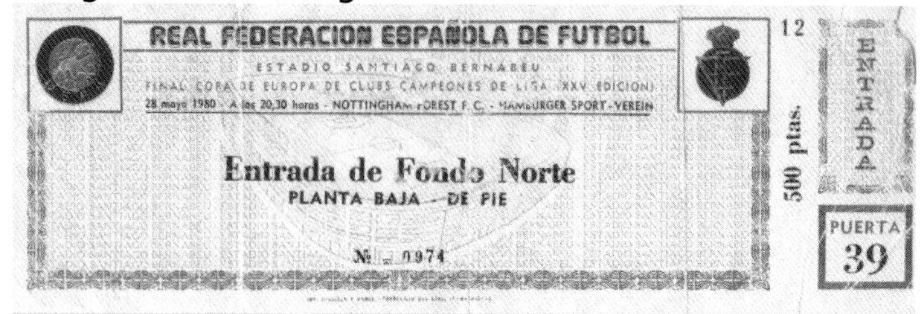

Kenny Burns' main job on the night was to keep Kevin Keegan quiet. 'Players that played against me knew they were going to get kicked,' he says. 'I'd kick them, apologize to the ref and then go and help them up. As I did so I'd say "I'm gonna kick you again next time!"' He clattered Keegan several times in the first half. 'He kept getting further back till he was almost at the half-way line,' recalls Burns. 'If it's him or anybody, the ball's there to be won and if he gets in the way I'll kick him and that's the way it is. I've cracked Kevin a couple of times when we went in for a fifty-fifty ball and it was a crunching tackle where both of us hit each other and we both went down, but we just got up and got on with it, and Keegan came back for some more, so all credit to him.'

Larry Lloyd also kept a close eye on Keegan and it was his foul on the permed one that gave Hamburg a free-kick on the edge of the area. Shilton made the first of several memorable saves from the ensuing shot. With just ten minutes gone Forest had had very little possession in the Hamburg half and Gary Mills was pulled back into midfield as Forest reverted to a 4-5-1 formation with Birtles left alone as the only striker. Clough and Taylor were looking very pensive on the bench and it wasn't until the sixteenth minute that Forest had a shot, when Birtles cut inside and fired wide and the near post. Three minutes later came the key moment of the match.

Frank Gray moved forward with the ball over the halfway line and then played it into the feet of Mills. Gray continued his diagonal run and took a defender with him. Mills was tackled but the ball came out to Robertson who immediately moved inside Kaltz and shrugged him off as he kept heading for the D of the German box. He played a one-two with Birtles, who was on the ground with his back to goal. Just as Robertson got it back from Birtles he managed to take it off the foot of Keegan, who'd chased back, and shot into the bottom corner of the goal from edge of area. Despite Hamburg having nine defenders packed around their goal area, Forest had scored.

Right from the restart Hamburg attacked and within seconds the ball was ricocheting around the Forest area. A shot came in from Kaltz on the edge of the box and Shilton saved, but the rebound landed at Milewski and he fired into the Forest net. Luckily Keegan was standing in an offside position and the goal was wiped out. After thirty-three minutes Shilton pulled off what he later said was his best save of the match. Keegan chested a long ball down eighteen yards out and the on-rushing forward unleashed a vicious volley that Shilton somehow got his left hand to when it looked like it was in. Forest finally forced their first corner of the match after forty minutes and the half finished with a number of tackles flying about but no further scoring.

Hamburg had tried to pass it through Forest in the first half to no avail so in the second half they decide to go for more of a 'route one' approach and threw on their big, burly striker Hrubesch to try and unsettle Forest in the air. Burns and Lloyd were too good though and comfortably dealt with this change of approach. 'I got on for about the last half hour to replace Gary Mills,' remembers John O'Hare. 'I basically had to play a defensive role, getting blocks in and trying to keep possession when we got it. I could remember watching Real Madrid and Benfica when I was a kid and the European Cup was about those clubs, not Nottingham Forest. So playing in the Final in Madrid was something I'll always remember.'

The Germans were increasingly having to rely on long-range efforts as they began to run out of ideas. Kaltz hit the outside of the post and a thirty yard shot from Nogly needed a Shilton save at full stretch to push it out for a corner. It was a backs to the wall situation but Gray was struggling. Clough told him to stay on but a couple of minutes later Burns gestured to the bench that Gray would have to come off. Peter Taylor famously turned to Brian Clough and said 'Who've we got to replace Gray?' When Clough replied that Bryn Gunn was the only full-back on the bench Taylor sighed 'Well we are in the s**t then!'

'I went off injured,' explains Gray, 'I got a knock a couple of weeks before the Final in one of the last league games. It was a calf strain I had and I didn't do much training before the game and I was a little bit doubtful in the week before but I was OK to play the game. But as the game went on it ached a little bit and I just couldn't make it that last seven or eight minutes. If at all possible I would have stayed on but I realized that they were putting the pressure on and could have been a little bit vulnerable because I knew that I couldn't get around as I would like to have done in the later stages. I think Hamburg themselves realised that as well and I thought it would probably better for us if I came off and Bryn Gunn went on. We hung on, it was a bit nerve-racking, I didn't actually watch the last the few minutes. I stayed in the tunnel for most of it and caught glimpses of it.'

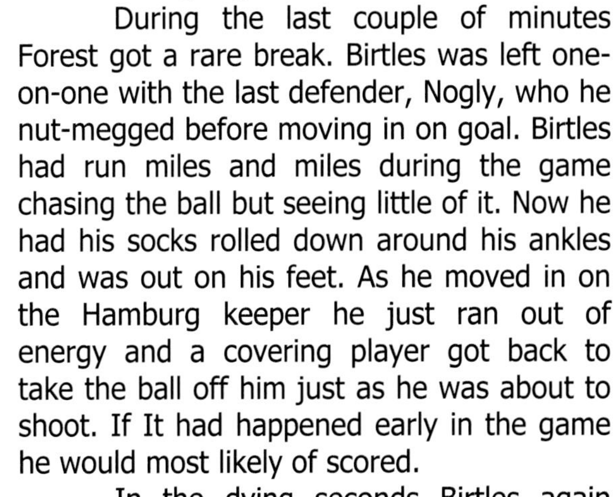

During the last couple of minutes Forest got a rare break. Birtles was left one-on-one with the last defender, Nogly, who he nut-megged before moving in on goal. Birtles had run miles and miles during the game chasing the ball but seeing little of it. Now he had his socks rolled down around his ankles and was out on his feet. As he moved in on the Hamburg keeper he just ran out of energy and a covering player got back to take the ball off him just as he was about to shoot. If It had happened early in the game he would most likely of scored.

In the dying seconds Birtles again had the ball in the Hamburg half, this time

he took it to the corner flag to waste a few more seconds. Keegan had chased him back and couldn't control his frustration that Birtles kept the ball from him. Eventually he gave away a free-kick to Forest and man-handled the linesman. Seconds later the game was over. Or was it. The referee had actually given a another throw-in although most of the players had started celebrating,. There then followed a few nervous moments as they had to concentrate again. It wasn't long before he did blow his whistle for good. ITV commentator Brian Moore couldn't contain his excitement and mistakenly shouted 'Hamburg are the champions of Europe again!'

Clough and Taylor disappeared down the tunnel and left the players to celebrate. Unlike the muted atmosphere after beating Malmo, the players really got excited. John McGovern was presented with the cup for the second year running from a makeshift table at the side of the pitch. 'It's not heavy,' he says, 'you could put an elephant in it and still lift it such is the elation. I always passed the cup on to let the others enjoy it because it was a team effort.' The Forest players took in a lap of honour while Keegan dejectedly led the Hamburg players off.

Shilton had once again proved to be world's best goalkeeper. The defence had been superb, the midfield and Birtles had run and run and run all night long. Martin O'Neill put the anguish of missing the previous final out of his mind. Frank Gray had put the misery of losing a European Cup final with Leeds behind him.

Trevor Francis watched it all on television. Clough had told Francis not to travel with the team in case it disrupted the preparations and so the injured striker was on holiday in the South of France. 'I would like to have gone but the manager wouldn't allow me to' says Francis. 'He felt that psychologically it wasn't good to have me around the players. He felt it would be a distraction and he was not willing for me to be there. I watched it in a TV room in a hotel in Cannes. Some people recognized me, then I remember going out afterwards in Cannes and having something to eat and a drink. To say it was strange sort of being sat there watching the game is an understatement.'

'We won the game on discipline and determination,' says Ian Bowyer. 'We refused to give it up, so it gave us a degree more satisfaction than the Malmo game. They tried to bombard us in the air, they tried to pass it round us and John McGovern was everywhere all over the pitch closing them down. We'd beaten the Dutch champions and the German champions – those countries were the strongest then, not the Italian or Spanish teams.'

Brian Clough: 'We were glad that we didn't go as favourites, and when we won of course once again it was played down a little bit. Even young Kevin Keegan came out with something. He was disappointed the way Forest played. Well what did he expect us to do, throw bloody nine in their box so that they could beat us five nil?'

The players got another massive reception when they returned to East Midlands Airport again and again Forest were given a civic reception at the Council House. Crowds began filling the Old Market Square at lunchtime for that evening's parade. 'We felt like we'd been diplomats and we ruled Europe for two years with exciting, attacking football,' says John McGovern. 'There was no trouble on our travels, everything was done in a professional manner. We weren't superstars like today, we could still rub shoulders with the supporters and mix with them when they'd spent a lot of money following us around the country and beyond – we had magnificent travelling support.' In four years Forest had played in seven finals and won six of them to go with the League Championship and a record forty-two game unbeaten run. John Robertson had made the winner for Francis in 1979 and scored the winner himself in 1980. He summed up the heights that Forest were now reaching when he said, 'As I boy I wanted to be a footballer, but I never dreamed I'd be anywhere near a European Cup final.'

July 1979				
30	Holsterbro B.K., Denmark	A	5-1	PSF
August				
1	Bayern Munich, W.Germany	A	0-5	PSF
9	Botafogo, Brazil	A	2-1	PSF*
10	Dynamo Bucharest, Romania	A	2-1	PSF*
14	Montpelier, France	A	1-0	PSF
18	Ipswich Town	A	1-0	
22	Stoke City	H	1-0	
25	Coventry City	H	4-1	
29	Blackburn Rovers	A	1-1	LC2-1
September				
1	West Bromwich Albion	A	5-1	
5`	Blackburn Rovers	H	6-1	LC2-2
8	Leeds United	H	0-0	
15	Norwich City	A	1-3	
19	Oesters Vaxjo, Sweden	H	2-0	EC1-1
22	Bristol City	A	1-1	
25	Middlesbrough	A	3-1	LC3
29	Liverpool	H	1-0	
October				
3	Oesters Vaxjo, Sweden	A	1-1	EC1-2
6	Wolverhampton Wanderers	H	3-1	
10	Stoke City	A	1-1	
13	Manchester City	A	0-1	
20	Bolton Wanderers	H	5-2	
24	Arges Pitesti, Romania	H	2-0	EC2-1
27	Tottenham Hotspur	A	0-1	
30	Bristol City	A	1-1	LC4
November				
3	Ipswich Town	H	2-0	
7	Arges Pitesti, Romania	A	2-1	EC2-2
10	Southampton	A	1-4	
12	Plymouth Argyle	A	2-1	F*2
14	Bristol City	H	3-0	LC4R
17	Brighton & Hove Albion	H	0-1	
24	Derby County	A	1-4	
27	Cairo Select XI, Egypt	A	3-1	F
December				
1	Arsenal	H	1-1	
4	West Ham United	A	0-0	LC5
8	Crystal Palace	A	0-1	
12	West Ham United	A	3-0	LC5R
18	Cologne, West Germany	A	1-1	F
22	Manchester United	A	0-3	
26	Aston Villa	H	2-1	
29	Coventry City	A	3-0	
January 1980				
1	Everton	A	0-1	
5	Leeds United	A	4-1	FAC3
8	Gravesend & Northfleet	A	1-2	
12	West Bromwich Albion	H	3-1	
19	Leeds United	A	2-1	

22	Liverpool	H	1-0	LCSF-1
26	Liverpool	H	0-2	FAC4
30	Barcelona	H	1-0	SCF-1
February				
5	Barcelona	A	1-1	SCF-2
9	Bristol City	H	0-0	
12	Liverpool	A	1-1	LCSF-2
16	Middlesbrough	H	2-2	
19	Liverpool	A	0-2	
23	Manchester City	H	4-0	
March				
1	Bolton Wanderers	A	0-1	
5	Dynamo Berlin, E. Germany	H	0-1	EC3-1
11	Tottenham Hotspur	H	4-0	
15	Wolverhampton Wanderers	N	0-1	LCF*3
19	Dynamo Berlin, E. Germany	A	3-1	EC3-2
22	Southampton	H	2-0	
29	Brighton & Hove Albion	A	0-1	
April				
2	Manchester United	H	2-0	
5	Aston Villa	A	2-3	
9	Ajax, Holland	H	2-0	ECSF-1
11	Emirates S.C., UAE	A	4-0	F
13	Murrahaq S.C., Bahrain	A	8-2	F
16	Lincoln City	A	1-2	F*4
19	Derby County	H	1-0	
23	Ajax, Holland	A	0-1	ECSF-2
26	Middlesbrough	A	0-0	
30	Norwich City	H	2-0	
May				
3	Crystal Palace	H	4-0	
5	Arsenal	A	0-0	
6	Notts County	A	2-1	CCF
9	Everton	H	1-0	
10	Stade Brestois, France	A	1-0	F
12	Wolverhampton Wanderers	A	1-3	
16	Leicester City	H	0-0	F*5
28	Hamburg SV, West Germany	N	1-0	ECF*6

	Pld	W	D	L	F	A	PTS	GD
Home	31	23	5	3	61	14	51	+47
Away	49	21	11	17	78	61	53	+17
League	42	20	8	14	63	43	48	+20
League Cup	10	5	4	1	19	6	14	+13
FA Cup	2	1	0	1	4	3	2	+1
European Cup	9	6	1	2	13	5	13	+8
Super Cup	2	1	1	0	2	1	3	+1
County Cup	1	1	0	0	2	1	2	+1
Friendlies	14	10	2	2	36	16	22	+20
Total	**80**	**44**	**16**	**20**	**139**	**75**	**104**	**+64**

* = Bilbao Tournament in Spain / *2 = at Ellis Stuttard's testimonial / *3 = at Wembley / *4 = Bert Loxley's testimonial / *5 = John Robertson's testimonial / *6 = at the Bernabeu Stadium, Madrid, Spain

Back Row (left to Right): Mills, Robertson, Bowyer, Barrett, Needham, Anderson, Burns
Middle Row (left to Right): O'Neill, O'Hare, Montgomery, Shilton, Lloyd, Gordon
Front Row (left to right): Birtles, Woodcock, McGovern, Taylor, Clough, Francis, Gray

1979-80 Player Statistics

	Lge	FAC	LCup	SC	EC	CC	F	Totals
John Robertson	42-11	2-1	10-4	2	9-3	1-1	13-5	79-25
Viv Anderson	41-3	2	10-1	2	8	1	13	77-4
Frank Gray	41-2	2-1	10-1	2	9	1	13	77-4
Peter Shilton	42	2	10	2	9	0	12	77
Garry Birtles	42-12	2-1	9-1	2	9-2	0	12-7	76-23
Larry Lloyd	42-3	2	9-1	2	9	1	10(1)-1	75(1)-5
John McGovern	41-2	2	8	1	9	0	12-1	72-3
Kenny Burns	34-1	1(1)	8	2-1	8	1	10-1	64(1)-3
Martin O'Neill	28-3	1	8(1)-2	1	7	1	13-3	59(1)-8
Trevor Francis	30-14	2	6	2	4-3	0	7-8	51-25
Ian Bowyer	12(7)-1	2-1	7-2	1	6-3	1	5(5)	34(12)-7
Tony Woodcock	16-4	0	5-5	0	4-2	0	6-2	31-13
Stan Bowles	19-2	1	0	1	2	1	6	30-2
David Needham	8(2)-1	1	3	0	1	1	8(2)-2	22(4)-3
Gary Mills	10(3)-1	0	3	0	3(1)	0	3(7)-2	19(11)-3
John O'Hare	7-1	0	4-2	0	1(1)	1-1	3(3)-1	16(4)-5
Asa Hartford	3	0	0	0	0	0	5	8
Charlie George	2	0	0	2-1	0	0	0	4-1
Bryn Gunn	2	0	0	0	1(1)	0	(5)	3(6)
Jim Montgomery	0	0	0	0	0	1	2	3

Also played: Colin Barrett (1(4)F), Stuart Gray ((2)F), Colin Smith ((1)F)

The 1980 - 81 Season

The 1980-81 season proved to be a turning point at Nottingham Forest. Inconsistencies that had crept in during the previous season were more obvious this time around as the club finished seventh in the First Division. The League Cup magic finally ran out with a fourth round loss at Watford. Some exciting FA Cup ties took the Reds to the quarter finals but they bowed out to Ipswich after a replay. The biggest disappointment was going out of the European Cup in the first round, just as Liverpool had done after winning it two years running.

On the face of it, the draw didn't seem too unkind: a tie against Bulgaria's champions CSKA Sofia. Forest were drawn away in the first leg for only the second time in nine ties. 'We played reasonably well and kept them down to a few chances,' says Dave Needham about the first leg. 'We had one or two chances ourselves and came away with like a 1-0 defeat and we thought we could do a good job in the return leg. But it was one of those nights where it just didn't click. We didn't score early on so that put the pressure on a little bit. Then we had to sort of leave ourselves a little bit open going for the goal and of course we got punished.' It might have been different if John Robertson's shot in the first leg hadn't come back off the inside of the post (which was square and not round).

The pair of 1-0 defeats came as a crushing blow so early in the season and the radical team changes that had started in the summer took off again. The likes of Ian Wallace and Raimondo Ponte had joined over the summer, youngsters like Stuart Gray, Bryn Gunn and Colin Walsh were also pushing for first team places.

ABSOLUTE DISASTER

PETER SHILTON — shattered by defeat

JOHN ROBERTSON — frustrated

LARRY LLOYD — resigned

JOHN McGOVERN — tired but unbowed

WHAT THE STARS SAID

CLOUGH—OUR FATAL MISTAKE

"IT WAS an absolute disaster," said manager Brian Clough after his Nottingham Forest side were stunningly dethroned as

Bulgarian coach wants Liverpool

European Cup action ★ European Cup

NIGHTMARE END TO THE DREAM RIDE

FOREST 0, CSKA SOFIA 1

Above and left:
the Evening Post spells out the end of the European Cup run.

Left:
John Robertson looks stunned as he walks off after Forest had just crashed out of the European Cup.

Above:
Forest did still have the World Club Championship to play for in Tokyo.

Left:
John McGovern before the game against Nacional, which he missed through injury.

The World Club Championship in Tokyo paired Forest with the South American champions, Nacional of Uruguay. Despite dominating the game, the Reds lost out to a single goal.

Frank Gray: 'That was a long to trip to Tokyo. It was another, a good game to play in. We felt we were unlucky not to win that night as well. We played quite well. We had enough chances it just wasn't to be.'

Kenny Burns: 'They got a stupid goal but we absolutely murdered them. We hit the cross-bar with a couple of good headers and we murdered them. Cloughy came to me at the end of the match and he said, "You were superb tonight, you're Man of the Match by far." But they gave it to the goalkeeper who never got a kick, but that's life.'

John Robertson: 'It was difficult for us because I think we travelled on the Sunday or Monday and we'd to play the game on the Wednesday. It wasn't the greatest of preparations but unfortunately we couldn't do anything about that because we had to play on the [following] Saturday. I don't think we

'We lost 1-0 in Tokyo, that was my last game for Forest. My next game in professional football was as player-manager for Wigan Athletic against bleeding Rochdale. I went from the World Club Championship to Rochdale in the old Fourth Division. And we even lost that 1-0!'

- Larry Lloyd

took it particularly seriously although looking back now, I'm not talking about management they obviously took it seriously, but I'm talking about players. Looking back we should have done better in the game. We should have won the match because we were the better side by a long way and they got the goal. I missed a sitter in the last two or three minutes that I should have scored and equalised but looking back maybe I regret that. I suppose that you could have been saying ten years down the line to your kids that you were a World Champion.'

Garry Birtles was sold to Manchester United, Martin O'Neill to Norwich, John O'Hare retired, Larry Lloyd moved on into management, Ian Bowyer went to join Frank Clark at Sunderland and Kenny Burns and Frank Gray both went to Leeds at the start of the next season and John McGovern left at he end of it with Peter Shilton. The Forest Giants had well and truly been broken up. It would take a few years to rebuild, but Forest did get back into Europe, via the UEFA Cup in 1983. They have never since played in the European Cup.

First Division , Final Table 1980-81

	Pld	Pts	GD
Aston Villa	42	60	+32
Ipswich Town	42	56	+34
Arsenal	42	53	+16
West Bromwich Albion	42	52	+18
Liverpool	42	51	+20
Southampton	42	50	+20
FOREST	**42**	**50**	**+18**
Manchester United	42	48	+15
Leeds United	42	44	-8
Tottenham Hotspur	42	43	+2
Stoke City	42	42	-9
Manchester City	42	39	-3
Birmingham City	42	38	-11
Middlesbrough	42	37	-8
Everton	42	36	-3
Coventry City	42	36	-20
Sunderland	42	35	-1
Wolverhampton Wanderers	42	35	-12
Brighton & Hove Albion	42	35	-13
Norwich City	42	33	-24
Leicester City	42	32	-27
Crystal Palace	42	19	-36

Left:
David Needham with Forest's only trophy of the season – The County Cup.

Above:
John McGovern takes a break in Alaska en route to Tokyo for the World Club Championship.

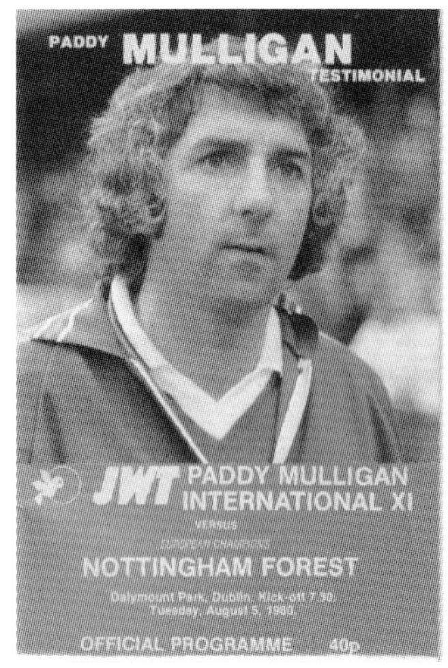

July 1980

23	Vancouver Whitecaps, Canada	A	1-1	PSF
25	Tampa Bay Rowdies, USA	A	0-0	PSF
27	Columbia national team	A	0-5	PSF
31	Toronto Blizzard, Canada	A	3-1	PSF

August

5	Paddy Mulligan select XI, Ireland	A	3-2	PSF*
8	Alkmar AZ67, Denmark	A	1-2	PSF
10	Bayern Munich, West Germany	A	0-3	PSF
11	Grasshoppers Zurich, Switzerland	A	0-0	PSF
16	Tottenham Hotspur	A	0-1	
20	Birmingham City	H	2-1	
23	Everton	A	0-0	
27	Peterborough United	H	3-0	LC2-1
30	Stoke City	H	5-0	

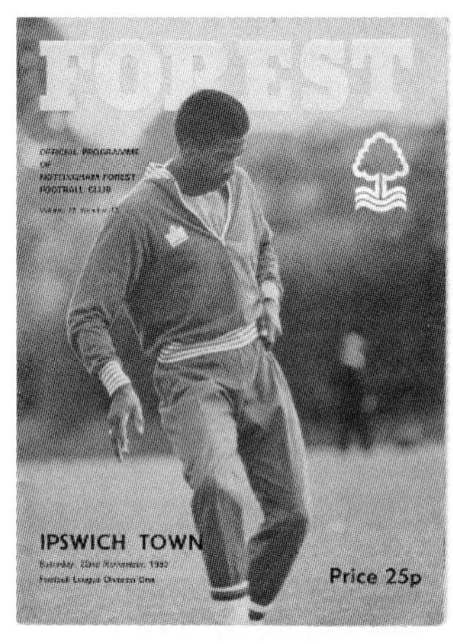

September

3	Peterborough United	A	1-1	LC2-2
6	Middlesbrough	A	0-0	
13	Manchester City	H	3-2	
17	CSKA Sofia, Bulgaria	A	0-1	EC1-1
20	Leicester City	H	5-0	
23	Bury	A	7-0	LC3
27	Arsenal	A	0-1	

October

1	CSKA Sofia, Bulgaria	H	0-1	EC1-2
4	Manchester United	H	1-2	
8	Sunderland	A	2-2	
11	Brighton & Hove Albion	H	1-0	
13	Tampa Bay Rowdies, USA	H	7-1	F
18	West Bromwich Albion	H	2-1	
22	Leeds United	H	2-1	
25	Norwich City	A	1-1	
28	Watford	A	1-4	LC4

November

1	Southampton	H	2-1	
8	Liverpool	A	0-0	
11	Birmingham City	A	0-2	
15	Tottenham Hotspur	A	0-3	
22	Ipswich Town	A	1-2	
25	Valencia, Spain	H	2-1	SCF-1
29	Coventry City	A	1-1	

December

6	Crystal Palace	H	3-0	
10	Grantham	A	6-0	F
13	Leeds United	A	0-1	
17	Valencia, Spain	A	0-1	SCF-2
20	Sunderland	A	3-1	
26	Wolverhampton Wanderers	A	4-1	
27	Aston Villa	H	2-2	

January 1981

3	Bolton Wanderers	H	3-3	FAC3
6	Bolton Wanderers	A	1-0	FAC3R
10	Ipswich Town	A	0-2	

11 Paris St Germain A 0-2 F
24 Manchester United H 1-0 FAC4
31 Everton H 1-0

February

4 Red Star Belgrade H 1-3 F
7 Manchester City A 1-1
11 Nacional, Uruguay A 0-1 WCC*2
14 Bristol City H 2-1 FAC5
18 Stoke City A 2-1
21 Arsenal H 3-1
28 Leicester City A 1-1

March

3 Middlesbrough H 1-0
7 Ipswich Town H 3-3 FAC6
10 Ipswich Town H 0-1 FAC6R
14 Brighton & Hove Albion A 4-1
18 Manchester United A 1-1
21 West Bromwich Albion H 1-2
28 Norwich City A 2-1

April

4 Southampton A 0-2
7 Kettering Town A 5-2 F
11 Liverpool H 0-0
14 Cardiff City A 2-1 F
18 Aston Villa A 0-2
20 Wolverhampton Wanderers H 1-0
25 Crystal Palace A 3-1

May

2 Coventry City H 1-1
4 Mansfield Town H 2-1 CCF
7 Notts County H 3-0 F*3
10 Real Madrid, Spain A 0-2 F
19 Real Mallorca A 5-0 F

Overall Record

	Pld	W	D	L	F	A	PTS	GD
Home	31	21	5	5	62	28	47	+34
Away	44	13	13	18	63	60	39	+3
League	42	19	12	11	62	44	50	+18
League Cup	4	2	1	1	12	5	5	+7
FA Cup	6	3	2	1	10	8	8	+2
European Cup	2	0	0	2	0	2	0	-2
World Club Champ.	1	0	0	1	0	1	0	-1
Super Cup	2	1	0	1	2	2	2	0
County Cup	1	1	0	0	2	1	2	+1
Friendlies	17	8	3	6	37	25	19	+12
Total	75	34	18	23	125	88	86	+37

* = Paddy Mulligan's testimonial / *2 = in Tokyo, Japan / *3 = Jimmy Gordon's testimonial

Back row (left to right): Anderson, O'Neill, Lloyd, Burns, Shilton, Francis
Front Row (left to right): Robertson, Wallace, Frank Gray, Stuart Gray, Ponte

1980-81 Player Statistics

	Lge	FAC	LCup	SC	EC	WCC	CC	F	Totals
Peter Shilton	40	6	3	2	2	1	1	14	69
Frank Gray	40-3	6	4-1	1	2	1	1	10	65-4
John Robertson	38-6	6-2	4-1	1	2	1	1	10-4	63-13
Ian Wallace	37-11	5-1	2-1	2	2	1	0	11-7	60-20
Kenny Burns	30-5	5	3	2	1	1	1	10(1)-1	53(1)-6
Viv Anderson	31-1	5	3	2	2	1	0	9-1	53-2
John McGovern	27	3	2	2	2	0	0	12-1	48-1
Raimondo Ponte	17(4)-3	3(1)-1	3-3	1(1)	0(1)	1	0	10-2	45(7)-9
Bryn Gunn	26	5	1	0	0	0	1	10(2)	43(2)
Gary Mills	23(4)-5	2	3-2	1	0	0	1	10(2)-4	40(6)-11
Martin O'Neill	21(3)-3	2	3	1	2	1	0	8(1)	38(4)-3
Larry Lloyd	18	2	2	2	1(1)	1	0	8	35(1)
Ian Bowyer	19(2)-3	1	3	1-2	2	0	0	6(2)	32(4)-5
Trevor Francis	18-6	6-5	0	1	0	1	0	5-5	31-16
David Needham	17	1	3	0	2	0	1	7-3	31-3
Colin Walsh	15(1)-4	4-1	0	1	0	0	1	6	27(1)-5
Peter Ward	14(2)-2	1(1)	0	1	0	(1)	1-1	5(2)-4	22(6)-7
Stuart Gray	14-1	3	0	0	0	1	1-1	3(3)-1	22(3)-3
Garry Birtles	9-6	0	3-3	0	2	0	0	7(1)-3	21(1)-12
Einar Aas	6(1)-1	0	0	0	0	0	1	3	10(1)-1
John O'Hare	0	0	1	0	0	0	0	2(1)	3(1)
Steve Sutton	1	0	1	0	0	0	0	1	3
Lee Smelt	1	0	0	0	0	0	0	1	2

Also played in friendlies: C. Smith 1(2), C. Plummer (1), C. Fairclough 1, S.Hodge 1, N. Thrower (1)
Note: team versus Cardiff City, April 1981, Friendly is unknown.
WCC = World Club Championship

Appendices: Statistical Records 1974-75 to 1980-81

The following pages contain records of all matches played in the aforementioned period with details of teams and scores.

Key:

A = goals against
D = games drawn
F = goals scored
GD = goal difference
L = games lost
Pld = games played
Pts = points
W = games won

ChSh = Charity Shield
CC = County Cup
EC = European Cup
FA = Football Association
FAC, FACup = Football Association Cup
Gls, G = Goals
LC, LCup = Football League Cup
Lge = league
PSF = pre-season friendly
SC = UEFA Super Cup
WCC = World Club Championship

1974-75

Date	Versus	Comp.	Score	1	2	3	4	5	6	7	8	9	10	11
August 3, 1974	Port Vale	PSF	3-1	Peacock	O'Kane	Anderson	Chapman	Serella	Richardson	Dennehy	Lyall	Martin	O'Neill	Woodcock
August 6, 1974	Walsall	PSF	1-1	Peacock	Anderson	Dulson	Chapman	Serella	Richardson	Dennehy	Lyall	Martin	O'Neill	Bowyer
August 10, 1974	**Leicester City**	PSF	1-3	Peacock	Serella	O'Kane	Chapman	Cottam	Richardson	Dennehy	Lyall	Martin	O'Neill	Bowyer
August 17, 1974	**Bristol City**	Division 2	0-0	Peacock	O'Kane	Richardson	Chapman	Cottam	Jones	Dennehy	Lyall	Martin	Robertson	Bowyer
August 19, 1974	Millwall	Division 2	0-3	Peacock	O'Kane	Jones	Chapman	Cottam	Richardson	Dennehy	Lyall	Galley	Robertson	Woodcock
August 24, 1974	Portsmouth	Division 2	0-2	Peacock	O'Kane	Jones	Chapman	Cottam	Richardson	Dennehy	Lyall	Galley	Woodcock	Jackson
August 27, 1974	**Millwall**	Division 2	2-1	Peacock	O'Kane	Jones	Chapman	Cottam	Richardson	Dennehy	Lyall	Galley	Martin	Jackson
August 31, 1974	**Oxford United**	Division 2	1-2	Peacock	O'Kane	Jones	Chapman	Serella	Richardson	Jackson	Lyall	Martin	Bowyer	Dennehy
September 6, 1974	Manchester Utd	Division 2	2-2	Peacock	O'Kane	Jones	Chapman	Cottam	Richardson	Dennehy	Lyall	Martin	Bowyer	O'Neill
September 10, 1974	**Newcastle Utd**	LC2	1-1	Peacock	O'Kane	Jones	Chapman	Cottam	Richardson	Dennehy	Lyall	Galley	Bowyer	O'Neill
September 14, 1974	**Hull City**	Division 2	4-0	Peacock	O'Kane	Jones	Chapman	Cottam	Richardson	Dennehy	Lyall	Martin	Bowyer	O'Neill
September 17, 1974	**Portsmouth**	Division 2	1-2	Peacock	O'Kane	Jones	Chapman	Cottam	Robertson	Dennehy	Lyall	Martin	Bowyer	O'Neill
September 21, 1974	S. Wednesday	Division 2	3-2	Peacock	Anderson	Jones	O'Kane	Serella	Jackson	Dennehy	Lyall	Martin	Bowyer	O'Neill
September 25, 1974	Newcastle Utd	LC2R	0-3	Peacock	Anderson	Jones	O'Kane	Serella	Jackson	Dennehy	Lyall	Martin	Bowyer	O'Neill
September 28, 1974	**Sunderland**	Division 2	1-1	Peacock	Anderson	Jones	O'Kane	Serella	Richardson	Dennehy	Lyall	Martin	Bowyer	O'Neill
October 2, 1974	Aston Villa	Division 2	0-3	Peacock	Anderson	Jones	O'Kane	Serella	Richardson	Dennehy	Lyall	Butlin	Bowyer	O'Neill
October 5, 1974	Southampton	Division 2	1-0	Peacock	O'Kane	Greenwood	Chapman	Jones	Richardson	Dennehy	Martin	Butlin	Bowyer	Jackson
October 12, 1974	**Norwich City**	Division 2	1-3	Peacock	O'Kane	Jones	Chapman	G'wood	Richardson	Dennehy	Bowyer	Martin	Butlin	Jackson
October 19, 1974	WBA	Division 2	1-0	Middleton	O'Kane	Greenwood	Chapman	Jones	Richardson	Dennehy	Martin	Butlin	Bowyer	Lyall
October 26, 1974	**Bristol Rovers**	Division 2	1-0	Middleton	O'Kane	Greenwood	Serella	Jones	Richardson	Dennehy	Martin	Butlin	Lyall	Jackson
October 29, 1974	**Coventry City**	F	1-1	Peacock	G'wood	Anderson	Dulson	Cottam	Jones	Dennehy	Jackson	Middleton	McCann	Lyall
November 2, 1974	Bolton	Division 2	0-2	Peacock	O'Kane	Greenwood	Serella	Jones	Richardson	Jackson	Lyall	Martin	Butlin	Dennehy
November 9, 1974	**Oldham Athletic**	Division 2	1-0	Middleton	O'Kane	Greenwood	Cottam	Jones	Jackson	Dennehy	Lyall	Martin	Butlin	O'Neill
November 16, 1974	Cardiff City	Division 2	1-2	Middleton	O'Kane	Greenwood	Chapman	Jones	Jackson	Dennehy	Lyall	Martin	Butlin	O'Neill
November 23, 1974	**York City**	Division 2	2-1	Middleton	O'Kane	Greenwood	Chapman	Jones	Richardson	Jackson	Lyall	Martin	Bowyer	Dennehy
November 30, 1974	Orient	Division 2	1-1	Middleton	O'Kane	Greenwood	Chapman	Jones	Richardson	Jackson	Butlin	Martin	Bowyer	Dennehy
December 7, 1974	**Fulham**	Division 2	1-1	Middleton	O'Kane	Greenwood	Chapman	Jones	Jackson	Dennehy	Martin	Butlin	Bowyer	Richardson
December 14, 1974	Bristol City	Division 2	0-1	Middleton	O'Kane	Greenwood	Chapman	Jones	Richardson	Dennehy	Butlin	Martin	Bowyer	O'Neill
December 21, 1974	**Blackpool**	Division 2	0-0	Middleton	O'Kane	Greenwood	Chapman	Jones	Richardson	Dennehy	Lyall	Butlin	Bowyer	O'Neill
December 26, 1974	Hull City	Division 2	3-1	Middleton	Serella	O'Kane	Chapman	Jones	Richardson	McIntosh	Martin	Butlin	Bowyer	Lyall
December 28, 1974	**Notts County**	Division 2	0-2	Middleton	Serella	O'Kane	Chapman	Jones	Richardson	McIntosh	Butlin	Martin	Bowyer	Lyall
January 4, 1975	**Tottenham H**	FAC3	1-1	Middleton	Anderson	Greenwood	Chapman	Jones	O'Kane	Dennehy	Lyall	Butlin	Bowyer	Richardson
January 8, 1975	Tottenham H	FAC3R	1-0	Middleton	O'Kane	Greenwood	Chapman	Jones	Richardson	Lyall	Martin	Butlin	Bowyer	O'Neill
January 11, 1975	Fulham	Division 2	1-0	Middleton	O'Kane	Greenwood	Chapman	Jones	Richardson	Lyall	Martin	Butlin	Bowyer	O'Neill
January 18, 1975	**Orient**	Division 2	2-2	Middleton	O'Kane	Greenwood	Chapman	Jones	Richardson	Lyall	Martin	Butlin	Bowyer	O'Neill
January 28, 1975	Fulham	FAC4	0-0	Middleton	O'Kane	Greenwood	Chapman	Cottam	Robertson	Lyall	Butlin	Martin	Bowyer	O'Neill
February 1, 1975	Oldham Athletic	Division 2	0-2	Middleton	O'Kane	Greenwood	Chapman	Cottam	Robertson	Lyall	Butlin	Martin	Bowyer	O'Neill
February 3, 1975	**Fulham**	FAC4R	1-1	Middleton	Jackson	Greenwood	Chapman	Cottam	Robertson	Lyall	Butlin	Martin	Richardson	O'Neill
February 5, 1975	Fulham	FAC4R2	1-1	Middleton	O'Kane	Richardson	Chapman	Cottam	Robertson	Lyall	Butlin	Martin	Bowyer	O'Neill
February 8, 1975	**Bolton**	Division 2	2-3	Middleton	Jackson	Cottam	Richardson	Chapman	Robertson	Lyall	Anderson	Butlin	Bowyer	Dennehy
February 10, 1975	**Fulham**	FACR3	1-2	Middleton	O'Kane	Richardson	Chapman	Jones	Robertson	Dennehy	Lyall	Martin	Bowyer	O'Neill
February 14, 1975	York City	Division 2	1-1	Middleton	O'Kane	Richardson	Chapman	Jones	Robertson	Lyall	Anderson	Martin	Bowyer	O'Neill
February 22, 1975	**Cardiff City**	Division 2	0-0	Middleton	Anderson	Cottam	Richardson	O'Kane	McGovern	Lyall	Robertson	Martin	Bowyer	O'Neill
February 28, 1975	Oxford United	Division 2	1-1	Middleton	Anderson	Richardson	O'Kane	Jones	McGovern	Lyall	Robertson	O'Hare	Butlin	Bowyer
March 8, 1975	**Aston Villa**	Division 2	2-3	Middleton	Anderson	O'Kane	McGovern	Jones	Richardson	Lyall	Robertson	O'Hare	Butlin	Bowyer
March 15, 1975	Sunderland	Division 2	0-0	Middleton	Anderson	O'Kane	McGovern	Jones	Richardson	Lyall	Robertson	O'Hare	Butlin	Bowyer
March 22, 1975	Manchester Utd	Division 2	0-1	Middleton	Anderson	Richardson	McGovern	Jones	O'Kane	Lyall	Robertson	O'Hare	Butlin	Bowyer
March 25, 1975	Notts County	Division 2	2-2	Middleton	Anderson	Richardson	O'Kane	Jones	Chapman	Lyall	Robertson	O'Hare	Butlin	Bowyer
March 29, 1975	Blackpool	Division 2	0-0	Middleton	O'Kane	Richardson	Chapman	Jones	Robertson	Anderson	Lyall	O'Hare	Butlin	Bowyer
April 1, 1975	**S. Wednesday**	Division 2	1-0	Middleton	Anderson	Richardson	O'Kane	Jones	Robertson	Lyall	Chapman	O'Hare	Butlin	Woodcock
April 5, 1975	Bristol Rovers	Division 2	2-4	Middleton	O'Kane	Richardson	McGovern	Jones	Chapman	Lyall	Robertson	O'Hare	Butlin	Woodcock
April 12, 1975	**Southampton**	Division 2	0-0	Middleton	O'Kane	Richardson	Chapman	Cottam	Robertson	Lyall	McGovern	O'Hare	Butlin	Dennehy
April 14, 1975	Worksop Town	F	2-1	Middleton	Anderson	Jones	Chapman	Cottam	Robertson	Dennehy	Lyall	Bowery	O'Hare	Richardson
April 19, 1975	Norwich City	Division 2	0-3	Middleton	O'Kane	Richardson	Chapman	Cottam	Robertson	Dennehy	Lyall	O'Hare	Butlin	McGovern
April 21, 1975	Grantham	F	1-0	Middleton	Anderson	O'Kane	Chapman	Cottam	Robertson	Miller	Lyall	McCann	Butlin	Richardson
April 26, 1975	**WBA**	Division 2	2-1	Middleton	Anderson	O'Kane	Chapman	Cottam	Richardson	McIntosh	Butlin	McCann	O'Neill	Woodcock
April 28, 1975	Biggleswade	F	6-1	-	-	-	-	-	-	-	Butlin	McCann	O'Neill	Woodcock
May 8, 1975	**Notts County**	CCF	0-1	Wells	Anderson	O'Kane	Chapman	Cottam	McIntosh	Lyall	O'Neill	McCann	Butlin	Bowyer

home games in **bold**

1975-76

Date	Versus	Comp.	Score	1	2	3	4	5	6	7	8	9	10	11
July 29, 1975	TSV Geingen	PSF	2-0	Middleton	O'Kane	Clark	Chapman	Cottam	Richardson	McIntosh	McGovern	O'Hare	Butlin	Lyall
July 31, 1975	SV Kaufbeuren	PSF	1-1	Middleton	Anderson	Clark	O'Kane	Chapman	Richardson	Mills	McIntosh	McCann	Butlin	Woodcock
August 1, 1975	BC Aichach	PSF	1-0	Middleton	Anderson	McGovern	O'Kane	Cottam	McIntosh	Mills	Lyall	McCann	O'Hare	Woodcock
August 3, 1975	TSV Gamersheim	PSF	9-0	Middleton	Anderson	Clark	O'Kane	Chapman	Richardson	McIntosh	Lyall	O'Hare	Butlin	Woodcock
August 5, 1975	Stuttgart Kickers	PSF	0-1	Middleton	Anderson	Clark	O'Kane	Chapman	Richardson	McIntosh	Lyall	O'Hare	Butlin	McGovern
August 9, 1975	Ballymena	PSF	3-0	Middleton	Anderson	Clark	O'Kane	Chapman	Richardson	McIntosh	McGovern	O'Hare	Robertson	Bowyer
August 11, 1975	Coleraine	PSF	3-2	Middleton	Gunn	Clark	O'Kane	Chapman	Richardson	Lyall	McGovern	O'Hare	Robertson	Bowyer
August 16, 1975	**Plymouth Argyle**	Division 2	2-0	Middleton	Anderson	Clark	Chapman	O'Kane	McGovern	Lyall	Richardson	O'Hare	Robertson	Bowyer
August 19, 1975	Rotherham	LC1-1	2-1	Middleton	Anderson	Clark	O'Kane	Chapman	McGovern	Robertson	Richardson	O'Hare	Bowyer	Lyall
August 23, 1975	Portsmouth	Division 2	1-1	Middleton	Anderson	Clark	O'Kane	Chapman	Richardson	Robertson	McGovern	O'Hare	Bowyer	Lyall
August 27, 1975	**Rotherham**	LC1-2	5-1	Middleton	Anderson	Gunn	Clark	Chapman	Richardson	Robertson	McGovern	O'Hare	Bowyer	Lyall
August 30, 1975	**Notts County**	Division 2	0-1	Middleton	Anderson	Gunn	Clark	Chapman	Richardson	Curran	McGovern	O'Hare	Robertson	Bowyer
September 4, 1975	Chelsea	Division 2	0-0	Middleton	Anderson	Gunn	Chapman	Clark	Robertson	Curran	McGovern	O'Hare	Richardson	Bowyer
September 10, 1975	Plymouth Argyle	LC2	1-0	Middleton	Anderson	Gunn	Clark	Chapman	Richardson	O'Neill	McGovern	O'Hare	Bowyer	Robertson
September 13, 1975	**Hull City**	Division 2	1-2	Middleton	Anderson	Gunn	McGovern	Chapman	Clark	Curran	Richardson	O'Hare	Robertson	Bowyer
September 20, 1975	Oxford Utd	Division 2	1-0	Middleton	Anderson	Gunn	Clark	Chapman	Richardson	Curran	McGovern	O'Hare	Robertson	Robertson
September 24, 1975	**Charlton**	Division 2	1-2	Middleton	Anderson	Gunn	Clark	Chapman	Richardson	Curran	McGovern	Bowyer	Lyall	Robertson
September 27, 1975	**Bolton**	Division 2	1-2	Middleton	Gunn	Clark	McGovern	Cottam	Chapman	Curran	Richardson	Bowyer	Lyall	Robertson
October 4, 1975	Bristol R	Division 2	2-4	Middleton	Gunn	Clark	McGovern	Chapman	Cottam	Curran	Richardson	O'Hare	Robertson	Bowyer
October 8, 1975	Manchester City	LC3	1-2	Middleton	Gunn	Clark	Chapman	Cottam	Richardson	O'Neill	McGovern	O'Hare	Bowyer	Robertson
October 11, 1975	Fulham	Division 2	0-0	Middleton	Anderson	Clark	Chapman	Cottam	Richardson	Curran	McGovern	Sunley	Lyall	Bowyer
October 18, 1975	**Southampton**	Division 2	3-1	Middleton	Anderson	Clark	McGovern	Cottam	Richardson	Curran	O'Neill	O'Hare	Butlin	Bowyer
October 21, 1975	**Luton**	Division 2	0-0	Middleton	Anderson	Clark	McGovern	Cottam	Richardson	Curran	O'Neill	O'Hare	Butlin	Robertson
October 25, 1975	Oldham A	Division 2	0-0	Middleton	Anderson	Clark	McGovern	Cottam	Richardson	Curran	O'Neill	O'Hare	Butlin	Bowyer
November 1, 1975	**Carlisle Utd**	Division 2	4-0	Middleton	Anderson	Clark	McGovern	Cottam	Richardson	Curran	O'Neill	O'Hare	Butlin	Bowyer
November 4, 1975	Blackpool	Division 2	1-1	Middleton	Anderson	Clark	McGovern	Cottam	Richardson	Robertson	O'Neill	O'Hare	Butlin	Bowyer
November 8, 1975	Sunderland	Division 2	0-3	Middleton	Anderson	Clark	McGovern	Chapman	Richardson	O'Neill	Robertson	O'Hare	Butlin	Bowyer
November 15, 1975	**Bristol City**	Division 2	1-0	Middleton	Anderson	Clark	McGovern	Chapman	Richardson	O'Neill	Robertson	O'Hare	Butlin	Bowyer
November 17, 1975	Hartlepool	F	0-0	Middleton	Anderson	Clark	McGovern	Chapman	Richardson	Robertson	Lyall	O'Hare	Butlin	Bowyer
November 22, 1975	Southampton	Division 2	3-0	Middleton	Anderson	Clark	McGovern	Chapman	Richardson	O'Neill	Robertson	O'Hare	Butlin	Bowyer
November 29, 1975	**York**	Division 2	1-0	Wells	Anderson	Clark	McGovern	Chapman	Richardson	O'Neill	Robertson	O'Hare	Butlin	Bowyer
December 6, 1975	Orient	Division 2	0-0	Wells	Anderson	Clark	McGovern	Chapman	Robertson	Curran	O'Neill	O'Hare	Butlin	Bowyer
December 9, 1975	Qatar XI	F	1-1	Wells	Gunn	Clark	McGovern	Cottam	Robertson	Lyall	O'Neill	O'Hare	Butlin	Richardson
December 13, 1975	**Portsmouth**	Division 2	0-1	Wells	Anderson	Clark	McGovern	Chapman	Robertson	Curran	O'Neill	O'Hare	Butlin	Bowyer
December 20, 1975	Plymouth Argyle	Division 2	0-1	Wells	Anderson	Clark	McGovern	Chapman	Richardson	Curran	O'Neill	O'Hare	Butlin	Bowyer
December 26, 1975	**WBA**	Division 2	0-2	Wells	O'Kane	Clark	McGovern	Chapman	Richardson	Curran	O'Neill	O'Hare	Butlin	Robertson
December 27, 1975	Blackburn R	Division 2	4-1	Wells	O'Kane	Clark	McGovern	Chapman	Robertson	McIntosh	Bowery	O'Hare	Butlin	Bowyer
January 1, 1976	**Peterborough U**	FAC3	0-0	Wells	O'Kane	Clark	McGovern	Chapman	Bowyer	McIntosh	Bowery	O'Hare	Butlin	Robertson
January 7, 1976	Peterborough U	FAC3R	0-1	Wells	O'Kane	Clark	McGovern	Chapman	Richardson	McIntosh	Bowery	O'Hare	Butlin	Bowyer
January 10, 1976	Hull City	Division 2	0-1	Wells	Anderson	Clark	McGovern	Chapman	Richardson	O'Neill	Robertson	O'Hare	Butlin	Bowyer
January 17, 1976	**Chelsea**	Division 2	1-3	Wells	O'Kane	Gunn	Clark	Chapman	Richardson	Curran	Bowyer	O'Hare	Butlin	Robertson
January 23, 1976	**Mansfield**	CCSF	2-1	Wells	Saunders	Clark	McGovern	Chapman	Richardson	Curran	O'Neill	Bowyer	Bowery	Robertson
January 31, 1976	Luton	Division 2	1-1	Wells	O'Kane	Clark	McGovern	Chapman	Bowyer	Curran	O'Neill	O'Hare	Butlin	Robertson
February 2, 1976	Corby	F	2-1	Wells	O'Kane	Gunn	McGovern	Chapman	Bowyer	Curran	O'Neill	O'Hare	Butlin	Robertson
February 7, 1976	**Blackpool**	Division 2	3-0	Wells	O'Kane	Clark	McGovern	Chapman	Bowyer	Curran	O'Neill	O'Hare	Butlin	Robertson
February 21, 1976	Bristol City	Division 2	2-0	Wells	O'Kane	Clark	McGovern	Chapman	Bowyer	Curran	O'Neill	O'Hare	Butlin	Robertson
February 24, 1976	Charlton	Division 2	2-2	Wells	Gunn	Clark	McGovern	Chapman	Bowyer	Curran	O'Neill	O'Hare	Butlin	Robertson
February 28, 1976	**Oldham**	Division 2	4-3	Wells	Gunn	Clark	McGovern	Chapman	Bowyer	Curran	O'Neill	O'Hare	Butlin	Robertson
March 6, 1976	Carlisle Utd	Division 2	1-1	Middleton	Gunn	Clark	McGovern	Chapman	Bowyer	Curran	McCann	O'Hare	Butlin	Robertson
March 13, 1976	**Fulham**	Division 2	1-0	Wells	Chapman	Clark	McGovern	Barrett	Bowyer	Curran	O'Neill	O'Hare	Butlin	Robertson
March 17, 1976	**Sunderland**	Division 2	2-1	Wells	Barrett	Clark	McGovern	Chapman	Bowyer	Curran	O'Neill	O'Hare	Butlin	Robertson
March 20, 1976	York	Division 2	2-3	Wells	Barrett	Clark	McGovern	Chapman	Bowyer	Curran	O'Neill	O'Hare	Butlin	Robertson
March 27, 1976	**Orient**	Division 2	1-0	Wells	Barrett	Clark	McGovern	Chapman	Bowyer	Curran	O'Neill	O'Hare	Butlin	Robertson
April 3, 1976	Bolton	Division 2	0-0	Wells	Barrett	Clark	McGovern	Chapman	Bowyer	Curran	O'Neill	O'Hare	Butlin	Robertson
April 6, 1976	Louth	F	6-0	Wells	Barrett	Gunn	McGovern	Chapman	Bowyer	Curran	O'Neill	O'Hare	McCann	Robertson
April 10, 1976	**Oxford Utd**	Division 2	4-0	Wells	Barrett	Clark	McGovern	Chapman	Bowyer	Curran	O'Neill	O'Hare	Butlin	Robertson
April 13, 1976	Notts County	Division 2	0-0	Wells	Barrett	Clark	McGovern	Chapman	Bowyer	Curran	O'Neill	O'Hare	Butlin	Robertson
April 17, 1976	WBA	Division 2	0-2	Wells	Barrett	Clark	McGovern	Chapman	Bowyer	Curran	O'Neill	O'Hare	Butlin	Robertson
April 20, 1976	**Blackburn R**	Division 2	1-0	Wells	Barrett	Clark	McGovern	Chapman	Bowyer	Curran	O'Neill	O'Hare	Butlin	Robertson
April 24, 1976	**Bristol R**	Division 2	3-0	Wells	Barrett	Clark	McGovern	Chapman	Bowyer	Curran	O'Neill	O'Hare	Butlin	Robertson
April 26, 1976	**Don Revie's All-Stars**	F	3-2	Middleton	Barrett	Clark	McGovern	Chapman	Bowyer	Curran	O'Neill	Baker	McKenzie	Robertson
April 30, 1976	CD Severence	F	10-0	Wells	Barrett	Saunders	McGovern	Chapman	Richardson	Curran	O'Neill	Bowyer	Butlin	Robertson

1976-77

Date	Versus	Comp.	Score	1	2	3	4	5	6	7	8	9	10	11
July 27, 1976	SV Furth	PSF	2-3	Wells	Barrett	Clark	McGovern	Chapman	Bowyer	Curran	O'Neill	O'Hare	Butlin	Robertson
July 28, 1976	Jahn Regensburg	PSF	5-0	Wells	Barrett	Saunders	McGovern	Chapman	Bowyer	Curran	O'Neill	O'Hare	Bannon	Robertson
July 30, 1976	Augsburg	PSF	1-0	Wells	Barrett	Clark	McGovern	Chapman	Bowyer	Curran	Haslegrave	O'Hare	Butlin	Robertson
August 1, 1976	Furstenfeldbruck	PSF	4-2	Wells	Saunders	Barrett	Richardson	Chapman	Wignall	Robertson	Bannon	O'Hare	O'Neill	Haslegrave
August 3, 1976	HSB Heidenheim	PSF	3-1	Wells	Barrett	Clark	McGovern	Wignall	Richardson	Curran	O'Neill	O'Hare	Butlin	Bowyer
August 7, 1976	Notts County	ASC	0-0	Wells	Saunders	Barrett	McGovern	Chapman	Bowyer	Curran	Haslegrave	O'Hare	Butlin	Robertson
August 11, 1976	**WBA**	ASC	3-2	Wells	Saunders	Clark	Barrett	Chapman	Bowyer	Curran	Haslegrave	O'Hare	Butlin	Robertson
August 14, 1976	**Bristol City**	ASC	4-2	Wells	Saunders	Clark	McGovern	Barrett	Bowyer	Curran	Haslegrave	O'Hare	Butlin	Robertson
August 21, 1976	Fulham	Division 2	0-0	Wells	Saunders	Clark	McGovern	Chapman	Bowyer	Curran	Haslegrave	O'Hare	Butlin	Robertson
August 25, 1976	**Charlton**	Division 2	1-1	Wells	Saunders	Clark	McGovern	Chapman	Bowyer	Curran	Richardson	O'Hare	Butlin	Robertson
August 28, 1976	**Wolves**	Division 2	1-3	Wells	Saunders	Clark	McGovern	Chapman	Bowyer	Curran	Barrett	O'Hare	Butlin	Robertson
August 31, 1976	Walsall	LC2	4-2	Middleton	Barrett	Clark	McGovern	Chapman	Bowyer	Curran	O'Neill	O'Hare	Butlin	Robertson
September 4, 1976	Luton	Division 2	1-1	Middleton	Barrett	Clark	McGovern	Chapman	Bowyer	Curran	O'Neill	O'Hare	Butlin	Robertson
September 11, 1976	**Hereford**	Division 2	4-3	Wells	Barrett	Clark	McGovern	Chapman	Bowyer	Curran	O'Neill	O'Hare	Butlin	Robertson
September 14, 1976	**Kilmarnock**	ASC	2-1	Wells	Barrett	Clark	Anderson	Chapman	Haslegrave	Curran	O'Neill	O'Hare	Butlin	Robertson
September 18, 1976	Southampton	Division 2	1-1	Middleton	Barrett	Clark	Anderson	Chapman	Bowyer	Curran	O'Neill	O'Hare	Butlin	Robertson
September 21, 1976	**Coventry**	LC3	0-3	Wells	Barrett	Clark	McGovern	Chapman	Bowyer	Curran	O'Neill	O'Hare	Butlin	Robertson
September 25, 1976	**Carlisle Utd**	Division 2	5-1	Middleton	Barrett	Clark	McGovern	Chapman	Bowyer	Curran	O'Neill	O'Hare	Withe	Robertson
September 28, 1976	Kilmarnock	ASC	2-2	Middleton	Anderson	Clark	McGovern	Chapman	Bowyer	Curran	O'Neill	O'Hare	Withe	Robertson
October 2, 1976	Hull City	Division 2	0-1	Middleton	Barrett	Clark	McGovern	Lloyd	Bowyer	Curran	O'Neill	O'Hare	Withe	Robertson
October 9, 1976	**Sheffield Utd**	Division 2	6-1	Middleton	Anderson	Clark	McGovern	Lloyd	Bowyer	Curran	O'Neill	Withe	Butlin	Robertson
October 13, 1976	Grantham	F	3-0	Middleton	Anderson	Clark	McGovern	Barrett	Bowyer	Curran	Haslegrave	Withe	Butlin	Robertson
October 16, 1976	Blackpool	Division 2	0-1	Middleton	Anderson	Clark	McGovern	Lloyd	Bowyer	Curran	O'Neill	Withe	Butlin	Robertson
October 20, 1976	**Ayr United**	ASCSF-1	2-1	Middleton	Anderson	Clark	McGovern	Lloyd	Bowyer	Haslegrave	O'Neill	Withe	Butlin	Robertson
October 23, 1976	**Burnley**	Division 2	5-2	Middleton	Anderson	Clark	McGovern	Lloyd	Bowyer	Curran	O'Neill	Withe	Butlin	Robertson
October 26, 1976	Notts County	CCF	0-1	Middleton	Saunders	Clark	McGovern	Chapman	Bowyer	Haslegrave	O'Neill	Withe	Butlin	Barrett
October 30, 1976	Oldham	Division 2	0-1	Middleton	Saunders	Clark	McGovern	Lloyd	Bowyer	Barrett	O'Neill	Withe	Butlin	Robertson
November 3, 1976	Ayr United	ASCSF-2	2-0	Middleton	Anderson	Clark	McGovern	Lloyd	Bowyer	Haslegrave	O'Neill	Withe	Woodcock	Robertson
November 6, 1976	**Blackburn R**	Division 2	3-0	Middleton	Anderson	Clark	McGovern	Chapman	Bowyer	Haslegrave	O'Neill	Withe	Woodcock	Robertson
November 13, 1976	Orient	Division 2	1-0	Middleton	Anderson	Clark	McGovern	Chapman	Bowyer	Haslegrave	O'Neill	Withe	Woodcock	Robertson
November 20, 1976	**Chelsea**	Division 2	1-1	Middleton	Anderson	Clark	McGovern	Chapman	Bowyer	Haslegrave	O'Neill	Withe	Woodcock	Robertson
November 27, 1976	Cardiff	Division 2	3-0	Middleton	Anderson	Clark	McGovern	Chapman	Bowyer	O'Hare	O'Neill	Withe	Woodcock	Robertson
December 4, 1976	**Bristol Rovers**	Division 2	4-2	Middleton	Anderson	Clark	McGovern	Lloyd	Bowyer	O'Hare	O'Neill	Withe	Woodcock	Robertson
December 11, 1976	Millwall	Division 2	3-0	Middleton	Anderson	Clark	McGovern	Lloyd	Bowyer	O'Hare	O'Neill	Withe	Woodcock	Robertson
December 13, 1976	Orient	ASCF1	1-1	Middleton	Anderson	Clark	McGovern	Lloyd	Bowyer	O'Hare	O'Neill	With	Woodcock	Robertson
December 15, 1976	**Orient**	ASCF2	4-0	Middleton	Anderson	Clark	McGovern	Lloyd	Chapman	O'Neill	Barrett	Bowery	Bowyer	Robertson
December 18, 1976	**Plymouth Argyle**	Division 2	1-1	Middleton	Anderson	Clark	Barrett	Lloyd	Bowyer	O'Neill	O'Hare	Bowery	Chapman	Woodcock
December 27, 1976	Bolton	Division 2	1-1	Middleton	Anderson	Clark	McGovern	Lloyd	Bowyer	O'Hare	O'Neill	Withe	Woodcock	Robertson
January 1, 1977	Blackburn R	Division 2	3-1	Middleton	Anderson	Clark	McGovern	Lloyd	Bowyer	O'Hare	O'Neill	Withe	Woodcock	Robertson
January 3, 1977	**Bristol Rovers**	FAC3	1-1	Middleton	Anderson	Clark	McGovern	Lloyd	Bowyer	O'Hare	O'Neill	Withe	Woodcock	Robertson
January 11, 1977	Bristol Rovers	FAC3R	1-1	Middleton	Anderson	Clark	Chapman	Lloyd	Bowyer	O'Hare	O'Neill	Withe	Woodcock	Robertson
January 14, 1977	Charlton	Division 2	1-2	Middleton	Anderson	Clark	McGovern	Lloyd	Bowyer	Chapman	O'Neill	Withe	Woodcock	Robertson
January 18, 1977	Bristol Rovers	FAC3R2	6-0	Middleton	Anderson	Clark	Chapman	Lloyd	Bowyer	O'Hare	O'Neill	Withe	Woodcock	Robertson
January 22, 1977	**Fulham**	Division 2	3-0	Middleton	Anderson	Clark	McGovern	Lloyd	Bowyer	O'Hare	O'Neill	Withe	Woodcock	Robertson
January 29, 1977	**Southampton**	FAC4	3-3	Middleton	Anderson	Clark	McGovern	Lloyd	Bowyer	O'Hare	O'Neill	Withe	Woodcock	Robertson
February 1, 1977	Southampton	FAC4R	1-2	Middleton	Anderson	Clark	McGovern	Lloyd	Bowyer	O'Hare	O'Neill	Withe	Woodcock	Robertson
February 5, 1977	Wolves	Division 2	1-2	Middleton	Anderson	Clark	McGovern	Lloyd	Bowyer	O'Hare	O'Neill	Withe	Woodcock	Robertson
February 12, 1977	**Luton**	Division 2	1-2	Middleton	Anderson	Clark	McGovern	Lloyd	Bowyer	Chapman	Haslegrave	O'Hare	Woodcock	Robertson
March 2, 1977	Hereford	Division 2	1-0	Middleton	Anderson	Clark	Barrett	Chapman	Bowyer	Curran	O'Neill	Withe	Woodcock	Robertson
March 5, 1977	Carlisle Utd	Division 2	1-1	Middleton	Anderson	Clark	McGovern	Chapman	Barrett	O'Hare	O'Neill	Curran	Woodcock	Robertson
March 8, 1977	**Notts County**	Division 2	1-2	Middleton	Anderson	Clark	McGovern	Chapman	Bowyer	O'Hare	O'Neill	Withe	Woodcock	Robertson
March 12, 1977	**Hull City**	Division 2	2-0	Middleton	Anderson	Clark	McGovern	Chapman	Bowyer	Birtles	O'Neill	Withe	Woodcock	Robertson
March 16, 1977	Grantham	F	2-0	Middleton	Anderson	Clark	Chapman	Lloyd	McGovern	Birtles	O'Hare	Withe	Woodcock	Burke
March 19, 1977	Sheffield Utd	Division 2	0-2	Middleton	Anderson	Clark	Chapman	Lloyd	Bowyer	McGovern	O'Neill	Withe	Woodcock	Robertson
March 22, 1977	**Southampton**	Division 2	2-1	Middleton	Anderson	Clark	Chapman	Lloyd	Bowyer	McGovern	O'Neill	Withe	Woodcock	Robertson
March 26, 1977	**Blackpool**	Division 2	3-0	Middleton	Anderson	Clark	Chapman	Lloyd	Bowyer	McGovern	O'Neill	With	Woodcock	Robertson
March 29, 1977	**Orient**	Division 2	3-0	Middleton	Anderson	Clark	Chapman	Lloyd	Bowyer	McGovern	O'Neill	With	Woodcock	Robertson
April 2, 1977	Burnley	Division 2	1-0	Middleton	Anderson	Clark	Chapman	Lloyd	Bowyer	McGovern	O'Neill	With	Woodcock	Robertson
April 6, 1977	**Bolton**	Division 2	3-1	Middleton	Anderson	Clark	Chapman	Lloyd	Bowyer	McGovern	O'Neill	With	Woodcock	Robertson
April 9, 1977	Notts County	Division 2	1-1	Middleton	Anderson	Clark	Chapman	Lloyd	Bowyer	McGovern	O'Neill	Withe	Woodcock	Robertson
April 16, 1977	Chelsea	Division 2	1-2	Middleton	Anderson	Clark	Chapman	Lloyd	Bowyer	McGovern	O'Neill	Withe	Woodcock	Robertson
April 23, 1977	**Cardiff**	Division 2	0-1	Middleton	Anderson	Clark	Chapman	Lloyd	Bowyer	McGovern	O'Neill	With	Woodcock	Robertson
April 27, 1977	**Oldham**	Division 2	3-0	Middleton	Anderson	Clark	Chapman	Lloyd	Bowyer	McGovern	O'Neill	Withe	Woodcock	Robertson
April 30, 1977	Bristol Rovers	Division 2	1-1	Middleton	Anderson	Clark	Chapman	Lloyd	Bowyer	McGovern	O'Neill	Withe	Woodcock	Robertson
May 2, 1977	Plymouth Argyle	Division 2	2-1	Middleton	Anderson	Clark	Chapman	Lloyd	Bowyer	McGovern	O'Neill	Withe	Woodcock	Robertson
May 7, 1977	**Millwall**	Division 2	1-0	Middleton	Anderson	Clark	Chapman	Lloyd	Bowyer	McGovern	O'Neill	Withe	Woodcock	Robertson
May 9, 1977	Derby County	F	0-1	Middleton	Anderson	Clark	Chapman	Lloyd	Bowyer	McGovern	O'Neill	Withe	Woodcock	Robertson
May 10, 1977	Mansfield	CCSF	2-1	Middleton	Anderson	Clark	Chapman	Lloyd	Bowyer	McGovern	O'Neill	Withe	Woodcock	Robertson
May 12, 1977	Peterborough U	F	5-2	Middleton	Anderson	Clark	Chapman	Lloyd	Bowyer	Barrett	O'Neill	Withe	Woodcock	Robertson

1977-78

Date	Opponents	Comp	Score	1	2	3	4	5	6	7	8	9	10	11
August 1, 1977	St Gallen	PSF	3-2	Middleton	Anderson	Clark	McGovern	Lloyd	Burns	Curran	Bowyer	Withe	Woodcock	Robertson
August 3, 1977	Innsbruck	PSF	2-0	Middleton	Anderson	Clark	McGovern	Lloyd	Burns	Curran	Bowyer	Withe	Woodcock	Robertson
August 5, 1977	SV Plattling	PSF	5-1	Middleton	Anderson	Gunn	Barrett	Lloyd	Burns	Curran	O'Neill	Elliott	Birtles	Haslegrave
August 6, 1977	Neuburg	PSF	5-1	Middleton	Gunn	Clark	McGovern	Barrett	Haslegrave	O'Neill	Birtles	Elliott	Woodcock	Robertson
August 9, 1977	SW Bregenz	PSF	3-0	Middleton	Anderson	Clark	Bowyer	Lloyd	Burns	Curran	O'Neill	Elliott	Woodcock	Robertson
August 13, 1977	Skegness T	PSF	4-0	Middleton	Anderson	Clark	McGovern	Barrett	Burns	Curran	Bowyer	Elliott	Woodcock	Robertson
August 15, 1977	**Notts C**	CCF	1-1	Middleton	Anderson	Clark	McGovern	Lloyd	Burns	O'Neill	Bowyer	Withe	Woodcock	Robertson
August 20, 1977	Everton	Division 1	3-1	Middleton	Anderson	Clark	McGovern	Lloyd	Burns	O'Neill	Bowyer	Withe	Woodcock	Robertson
August 23, 1977	**Bristol C**	Division 1	1-0	Middleton	Anderson	Clark	McGovern	Lloyd	Burns	O'Neill	Bowyer	Withe	Woodcock	Robertson
August 27, 1977	**Derby C**	Division 1	3-0	Middleton	Anderson	Clark	McGovern	Lloyd	Burns	O'Neill	Bowyer	With	Woodcock	Robertson
August 30, 1977	**West Ham U**	LC2	5-0	Middleton	Anderson	Clark	McGovern	Lloyd	Burns	O'Neill	Bowyer	Withe	Woodcock	Robertson
September 3, 1977	Arsenal	Division 1	0-3	Middleton	Anderson	Clark	McGovern	Lloyd	Burns	O'Neill	Bowyer	Withe	Woodcock	Robertson
September 10, 1977	Wolves	Division 1	3-2	Middleton	Anderson	Barrett	McGovern	Lloyd	Burns	O'Neill	Bowyer	Withe	Woodcock	Robertson
September 12, 1977	**Leicester C**	F	0-0	Middleton	O'Kane	Barrett	McGovern	Burns	Todd	O'Neill	Gemmill	Withe	McKenzie	Robertson
September 17, 1977	**Aston Villa**	Division 1	2-0	Shilton	Anderson	Barrett	McGovern	Lloyd	Burns	O'Neill	Bowyer	Withe	Woodcock	Robertson
September 24, 1977	Leicester C	Division 1	3-0	Shilton	Anderson	Barrett	McGovern	Lloyd	Burns	O'Neill	Bowyer	O'Hare	Woodcock	Robertson
October 1, 1977	**Norwich C**	Division 1	1-1	Shilton	Anderson	Barrett	Bowyer	Lloyd	Burns	O'Neill	Gemmill	Withe	Woodcock	Robertson
October 4, 1977	**Ipswich T**	Division 1	4-0	Shilton	Anderson	Barrett	McGovern	Lloyd	Burns	O'Neill	Bowyer	Withe	Woodcock	Robertson
October 8, 1977	West Ham U	Division 1	0-0	Shilton	Anderson	Barrett	McGovern	Lloyd	Burns	O'Neill	Bowyer	Withe	Woodcock	Robertson
October 15, 1977	**Man City**	Division 1	2-1	Shilton	Anderson	Barrett	McGovern	Lloyd	Burns	O'Neill	Bowyer	Withe	Woodcock	Robertson
October 17, 1977	Sheff U	F	6-1	Shilton	Anderson	Barrett	McGovern	Lloyd	Burns	Gemmill	Bowyer	Withe	Woodock	Robertson
October 22, 1977	QPR	Division 1	2-0	Shilton	Anderson	Barrett	Gemmill	Lloyd	Burns	O'Neill	Bowyer	Withe	Woodcock	Robertson
October 25, 1977	**Notts C**	LC3	4-0	Woods	Anderson	Barrett	McGovern	Lloyd	Burns	O'Neill	Bowyer	Withe	Woodcock	Robertson
October 29, 1977	**Middlesbrough**	Division 1	4-0	Shilton	Anderson	Barrett	McGovern	Lloyd	Burns	Gemmill	Bowyer	Withe	Woodcock	Robertson
November 5, 1977	Chelsea	Division 1	0-1	Shilton	Anderson	Barrett	McGovern	Lloyd	Burns	Gemmill	Bowyer	Withe	Woodcock	Robertson
November 12, 1977	**Man U**	Division 1	2-1	Shilton	Anderson	Barrett	McGovern	Lloyd	Burns	Gemmill	Bowyer	Withe	Woodcock	Robertson
November 14, 1977	Hartlepool U	F	2-2	Shilton	Anderson	Barrett	Birtles	Lloyd	Burns	McGovern	Gemmill	Withe	Woodcock	Robertson
November 19, 1977	Leeds U	Division 1	0-1	Shilton	Anderson	Barrett	McGovern	Lloyd	Burns	Gemmill	Bowyer	Withe	Woodcock	Robertson
November 22, 1977	Aviv	F	6-1	Shilton	Anderson	Barrett	McGovern	Lloyd	Burns	Gemmill	O'Neill	Withe	Woodcock	Robertson
November 26, 1977	**WBA**	Division 1	0-0	Shilton	Anderson	Barrett	McGovern	Lloyd	Burns	O'Neill	Gemmill	Withe	Woodcock	Robertson
November 29, 1977	**Aston Villa**	LC4	4-2	Woods	Anderson	Barrett	McGovern	Lloyd	Burns	O'Neill	Bowyer	Withe	Woodcock	Robertson
December 3, 1977	Birmingham C	Division 1	2-0	Shilton	Anderson	Barrett	McGovern	Lloyd	Burns	O'Neill	Gemmill	Withe	Woodcock	Robertson
December 10, 1977	**Coventry C**	Division 1	2-0	Shilton	Anderson	Barrett	McGovern	Lloyd	Burns	O'Neill	Gemmill	Withe	Woodcock	Robertson
December 17, 1977	Man U &	Division 1	4-0	Shilton	Anderson	Barrett	McGovern	Needham	Burns	O'Neill	Gemmill	Withe	Woodcock	Robertson
December 26, 1977	**Liverpool**	Division 1	1-1	Shilton	Anderson	Barrett	McGovern	Needham	Burns	O'Neill	Gemmill	Withe	Woodcock	Robertson
December 28, 1977	Newcastle U	Division 1	2-0	Shilton	Anderson	Barrett	McGovern	Needham	Burns	O'Neill	Gemmill	Withe	Woodcock	Robertson
December 31, 1977	Bristol C	Division 1	3-1	Shilton	Anderson	Barrett	McGovern	Needham	Burns	O'Neill	Gemmill	Withe	Woodcock	Robertson
January 2, 1978	**Everton**	Division 1	1-1	Shilton	Anderson	Barrett	McGovern	Needham	Burns	O'Neill	Gemmill	Withe	Woodcock	Robertson
January 7, 1978	**Swindon T**	FAC3	4-1	Shilton	Anderson	Barrett	McGovern	Needham	Burns	O'Neill	Gemmill	Withe	Woodcock	Robertson
January 14, 1978	Derby C	Division 1	0-0	Shilton	Anderson	Barrett	McGovern	Needham	Burns	O'Neill	Gemmill	Withe	Woodcock	Robertson
January 17, 1978	Bury	LC5	3-0	Woods	Anderson	Clark	McGovern	Barrett	Burns	O'Neill	Bowyer	Withe	Woodcock	Robertson
January 21, 1978	**Arsenal**	Division 1	2-0	Shilton	Anderson	Barrett	McGovern	Needham	Burns	O'Neill	Gemmill	Withe	Woodcock	Robertson
January 24, 1978	**Man C**	FAC4	2-1	Shilton	Anderson	Barrett	McGovern	Needham	Burns	O'Neill	Gemmill	Withe	Woodcock	Robertson
February 4, 1978	**Wolves**	Division 1	2-0	Shilton	Anderson	Barrett	McGovern	Needham	Burns	O'Neill	Gemmill	Withe	Woodcock	Robertson
February 8, 1978	Leeds U	LCSF-1	3-1	Woods	Anderson	Barrett	McGovern	Burns	O'Hare	O'Neill	Bowyer	Withe	Woodcock	Robertson
February 18, 1978	QPR	FAC5	1-1	Shilton	Anderson	Barrett	McGovern	Needham	Burns	O'Neill	Gemmill	Withe	Woodcock	Robertson
February 22, 1978	**Leeds U**	FLCSF-2	4-2	Woods	Anderson	Barrett	McGovern	Lloyd	Burns	O'Neill	Bowyer	Withe	Woodcock	Robertson
February 25, 1978	Norwich C	Division 1	3-3	Shilton	Anderson	Barrett	McGovern	Needham	Burns	O'Neill	Gemmill	Withe	Woodcock	Robertson
February 27, 1978	**QPR**	FAC5R	1-1	Shilton	Anderson	Clark	Needham	Lloyd	Burns	O'Neill	Bowyer	Withe	Woodcock	Robertson
March 2, 1978	**QPR**	FAC5R2	3-1	Shilton	Anderson	Clark	Needham	Lloyd	Burns	O'Neill	Bowyer	Withe	Woodcock	Robertson
March 4, 1978	**West Ham**	Division 1	2-0	Shilton	Bowyer	Clark	O'Hare	Needham	Burns	O'Neill	Gemmill	Withe	Woodcock	Robertson
March 11, 1978	WBA	FAC6	0-2	Shilton	Bowyer	Clark	McGovern	Needham	Burns	O'Neill	Gemmill	Withe	Woodcock	Robertson
March 14, 1978	**Leicester C**	Division 1	1-0	Shilton	Anderson	Clark	O'Hare	Needham	Burns	O'Neill	Gemmill	Bowyer	Woodcock	Robertson
March 18, 1978	Liverpool	LCF	0-0	Woods	Anderson	Clark	McGovern	Lloyd	Burns	O'Neill	Bowyer	Withe	Woodcock	Robertson
March 22, 1978	Liverpool	LCFR	1-0	Woods	Anderson	Clark	O'Hare	Lloyd	Burns	O'Neill	Bowyer	Withe	Woodcock	Robertson
March 25, 1978	**Newcastle U**	Division 1	2-0	Shilton	Anderson	Clark	O'Hare	Needham	Burns	O'Neill	Gemmill	Withe	Woodcock	Robertson
March 29, 1978	Middlesbrough	Division 1	2-2	Shilton	Bowyer	Clark	O'Hare	Needham	Burns	O'Neill	Gemmill	Withe	Woodcock	Robertson
April 1, 1978	**Chelsea**	Division 1	3-1	Shilton	Bowyer	Clark	O'Hare	Lloyd	Burns	O'Neill	Gemmill	Withe	Woodcock	Robertson
April 3, 1978	Derby C	F	2-1	Shilton	Anderson	Barrett	O'Hare	Lloyd	Burns	O'Neill	Gemmill	Bowyer	Woodcock	Robertson
April 5, 1978	Aston Villa	Division 1	1-0	Shilton	Anderson	Barrett	O'Hare	Lloyd	Burns	O'Neill	Gemmill	Withe	Woodcock	Robertson
April 11, 1978	Man C	Division 1	0-0	Shilton	Anderson	Barrett	O'Hare	Lloyd	Burns	O'Neill	Gemmill	Withe	Woodcock	Robertson
April 12, 1978	Notts C	F	1-0	Shilton	Barrett	Clark	McGovern	Needham	Burns	Gemmill	Bowyer	Withe	Woodcock	Robertson
April 15, 1978	**LeedsU**	Division 1	1-1	Shilton	Barrett	Clark	McGovern	Lloyd	Burns	O'Neill	Gemmill	Withe	Bowyer	Robertson
April 18, 1978	**QPR**	Division 1	1-0	Shilton	Barrett	Clark	McGovern	Lloyd	Burns	O'Neill	Gemmill	Withe	Bowyer	Robertson
April 22, 1978	Coventry C	Division 1	0-0	Shilton	Anderson	Barrett	O'Hare	Needham	Burns	O'Neill	Bowyer	Withe	Gemmill	Robertson
April 25, 1978	Ipswich T &	Division 1	2-0	Shilton	Anderson	Barrett	O'Hare	Needham	Burns	O'Neill	Bowyer	Withe	Gemmill	Robertson
April 29, 1978	**Birmingham C**	Division 1	0-0	Shilton	Anderson	Barrett	McGovern	Needham	Burns	O'Neill	Gemmill	Withe	Woodcock	Robertson
May 1, 1978	**Derby C**	F	2-1	Shilton	Anderson	Barrett	McGovern	Lloyd	Burns	O'Neill	Elliott	Withe	Needham	Robertson
May 2, 1978	WBA	Division 1	2-2	Shilton	Anderson	Barrett	McGovern	Lloyd	Burns	O'Neill	Gemmill	Withe	Bowyer	Robertson
May 4, 1978	Liverpool	Division 1	0-0	Shilton	Anderson	Barrett	McGovern	Lloyd	Clark	O'Neill	Gemmill	Withe	Bowyer	Robertson

1978-1979

Date	Versus	Comp.	Score	1	2	3	4	5	6	7	8	9	10	11
July 25, 1978	Red Star Belgrade	PSF	2-3	Shilton	Anderson	Barrett	McGovern	Lloyd	Burns	O'Neill	Gemmill	Withe	Woodcock	Robertson
July 27, 1978	Dynamo Zagreb	PSF	1-1	Shilton	Anderson	Barrett	McGovern	Lloyd	Burns	O'Neill	Gemmill	Withe	Woodcock	Robertson
July 30, 1978	SK Osijek	PSF	1-1	Shilton	Anderson	Barrett	McGovern	Lloyd	Burns	O'Neill	Gemmill	Withe	Woodcock	Robertson
August 2, 1978	AEK Athens	PSF	1-1	Shilton	Anderson	Barrett	McGovern	Lloyd	Burns	O'Neill	Gemmill	Withe	Woodcock	Robertson
August 12, 1978	Ipswich	ChSh	5-0	Shilton	Anderson	Barrett	McGovern	Lloyd	Burns	O'Neill	Gemmill	Withe	Woodcock	Robertson
August 14, 1978	Celta Vigo	PSF	1-1	Shilton	Anderson	Barrett	McGovern	Lloyd	Burns	O'Neill	Gemmill	Withe	Woodcock	Robertson
August 16, 1978	FC Porto	PSF	0-1	Shilton	Anderson	Barrett	McGovern	Needham	Burns	O'Neill	Bowyer	Elliott	Woodcock	Robertson
August 19, 1978	**Tottenham H**	Division 1	1-1	Shilton	Anderson	Barrett	McGovern	Needham	Burns	O'Neill	Gemmill	Withe	Woodcock	Robertson
August 22, 1978	Coventry	Division 1	0-0	Shilton	Anderson	Barrett	McGovern	Needham	Burns	O'Neill	Gemmill	Elliott	Woodcock	Robertson
August 26, 1978	QPR	Division 1	0-0	Shilton	Anderson	Barrett	McGovern	Needham	Burns	O'Neill	Gemmill	Elliott	Woodcock	Robertson
August 29, 1978	Oldham	LC2	0-0	Shilton	Anderson	Barrett	McGovern	Needham	Burns	O'Neill	Gemmill	Elliott	Woodcock	Robertson
September 2, 1978	**WBA**	Division 1	0-0	Shilton	Anderson	Barrett	McGovern	Needham	Burns	O'Neill	Gemmill	Elliott	Woodcock	Robertson
September 4, 1978	Mansfield	F	6-1	Shilton	Anderson	Barrett	McGovern	Needham	Burns	O'Neill	Gemmill	Elliott	Woodcock	Robertson
September 6, 1978	**Oldham**	LC2R	4-2	Shilton	Anderson	Barrett	McGovern	Needham	Burns	O'Neill	Bowyer	Elliott	Woodcock	Robertson
September 9, 1978	**Arsenal**	Division 1	2-1	Shilton	Anderson	Barrett	McGovern	Lloyd	Burns	Mills	Bowyer	Birtles	Woodcock	Robertson
September 13, 1978	**Liverpool**	EC1-1	2-0	Shilton	Anderson	Barrett	McGovern	Lloyd	Burns	Gemmill	Bowyer	Birtles	Woodcock	Robertson
September 16, 1978	Manchester Utd	Division 1	1-1	Shilton	Anderson	Barrett	McGovern	Lloyd	Burns	Gemmill	Bowyer	Birtles	Woodcock	Robertson
September 19, 1978	**Mansfield**	CCF	4-0	Woods	Anderson	Barrett	McGovern	Needham	Burns	Mills	O'Hare	Elliott	Burke	Robertson
September 23, 1978	**Middlesbrough**	Division 1	2-2	Shilton	Anderson	Barrett	McGovern	Lloyd	Burns	O'Neill	Bowyer	Birtles	Woodcock	Robertson
September 27, 1978	Liverpool	EC1-2	0-0	Shilton	Anderson	Clark	McGovern	Lloyd	Burns	Gemmill	Bowyer	Birtles	Woodcock	Robertson
September 30, 1978	Aston Villa	Division 1	2-1	Shilton	Anderson	Bowyer	McGovern	Lloyd	Burns	O'Neill	Gemmill	Birtles	Woodcock	Robertson
October 4, 1978	Oxford Utd	LC3	5-0	Shilton	Anderson	Bowyer	McGovern	Lloyd	Burns	O'Neill	Gemmill	Birtles	Woodcock	Robertson
October 7, 1978	**Wolves**	Division 1	3-0	Shilton	Anderson	Clark	McGovern	Lloyd	Burns	O'Neill	Gemmill	Birtles	Woodcock	Robertson
October 14, 1978	Bristol City	Division 1	3-1	Shilton	Anderson	Clark	McGovern	Lloyd	Burns	O'Neill	Gemmill	Birtles	O'Hare	Robertson
October 18, 1978	AEK Athens	EC2-1	2-1	Shilton	Anderson	Clark	McGovern	Lloyd	Burns	Gemmill	Bowyer	Birtles	Woodcock	Robertson
October 21, 1978	**Ipswich**	Division 1	1-0	Shilton	Anderson	Clark	McGovern	Lloyd	Burns	O'Neill	Bowyer	Birtles	Woodcock	Robertson
October 28, 1978	Southampton	Division 1	0-0	Shilton	Anderson	Bowyer	McGovern	Lloyd	Burns	Gemmill	O'Hare	Birtles	Woodcock	Robertson
November 1, 1978	**AEK Athens**	EC2-2	5-1	Shilton	Anderson	Clark	O'Hare	Lloyd	Needham	Gemmill	Bowyer	Birtles	Woodcock	Robertson
November 4, 1978	**Everton**	Division 1	0-0	Shilton	Anderson	Bowyer	O'Hare	Lloyd	Burns	O'Neill	Gemmill	Birtles	Woodcock	Robertson
November 7, 1978	Everton	LC4	3-2	Shilton	Anderson	Bowyer	O'Hare	Lloyd	Burns	Gemmill	Needham	Birtles	Woodcock	Robertson
November 11, 1978	Tottenham H	Division 1	3-1	Shilton	Anderson	Bowyer	O'Hare	Lloyd	Needham	Gemmill	Mills	Birtles	Woodcock	Robertson
November 18, 1978	**QPR**	Division 1	0-0	Shilton	Anderson	Bowyer	Needham	Lloyd	O'Hare	Mills	Gemmill	Birtles	Woodcock	Robertson
November 25, 1978	Bolton	Division 1	1-0	Shilton	Anderson	Clark	Needham	Lloyd	Bowyer	O'Neill	Gemmill	Birtles	Woodcock	Robertson
December 5, 1978	Dinamo Zagreb	F	2-0	Shilton	Anderson	Clark	McGovern	Needham	Bowyer	O'Neill	Gemmill	Birtles	O'Hare	Robertson
December 9, 1978	Liverpool	Division 1	0-2	Shilton	Anderson	Clark	Needham	Lloyd	Bowyer	Gemmill	McGovern	Elliott	Birtles	Robertson
December 13, 1978	**Brighton & H.A.**	LC5	3-1	Shilton	Anderson	Clark	McGovern	Lloyd	Needham	Bowyer	Gemmill	Birtles	Woodcock	Robertson
December 16, 1978	**Birmingham**	Division 1	1-0	Shilton	Anderson	Clark	McGovern	Lloyd	Needham	Bowyer	Gemmill	Birtles	Woodcock	Robertson
December 23, 1978	Manchester City	Division 1	0-0	Shilton	Anderson	Clark	McGovern	Lloyd	Needham	O'Neill	Gemmill	Birtles	Woodcock	Robertson
December 26, 1978	**Derby**	Division 1	1-1	Shilton	Anderson	Clark	McGovern	Lloyd	Needham	O'Neill	Gemmill	Birtles	Woodcock	Robertson
January 10, 1979	Aston Villa	FAC3	2-0	Shilton	Anderson	Clark	McGovern	Lloyd	Needham	O'Neill	Gemmill	Birtles	Woodcock	Robertson
January 13, 1979	Arsenal	Division 1	1-2	Shilton	Anderson	Clark	McGovern	Lloyd	Needham	O'Neill	Gemmill	Birtles	Woodcock	Robertson
January 17, 1979	**Watford**	LCSF-1	3-1	Shilton	Anderson	Clark	McGovern	Lloyd	Needham	O'Neill	Bowyer	Birtles	Woodcock	Robertson
January 27, 1979	**York**	FAC4	4-1	Shilton	Anderson	Bowyer	McGovern	Lloyd	Burns	O'Neill	Gemmill	Birtles	Woodcock	Robertson
January 30, 1979	Watford	LCSF-2	0-0	Shilton	Anderson	Bowyer	McGovern	Lloyd	Burns	O'Neill	Gemmill	Birtles	Woodcock	Robertson
February 3, 1979	Middlesbrough	Division 1	3-1	Shilton	Anderson	Bowyer	McGovern	Lloyd	Burns	O'Neill	Gemmill	Birtles	Woodcock	Robertson
February 19, 1979	Exeter	F	5-0	Shilton	Anderson	Clark	McGovern	Lloyd	Needham	O'Neill	Gemmill	Birtles	Woodcock	Robertson
February 21, 1979	WBA	F	0-0	Shilton	Anderson	Clark	McGovern	Lloyd	Burns	O'Neill	Gemmill	Birtles	Woodcock	Robertson
February 24, 1979	**Bristol City**	Division 1	2-0	Shilton	Anderson	Clark	McGovern	Lloyd	Needham	O'Neill	Gemmill	Birtles	Woodcock	Robertson
February 26, 1979	**Arsenal**	FAC5	0-1	Shilton	Anderson	Clark	McGovern	Lloyd	Needham	O'Neill	Gemmill	Birtles	Woodcock	Robertson
February 3, 1979	Ipswich	Division 1	1-1	Shilton	Anderson	Clark	McGovern	Lloyd	Needham	O'Neill	Gemmill	Birtles	Francis	Robertson
March 7, 1979	**G. Zurich**	EC3-1	4-1	Shilton	Anderson	Clark	McGovern	Lloyd	Needham	O'Neill	Gemmill	Birtles	Woodcock	Robertson
March 10, 1979	Everton	Division 1	1-1	Shilton	Barrett	Bowyer	McGovern	Lloyd	Needham	Francis	O'Hare	Birtles	Woodcock	Robertson
March 14, 1979	**Norwich**	Division 1	2-1	Shilton	Barrett	Clark	McGovern	Lloyd	Needham	Francis	Gemmill	Birtles	Woodcock	Robertson
March 17, 1979	Southampton	LCF	3-2	Shilton	Barrett	Clark	McGovern	Lloyd	Needham	O'Neill	Gemmill	Birtles	Woodcock	Robertson
March 21, 1979	G. Zurich	EC3-2	1-1	Shilton	Anderson	Barrett	McGovern	Lloyd	Needham	O'Neill	Gemmill	Birtles	Woodcock	Robertson
March 24, 1979	**Coventry**	Division 1	3-0	Shilton	Anderson	Barrett	McGovern	Lloyd	Needham	O'Neill	Francis	Birtles	Woodcock	Robertson
March 28, 1979	**Chelsea**	Division 1	6-0	Shilton	Anderson	Bowyer	McGovern	Lloyd	Needham	O'Neill	Francis	Birtles	Woodcock	Robertson
March 31, 1979	**Bolton**	Division 1	1-1	Shilton	Anderson	Bowyer	McGovern	Lloyd	Needham	O'Neill	Francis	Birtles	Woodcock	Robertson
April 4, 1979	**Aston Villa**	Division 1	4-0	Shilton	Anderson	Bowyer	McGovern	Lloyd	Needham	O'Neill	Gemmill	Francis	Woodcock	Robertson
April 7, 1979	Chelsea	Division 1	3-1	Shilton	Anderson	Gunn	McGovern	Lloyd	Needham	O'Neill	Gemmill	Francis	Bowyer	Robertson
April 11, 1979	**Cologne**	ECSF-1	3-3	Shilton	Barrett	Bowyer	McGovern	Lloyd	Needham	O'Neill	Gemmill	Birtles	Woodcock	Robertson
April 14, 1979	Derby	Division 1	2-1	Shilton	Anderson	Clark	Bowyer	Needham	Burns	O'Neill	Francis	Birtles	Woodcock	Robertson
April 16, 1979	**Leeds**	Division 1	0-0	Shilton	Anderson	Clark	McGovern	Lloyd	Burns	O'Neill	Bowyer	Birtles	Francis	Robertson
April 18, 1979	**Manchester Utd**	Division 1	1-1	Shilton	Anderson	Barrett	McGovern	Lloyd	Burns	O'Neill	Bowyer	Francis	Woodcock	Robertson
April 21, 1979	Birmingham	Division 1	2-0	Shilton	Anderson	Clark	McGovern	Lloyd	Burns	O'Neill	Francis	Birtles	Woodcock	Robertson
April 25, 1979	Cologne	ECSF-2	1-0	Shilton	Anderson	Clark	McGovern	Lloyd	Burns	O'Neill	Bowyer	Birtles	Woodcock	Robertson
April 28, 1979	**Liverpool**	Division 1	0-0	Shilton	Anderson	Clark	McGovern	Lloyd	Burns	O'Neill	Francis	Birtles	Woodcock	Robertson
April 30, 1979	Wolves	Division 1	0-1	Shilton	Anderson	Bowyer	McGovern	Lloyd	Burns	O'Hare	Francis	Birtles	Woodcock	Robertson
May 2, 1979	**Southampton**	Division 1	1-0	Shilton	Anderson	Clark	McGovern	Lloyd	Burns	Francis	Bowyer	Birtles	Woodcock	Robertson
May 5, 1979	Norwich	Division 1	1-1	Shilton	Anderson	Clark	McGovern	Lloyd	Burns	Francis	Bowyer	Birtles	Woodcock	Robertson
May 9, 1979	**Manchester City**	Division 1	3-1	Shilton	Anderson	Clark	McGovern	Lloyd	Burns	O'Neill	Francis	Birtles	Woodcock	Robertson
May 11, 1979	Southampton	F	4-0	Shilton	Anderson	Clark	McGovern	Lloyd	Burns	Francis	Bowyer	Birtles	Woodcock	Robertson
May 15, 1979	Leeds	Division 1	2-1	Shilton	Anderson	Clark	O'Hare	Lloyd	Burns	Mills	Francis	Birtles	Bowyer	Robertson
May 18, 1979	WBA	Division 1	1-0	Shilton	Anderson	Bowyer	McGovern	Lloyd	Burns	O'Hare	Francis	Birtles	Woodcock	Robertson
May 23, 1979	**Mansfield**	CCF	3-1	Shilton	Anderson	Bowyer	McGovern	Lloyd	Burns	O'Hare	Francis	Birtles	Woodcock	Robertson
May 30, 1979	Malmo	ECF	1-0	Shilton	Anderson	Clark	McGovern	Lloyd	Burns	Francis	Bowyer	Birtles	Woodcock	Robertson

1979-80

Date	Versus	Comp.	Score	1	2	3	4	5	6	7	8	9	10	11
July 30, 1979	Holsterbro BK	PSF	5-1	Shilton	Anderson	Barrett	McGovern	Lloyd	Burns	O'Neill	Hartford	Birtles	Woodcock	Robertson
August 1, 1979	Bayern Munich	PSF	0-5	Shilton	Anderson	Gray	McGovern	Lloyd	Burns	O'Neill	Hartford	Birtles	Woodcock	Robertson
August 9, 1979	Botafogo	PSF	2-1	Shilton	Anderson	Gray	McGovern	Lloyd	Burns	O'Neill	Hartford	Birtles	Woodcock	Robertson
August 10, 1979	Dynamo Bucharest	PSF	2-1	Shilton	Anderson	Gray	McGovern	Lloyd	Burns	O'Neill	Hartford	Birtles	Woodcock	Robertson
August 14, 1979	Montpelier	PSF	1-0	Shilton	Anderson	Gray	McGovern	Lloyd	Burns	O'Neill	Hartford	Birtles	Woodcock	Robertson
August 18, 1979	Ipswich	Division 1	1-0	Shilton	Anderson	Gray	McGovern	Lloyd	Needham	O'Neill	Hartford	Birtles	Woodcock	Robertson
August 22, 1979	**Stoke**	Division 1	1-0	Shilton	Anderson	Gray	McGovern	Lloyd	Needham	O'Neill	Hartford	Birtles	Woodcock	Robertson
August 25, 1979	**Coventry**	Division 1	4-1	Shilton	Anderson	Gray	McGovern	Lloyd	Burns	O'Neill	Hartford	Birtles	Woodcock	Robertson
August 29, 1979	Blackburn R	LC2-1	1-1	Shilton	Anderson	Gray	McGovern	Lloyd	Burns	O'Neill	Mills	Bowyer	Woodcock	Robertson
September 1, 1979	WBA	Division 1	5-1	Shilton	Anderson	Gray	McGovern	Lloyd	Burns	O'Neill	Bowyer	Birtles	Woodcock	Robertson
September 5, 1979	**Blackburn R**	LC2-2	6-1	Shilton	Anderson	Gray	McGovern	Lloyd	Burns	O'Neill	Bowyer	Birtles	Woodcock	Robertson
September 8, 1979	**Leeds**	Division 1	0-0	Shilton	Anderson	Gray	McGovern	Lloyd	Burns	O'Neill	Bowyer	Birtles	Woodcock	Robertson
September 15, 1979	Norwich	Division 1	1-3	Shilton	Anderson	Gray	McGovern	Lloyd	Burns	O'Neill	Bowyer	Birtles	Woodcock	Robertson
September 19, 1979	**Osters Vaxjo**	EC1-1	2-0	Shilton	Anderson	Gray	McGovern	Lloyd	Burns	O'Neill	Bowyer	Birtles	Woodcock	Robertson
September 22, 1979	Bristol City	Division 1	1-1	Shilton	Anderson	Gray	McGovern	Lloyd	Burns	Mills	O'Hare	Birtles	Woodcock	Robertson
September 25, 1979	Middlesbrough	LC3	3-1	Shilton	Anderson	Gray	McGovern	Lloyd	Burns	Mills	O'Hare	Birtles	Woodcock	Robertson
September 29, 1979	**Liverpool**	Division 1	1-0	Shilton	Anderson	Gray	McGovern	Lloyd	Burns	O'Neill	O'Hare	Birtles	Woodcock	Robertson
October 3, 1979	Osters Vaxjo	EC1-2	1-1	Shilton	Anderson	Gray	McGovern	Lloyd	Burns	O'Neill	Mills	Birtles	Woodcock	Robertson
October 6, 1979	**Wolves**	Division 1	3-1	Shilton	Anderson	Gray	McGovern	Lloyd	Burns	Francis	O'Hare	Birtles	Woodcock	Robertson
October 10, 1979	Stoke	Division 1	1-1	Shilton	Anderson	Gray	McGovern	Lloyd	Burns	Francis	Mills	Birtles	Woodcock	Robertson
October 13, 1979	Manchester City	Division 1	0-1	Shilton	Anderson	Gray	McGovern	Lloyd	Burns	Francis	Mills	Birtles	Woodcock	Robertson
October 20, 1979	**Bolton**	Division 1	5-2	Shilton	Anderson	Gray	McGovern	Lloyd	Burns	Francis	Mills	Birtles	Woodcock	Robertson
October 24, 1979	**Arges Pitesti**	EC2-1	2-0	Shilton	Anderson	Gray	McGovern	Lloyd	Burns	Mills	Bowyer	Birtles	Woodcock	Robertson
October 27, 1979	Tottenham H	Division 1	0-1	Shilton	Anderson	Gray	McGovern	Lloyd	Burns	Mills	Francis	Birtles	Woodcock	Robertson
October 30, 1979	Bristol City	LC4		Shilton	Anderson	Gray	McGovern	Lloyd	Burns	O'Hare	Francis	Birtles	Woodcock	Robertson
November 3, 1979	**Ipswich**	Division 1	2-0	Shilton	Anderson	Gray	McGovern	Lloyd	Burns	Francis	O'Hare	Birtles	Woodcock	Robertson
November 7, 1979	Arges Pitesti	EC2-2	2-0	Shilton	Anderson	Gray	McGovern	Lloyd	Burns	O'Hare	Bowyer	Birtles	Woodcock	Robertson
November 10, 1979	Southampton	Division 1	1-4	Shilton	Anderson	Gray	McGovern	Lloyd	Burns	Francis	Bowyer	Birtles	Woodcock	Robertson
November 12, 1979	Plymouth Argyle	F	2-1	Shilton	Anderson	Gray	McGovern	Lloyd	Needham	O'Neill	Bowyer	Francis	Woodcock	Robertson
November 14, 1979	**Bristol C**	LC4R	3-0	Shilton	Anderson	Gray	McGovern	Lloyd	Needham	O'Neill	Francis	Birtles	Woodcock	Robertson
November 17, 1979	**Brighton & H.A.**	Division 1	0-1	Shilton	Anderson	Gray	McGovern	Lloyd	Needham	O'Neill	Francis	Birtles	Woodcock	Robertson
November 24, 1979	Derby County	Division 1	1-4	Shilton	Anderson	Gray	McGovern	Lloyd	Needham	O'Neill	O'Hare	Birtles	Francis	Robertson
November 27, 1979	Cairo XI	F	3-1	Shilton	Anderson	Gray	McGovern	Lloyd	Needham	O'Neill	Bowyer	Birtles	Francis	Robertson
December 1, 1979	**Arsenal**	Division 1	1-1	Shilton	Anderson	Gray	McGovern	Lloyd	Burns	O'Neill	O'Hare	Birtles	Francis	Robertson
December 4, 1979	West Ham	LC5	0-0	Shilton	Anderson	Gray	Bowyer	Lloyd	Burns	O'Neill	O'Hare	Birtles	Francis	Robertson
December 8, 1979	Crystal Palace	Division 1	0-1	Shilton	Anderson	Gray	Bowyer	Lloyd	Burns	O'Neill	O'Hare	Birtles	Francis	Robertson
December 12, 1979	**West Ham**	LC5R	3-0	Shilton	Anderson	Gray	Bowyer	Lloyd	Burns	O'Neill	O'Hare	Birtles	Francis	Robertson
December 18, 1979	Cologne	F	1-1	Shilton	Anderson	Gray	McGovern	Lloyd	Needham	O'Neill	Bowles	Birtles	Francis	Robertson
December 22, 1979	Manchester Utd	Division 1	0-3	Shilton	Anderson	Gray	McGovern	Lloyd	Burns	O'Neill	Bowles	Birtles	Francis	Robertson
December 26, 1979	**Aston Villa**	Division 1	2-1	Shilton	Anderson	Gray	McGovern	Lloyd	Burns	Bowyer	Bowles	Birtles	Francis	Robertson
December 29, 1979	Coventry	Division 1	3-0	Shilton	Anderson	Gray	McGovern	Lloyd	Burns	Francis	Bowles	Birtles	Bowyer	Robertson
January 1, 1980	Everton	Division 1	0-1	Shilton	Anderson	Gray	McGovern	Lloyd	Burns	Francis	Bowles	Birtles	Bowyer	Robertson
January 5, 1980	Leeds	FAC3	4-1	Shilton	Anderson	Gray	McGovern	Lloyd	Burns	Francis	Bowles	Birtles	Bowyer	Robertson
January 8, 1980	Gravesend	F	6-1	Montgomery	Anderson	Gray	McGovern	Needham	Burns	O'Neill	Bowles	Birtles	Francis	Robertson
January 12, 1980	**WBA**	Division 1	3-1	Shilton	Anderson	Gray	McGovern	Lloyd	Needham	O'Neill	Bowles	Birtles	Francis	Robertson
January 19, 1980	Leeds	Division 1	2-1	Shilton	Anderson	Gray	McGovern	Lloyd	Needham	Francis	George	Birtles	Bowles	Robertson
January 22, 1980	**Liverpool**	LCSF-1	1-0	Shilton	Anderson	Gray	McGovern	Lloyd	Needham	O'Neill	Bowyer	Birtles	Francis	Robertson
January 26, 1980	**Liverpool**	FAC4	0-2	Shilton	Anderson	Gray	McGovern	Lloyd	Needham	O'Neill	Bowyer	Birtles	Francis	Robertson
January 30, 1980	**Barcelona**	SC-1	1-0	Shilton	Anderson	Gray	O'Neill	Lloyd	Burns	Francis	Bowyer	Birtles	George	Robertson
February 5, 1980	Barcelona	SC-2	1-1	Shilton	Anderson	Gray	McGovern	Lloyd	Burns	Francis	Bowles	Birtles	George	Robertson
February 9, 1980	**Bristol City**	Division 1	0-0	Shilton	Anderson	Gunn	McGovern	Lloyd	Burns	O'Neill	Bowles	Birtles	George	Robertson
February 12, 1980	Liverpool	LCSF-2	1-1	Shilton	Anderson	Gray	McGovern	Lloyd	Burns	O'Neill	Mills	Birtles	Bowyer	Robertson
February 16, 1980	**Middlesbrough**	Division 1	2-2	Shilton	Anderson	Gray	McGovern	Lloyd	Burns	O'Neill	Bowles	Birtles	Francis	Robertson
February 19, 1980	Liverpool	Division 1	0-2	Shilton	Anderson	Gray	McGovern	Lloyd	Burns	O'Neill	Bowyer	Birtles	Francis	Robertson
February 23, 1980	**Manchester City**	Division 1	4-0	Shilton	Anderson	Gray	McGovern	Lloyd	Burns	O'Neill	Bowles	Birtles	Francis	Robertson
March 1, 1980	Bolton	Division 1	0-1	Shilton	Gunn	Gray	McGovern	Lloyd	Burns	O'Neill	Bowles	Birtles	Francis	Robertson
March 5, 1980	**Dynamo Berlin**	EC3-1	0-1	Shilton	Gunn	Gray	McGovern	Lloyd	Burns	O'Neill	Bowles	Birtles	Francis	Robertson
March 11, 1980	**Tottenham H**	Division 1	4-0	Shilton	Anderson	Gray	McGovern	Lloyd	Burns	Francis	Bowles	Birtles	O'Neill	Robertson
March 15, 1980	Wolves	LCF	0-1	Shilton	Anderson	Gray	McGovern	Needham	Burns	O'Neill	Bowyer	Birtles	Francis	Robertson
March 19, 1980	Dynamo Berlin	EC3-2	3-1	Shilton	Anderson	Gray	McGovern	Lloyd	Needham	O'Neill	Bowyer	Birtles	Francis	Robertson
March 22, 1980	**Southampton**	Division 1	2-0	Shilton	Anderson	Gray	McGovern	Lloyd	Burns	O'Neill	Bowles	Birtles	Francis	Robertson
March 29, 1980	Brighton & H.A.	Division 1	0-1	Shilton	Anderson	Gray	McGovern	Lloyd	Burns	O'Neill	Bowles	Birtles	Francis	Robertson
April 2, 1980	**Manchester Utd**	Division 1	2-0	Shilton	Anderson	Gray	McGovern	Lloyd	Burns	O'Neill	Bowles	Birtles	Francis	Robertson
April 5, 1980	Aston Villa	Division 1	2-3	Shilton	Anderson	Gray	McGovern	Lloyd	Burns	O'Neill	Bowles	Birtles	Francis	Robertson
April 9, 1980	**Ajax Amsterdam**	ECSF-1	2-0	Shilton	Anderson	Gray	McGovern	Lloyd	Burns	O'Neill	Bowles	Birtles	Francis	Robertson
April 11, 1980	Emirates SC	F	4-0	Shilton	Anderson	Gray	O'Hare	Needham	Burns	O'Neill	Bowles	Birtles	Francis	Robertson
April 13, 1980	Murrahaq SC	F	8-2	Shilton	Anderson	Gray	O'Hare	Needham	Burns	O'Neill	Bowles	Birtles	Francis	Robertson
April 16, 1980	Lincoln	F	1-2	Montgomery	Anderson	Gray	McGovern	Lloyd	Needham	O'Hare	Bowles	Bowyer	Francis	Robertson
April 19, 1980	**Derby County**	Division 1	1-0	Shilton	Anderson	Gray	McGovern	Lloyd	Needham	O'Neill	Bowles	Birtles	Francis	Robertson
April 23, 1980	Ajax	ECSF-2	0-1	Shilton	Anderson	Gray	McGovern	Lloyd	Burns	O'Neill	Bowyer	Birtles	Francis	Robertson
April 26, 1980	Middlesbrough	Division 1	0-0	Shilton	Anderson	Gray	McGovern	Lloyd	Needham	Mills	Bowyer	Birtles	Francis	Robertson
April 30, 1980	**Norwich**	Division 1	2-0	Shilton	Anderson	Gray	McGovern	Lloyd	Burns	Mills	Bowles	Birtles	Francis	Robertson
May 3, 1980	**C. Palace**	Division 1	4-0	Shilton	Anderson	Gray	McGovern	Lloyd	Burns	O'Neill	Bowles	Birtles	Francis	Robertson
May 5, 1980	Arsenal	Division 1	0-0	Shilton	Anderson	Gray	McGovern	Lloyd	Burns	O'Neill	Bowyer	Birtles	Mills	Robertson
May 6, 1980	Notts County	CCF	2-1	Montgomery	Anderson	Gray	Bowyer	Lloyd	Needham	O'Neill	O'Hare	Burns	Bowles	Robertson
May 9, 1980	**Everton**	Division 1	1-0	Shilton	Anderson	Gray	McGovern	Lloyd	Burns	O'Neill	Bowles	Birtles	Mills	Robertson
May 10, 1980	Stade Brestois	F	1-0	Shilton	Anderson	Gray	McGovern	Lloyd	Burns	O'Neill	Bowles	Birtles	Mills	Robertson
May 12, 1980	Wolves	Division 1	1-3	Shilton	Anderson	Gray	McGovern	Lloyd	Burns	O'Neill	Bowyer	Birtles	O'Hare	Robertson
May 16, 1980	**Leicester**	F	0-0	Shilton	Anderson	Gray	McGovern	Needham	Burns	O'Neill	Mills	Birtles	Bowyer	Robertson
May 28, 1980	Hamburg SV	ECF	1-0	Shilton	Anderson	Gray	McGovern	Lloyd	Burns	O'Neill	Bowyer	Birtles	Mills	Robertson

1980-81

Date	Opponents	Comp	Score	1	2	3	4	5	6	7	8	9	10	11
July 23, 1980	Vancouver Whitecaps	PSF	1-1	Shilton	Anderson	F Gray	McGovern	Lloyd	Burns	O'Neill	Bowyer	Birtles	Wallace	Robertson
July 25, 1980	Tampa Bay Rowdies	PSF	0-0	Shilton	Anderson	F Gray	McGovern	Lloyd	Burns	O'Neill	Bowyer	Birtles	Ponte	Mills
July 27, 1980	Colombia	PSF	0-5	Shilton	Anderson	F Gray	McGovern	Lloyd	Burns	O'Neill	Bowyer	Birtles	Ponte	Mills
July 31, 1980	Toronto Blizzard	PSF	3-1	Shilton	Anderson	F Gray	McGovern	Needham	Burns	O'Neill	Ponte	Birtles	Wallace	Mills
August 5, 1980	Paddy Mulligan XI	PSF	3-2	Shilton	Anderson	F Gray	McGovern	Needham	Burns	Ponte	Bowyer	Birtles	Wallace	Robertson
August 8, 1980	Alkmaar AZ67	PSF	1-2	Shilton	Gunn	F Gray	McGovern	Lloyd	Burns	O'Neill	Bowyer	Birtles	Wallace	Robertson
August 10, 1980	Bayern Munich	PSF	0-3	Shilton	Gunn	F Gray	O'Hare	Needham	Burns	O'Neill	Ponte	Birtles	Wallace	Robertson
August 11, 1980	Grasshopper Zurich	PSF	0-0	Shilton	Gunn	F Gray	McGovern	Needham	Burns	O'Neill	Ponte	O'Hare	Mills	Robertson
August 16, 1980	Tottenham H	Division 1	0-2	Shilton	Gunn	F Gray	McGovern	Needham	Burns	Ponte	Bowyer	Birtles	Wallace	Robertson
August 20, 1980	**Birmingham**	Division 1	2-1	Shilton	Anderson	F Gray	McGovern	Needham	Burns	O'Neill	Ponte	Birtles	Wallace	Robertson
August 23, 1980	Everton	Division 1	0-0	Shilton	Anderson	F Gray	McGovern	Needham	Burns	Ponte	Bowyer	Birtles	Wallace	Robertson
August 27, 1980	**Peterborough U**	LC2-1	3-0	Shilton	Anderson	F Gray	O'Hare	Lloyd	Needham	O'Neill	Bowyer	Birtles	Wallace	Robertson
August 30, 1980	**Stoke**	Division 1	5-0	Shilton	Anderson	F Gray	McGovern	Lloyd	Needham	O'Neill	Bowyer	Birtles	Wallace	Robertson
September 3, 1980	Peterborough U	LC2-2	3-0	Shilton	Anderson	F Gray	McGovern	Needham	Burns	Ponte	Bowyer	Birtles	Mills	Robertson
September 6, 1980	Middlesbrough	Division 1	0-0	Shilton	Anderson	F Gray	McGovern	Needham	Burns	O'Neill	Bowyer	Birtles	Wallace	Robertson
September 13, 1980	**Manchester City**	Division 1	3-2	Shilton	Anderson	F Gray	McGovern	Needham	Burns	O'Neill	Bowyer	Birtles	Wallace	Robertson
September 17, 1980	CSKA Sofia	EC1-1	0-1	Shilton	Anderson	F Gray	McGovern	Lloyd	Needham	O'Neill	Bowyer	Birtles	Wallace	Robertson
September 20, 1980	**Leicester**	Division 1	5-0	Shilton	Anderson	F Gray	McGovern	Needham	Burns	O'Neill	Ponte	Birtles	Wallace	Robertson
September 23, 1980	Bury	LC3	7-0	Shilton	Anderson	F Gray	McGovern	Needham	Burns	O'Neill	Ponte	Birtles	Mills	Robertson
September 27, 1980	Arsenal	Division 1	0-1	Shilton	Anderson	F Gray	McGovern	Needham	Burns	O'Neill	Ponte	Birtles	Mills	Robertson
October 2, 1980	**CSKA Sofia**	EC1-2	0-1	Shilton	Anderson	F Gray	McGovern	Needham	Burns	O'Neill	Bowyer	Birtles	Wallace	Robertson
October 4, 1980	**Manchester Utd**	Division 1	1-2	Shilton	Anderson	F Gray	McGovern	Lloyd	Needham	O'Neill	Bowyer	Birtles	Wallace	Robertson
October 8, 1980	Sunderland	Division 1	2-2	Shilton	Gunn	F Gray	McGovern	Lloyd	Needham	O'Neill	Bowyer	Mills	Wallace	Robertson
October 11, 1980	**Brighton & H.A.**	Division 1	1-0	Shilton	Gunn	F Gray	McGovern	Lloyd	Needham	O'Neill	Bowyer	Mills	Wallace	Robertson
October 13, 1980	**Tampa Bay Rowdies**	F	7-1	Sutton	Gunn	Bowyer	Ponte	Lloyd	Needham	Plummer	Smith	Burns	Wallace	Walsh
October 18, 1980	**WBA**	Division 1	2-1	Shilton	Gunn	F Gray	Ponte	Lloyd	Burns	O'Neill	Bowyer	Mills	Wallace	Robertson
October 22, 1980	**Leeds**	Division 1	2-1	Shilton	Gunn	F Gray	Ponte	Lloyd	Burns	O'Neill	Bowyer	Ward	Wallace	Robertson
October 25, 1980	Norwich	Division 1	1-1	Sutton	Gunn	F Gray	McGovern	Lloyd	Burns	O'Neill	Bowyer	Ward	Wallace	Robertson
October 28, 1980	Watford	LC4	1-4	Sutton	Gunn	F Gray	Ponte	Lloyd	Burns	O'Neill	Bowyer	Mills	Wallace	Robertson
November 1, 1980	**Southampton**	Division 1	2-1	Shilton	Anderson	F Gray	Ponte	Lloyd	Burns	O'Neill	Bowyer	Ward	Wallace	Robertson
November 8, 1980	Liverpool	Division 1	0-0	Shilton	Anderson	F Gray	McGovern	Lloyd	Burns	O'Neill	Bowyer	Ward	Wallace	Robertson
November 11, 1980	Birmingham	Division 1	0-2	Shilton	Gunn	F Gray	McGovern	Lloyd	Burns	O'Neill	Bowyer	Ward	Wallace	Robertson
November 15, 1980	**Tottenham H**	Division 1	0-3	Shilton	Anderson	F Gray	Bowyer	Lloyd	Burns	Mills	Ponte	Ward	Wallace	Robertson
November 22, 1980	**Ipswich**	Division 1	1-2	Shilton	Anderson	F Gray	McGovern	Lloyd	Burns	Mills	Bowyer	Ward	Wallace	Robertson
November 25, 1980	**Valencia**	SC-1	2-1	Shilton	Anderson	F Gray	McGovern	Lloyd	Burns	Mills	Bowyer	Ward	Wallace	Robertson
November 29, 1980	Coventry	Division 1	1-1	Shilton	Anderson	F Gray	Gunn	Lloyd	Ponte	Mills	Bowyer	Ward	Wallace	Robertson
December 6, 1980	**Crystal Palace**	Division 1	3-0	Shilton	Anderson	F Gray	McGovern	Lloyd	Gunn	Mills	Bowyer	Ward	Wallace	Walsh
December 10, 1980	Grantham	F	6-0	Shilton	Anderson	Ponte	O'Neill	Lloyd	Gunn	Mills	Walsh	Ward	Wallace	S Gray
December 13, 1980	Leeds	Division 1	0-1	Shilton	Anderson	F Gray	McGovern	Lloyd	Gunn	Mills	O'Neill	Ward	Wallace	Walsh
December 17, 1980	Valencia	SC-2	0-1	Shilton	Anderson	Gunn	McGovern	Lloyd	Burns	O'Neill	Ponte	Francis	Wallace	Walsh
December 20, 1980	Sunderland	Division 1	3-1	Shilton	Anderson	F Gray	McGovern	Lloyd	Gunn	O'Neill	Ponte	Francis	Wallace	Walsh
December 26, 1980	Wolves	Division 1	4-1	Shilton	Anderson	F Gray	McGovern	Lloyd	Gunn	O'Neill	Ponte	Francis	Wallace	Walsh
December 27, 1980	**Aston Villa**	Division 1	2-2	Shilton	Anderson	F Gray	McGovern	Lloyd	Gunn	O'Neill	Ponte	Francis	Wallace	Robertson
January 3, 1981	**Bolton**	FAC3	3-3	Shilton	Anderson	F Gray	McGovern	Lloyd	Gunn	O'Neill	Ponte	Francis	Wallace	Robertson
January 6, 1981	Bolton	FAC3R	1-0	Shilton	Anderson	F Gray	McGovern	Lloyd	Burns	O'Neill	Bowyer	Francis	Ward	Robertson
January 10, 1981	Ipswich	Division 1	0-2	Shilton	Anderson	F Gray	McGovern	Needham	Burns	O'Neill	Bowyer	Francis	Ward	Robertson
January 11, 1981	Paris St Germain	F	0-2	Shilton	Anderson	F Gray	McGovern	Needham	Gunn	Mills	Ponte	Francis	Ward	Robertson
January 24, 1981	**Manchester Utd**	FAC4	1-0	Shilton	Anderson	F Gray	McGovern	Burns	Gunn	Ponte	Wallace	Francis	Walsh	Robertson
January 31, 1981	**Everton**	Division 1	1-0	Shilton	Anderson	F Gray	McGovern	Burns	Gunn	Ponte	Wallace	Francis	Walsh	Robertson
February 4, 1981	**Red Star Belgrade**	F	1-3	Shilton	Anderson	F Gray	Gunn	Burns	Needham	Ponte	Wallace	Francis	Walsh	Robertson
February 7, 1981	Manchester City	Division 1	1-1	Shilton	Anderson	F Gray	S Gray	Burns	Gunn	Mills	Wallace	Francis	Walsh	Robertson
February 11, 1981	Nacional	WCC	0-1	Shilton	Anderson	F Gray	S Gray	Lloyd	Burns	O'Neill	Ponte	Francis	Wallace	Robertson
February 14, 1981	**Bristol**	FAC5	2-1	Shilton	Anderson	F Gray	S Gray	Burns	Gunn	Mills	Wallace	Francis	Walsh	Robertson
February 18, 1981	Stoke	Division 1	2-1	Shilton	Anderson	F Gray	S Gray	Burns	Gunn	Mills	Wallace	Francis	Walsh	Robertson
February 21, 1981	**Arsenal**	Division 1	3-1	Shilton	Anderson	F Gray	S Gray	Burns	Gunn	Mills	Wallace	Francis	O'Neill	Robertson
February 28, 1981	Leicester	Division 1	1-1	Shilton	Anderson	F Gray	S Gray	Burns	Gunn	Mills	Wallace	Francis	Walsh	Robertson
March 3, 1981	**Middlesbrough**	Division 1	1-0	Shilton	Anderson	F Gray	S Gray	Burns	Gunn	Mills	Wallace	Francis	Walsh	Robertson
March 7, 1981	**Ipswich**	FAC6	3-3	Shilton	Anderson	F Gray	S Gray	Burns	Gunn	Mills	Wallace	Francis	Walsh	Robertson
March 10, 1981	Ipswich	FAC6R	0-1	Shilton	Gunn	F Gray	S Gray	Needham	Burns	Ponte	Wallace	Francis	Walsh	Robertson
March 14, 1981	**Brighton & H.A.**	Division 1	4-1	Shilton	Gunn	F Gray	S Gray	Needham	Burns	Ponte	Wallace	Mills	Walsh	Robertson
March 18, 1981	Manchester Utd	Division 1	1-1	Shilton	Gunn	F Gray	S Gray	Needham	Burns	Ponte	Wallace	Mills	Walsh	Robertson
March 21, 1981	WBA	Division 1	1-2	Smelt	Gunn	F Gray	S Gray	Needham	Burns	Mills	Wallace	Francis	Walsh	Robertson
March 28, 1981	**Norwich**	Division 1	2-1	Shilton	Anderson	F Gray	S Gray	Needham	Burns	Ponte	Wallace	Francis	Walsh	Robertson
April 4, 1981	Southampton	Division 1	0-2	Shilton	Anderson	F Gray	S Gray	Aas	Burns	Mills	Wallace	Francis	Walsh	Robertson
April 7, 1981	Kettering Town	F	5-2	Shilton	Anderson	Gunn	McGovern	Needham	Aas	Ponte	Wallace	Francis	Walsh	Robertson
April 11, 1981	**Liverpool**	Division 1	0-0	Shilton	Anderson	F Gray	McGovern	Aas	Burns	Mills	S Gray	Francis	Ward	Robertson
April 14, 1981	Cardiff	F	2-1	-	-	-	-	-	-	-	-	-	-	-
April 18, 1981	Aston Villa	Division 1	0-2	Shilton	Anderson	Gunn	McGovern	Needham	Aas	Mills	S Gray	Francis	Ward	Robertson
April 20, 1981	**Wolves**	Division 1	1-0	Shilton	Anderson	F Gray	McGovern	Aas	Gunn	Mills	Ward	Francis	Walsh	Robertson
April 25, 1981	Crystal Palace	Division 1	3-1	Shilton	Anderson	Gunn	McGovern	Aas	Burns	Mills	Wallace	Francis	S Gray	Robertson
May 2, 1981	**Coventry**	Division 1	1-1	Shilton	Gunn	F Gray	McGovern	Aas	Burns	Mills	Wallace	Francis	S Gray	Robertson
May 4, 1981	**Mansfield**	CCF	2-1	Shilton	Gunn	F Gray	Needham	Aas	Walsh	Mills	Ward	Burns	S Gray	Robertson
May 7, 1981	**Notts County**	F	3-0	Shilton	Kendal	Gunn	McGovern	Needham	Aas	Mills	S Gray	Burns	Wallace	Robertson
May 10, 1981	Real Madrid	F	0-2	Shilton	Gunn	S Gray	McGovern	Burns	Aas	Mills	Ward	Francis	Walsh	Robertson
May 19, 1981	Real Mallorca	F	5-0	Smelt	Gunn	S Gray	McGovern	Fairclough	Smith	Mills	Wallace	Ward	Hodge	Walsh

Viv Anderson

Year	Pld	Gls
1976-77	49(3)	3
1977-78	60	5
1978-79	72	4
1979-80	77	4
1980-81	53	2
Totals	311(3)	18

Colin Barrett

Year	Pld	Gls
1976-77	22(6)	5
1977-78	38(3)	2
1978-79	23(3)	3
1979-80	1(4)	0
1980-81	-	-
Totals	84(16)	10

Garry Birtles

Year	Pld	Gls
1976-77	2(1)	0
1977-78	2(1)	1
1978-79	58	30
1979-80	76	23
1980-81	21(1)	12
Totals	159(3)	66

Ian Bowyer

Year	Pld	Gls
1976-77	64	16
1977-78	44(4)	15
1978-79	43(8)	10
1979-80	34(12)	7
1980-81	32(4)	5
Totals	217(28)	53

Kenny Burns

Year	Pld	Gls
1976-77	-	-
1977-78	67	6
1978-79	48	1
1979-80	64(1)	3
1980-81	53(1)	6
Totals	232(2)	16

Frank Clark

Year	Pld	Gls
1976-77	65	0
1977-78	26(1)	1
1978-79	36	0
1979-80	-	-
1980-81	-	-
Totals	127(1) 1	1

Trevor Francis

Year	Pld	Gls
1976-77	-	-
1977-78	-	-
1978-79	22(2)	8
1979-80	51	25
1980-81	31	16
Total	104(2)	49

Archie Gemmill

Year	Pld	Gls
1976-77	-	-
1977-78	39(2)	3
1978-79	51(1)	2
1979-80	-	-
1980-81	-	-
Totals	90(3)	5

Frank Gray

Year	Pld	Gls
1976-77	-	-
1977-78	-	-
1978-79	-	-
1979-80	77	4
1980-81	65	4
Totals	142	8

Larry Lloyd

Year	Pld	Gls
1976-77	37	4
1977-78	43	4
1978-79	65	5
1979-80	75(1)	5
1980-81	35(1)	0
Totals	255(2)	14

John McGovern

Year	Pld	Gls
1976-77	60	0
1977-78	52	6
1978-79	68	5
1979-80	72	3
1980-81	48	1
Totals	300	15

Gary Mills

Year	Pld	Gls
1976-77	-	-
1977-78	-	-
1978-79	5(3)	2
1979-80	19(11)	3
1980-81	40(6)	11
Totals	64(20)	16

David Needham

Year	Pld	Gls
1976-77	-	-
1977-78	24	4
1978-79	40(8)	6
1979-80	22(4)	3
1980-81	31	3
Totals	117(12)	16

John O'Hare

Year	Pld	Gls
1976-77	38(3)	7
1977-78	13(4)	3
1978-79	13(4)	0
1979-80	16(4)	5
1980-81	3(1)	0
Totals	83(16)	15

Martin O'Neill

Year	Pld	Gls
1976-77	58(3)	13
1977-78	60(3)	15
1978-79	52	16
1979-80	59(1)	8
1980-81	38(4)	3
Totals	247(11)	55

John Robertson

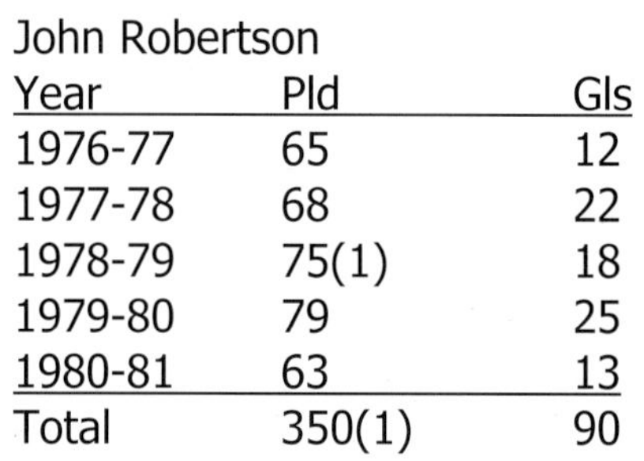

Year	Pld	Gls
1976-77	65	12
1977-78	68	22
1978-79	75(1)	18
1979-80	79	25
1980-81	63	13
Total	350(1)	90

Peter Shilton

Year	Pld	Gls
1976-77	-	-
1977-78	48	0
1978-79	75	0
1979-80	77	0
1980-81	69	0
Total	269	0

Peter Withe

Year	Pld	Gls
1976-77	47(1)	21
1977-78	62	25
1978-79	8	3
1979-80	-	-
1980-81	-	-
Totals	117(1)	49

Tony Woodcock

Year	Pld	Gls
1976-77	40	18
1977-78	60	27
1978-79	69	18
1979-80	31	13
1980-81	-	-
Totals	200	76

Combined Appearances: 1976-77 to 1980-81

No.	Name	Played	Goals
1	John Robertson	350(1)	90
2	Viv Anderson	311(3)	18
3	John McGovern	300	15
4	Peter Shilton	269	0
5	Larry Lloyd	255(2)	14
6	Martin O'Neill	247(11)	55
7	Kenny Burns	232(2)	16
8	Ian Bowyer	217(28)	53
9	Tony Woodcock	200	76
10	Garry Birtles	159(3)	66
11	Frank Gray	142	8
12	Frank Clark	127(1)	1
13	David Needham	117(12)	16
14	Peter Withe	117(1)	49
15	Trevor Francis	104(2)	49
16	Archie Gemmill	90(3)	5
17	Colin Barrett	84(16)	10
18	John O'Hare	83(16)	15
19	John Middleton	68	0
20	Gary Mills	64(20)	16

Honours: 1976-77 to 1980-81

Year	League	FACup	LCup	European Cup	Others
1976-77	3rd (Div. Two)	4th round	3rd round	-	**Anglo-Scottish winners**
1977-78	**champions**	6th round	**winners**	-	-
1978-79	runners-up	5th round	**winners**	**winners**	**Charity Shield winners**
1979-80	5th	4th round	finalists	**winners**	**Super Cup winners**
1980-81	7th	6th round	4th round	1st round	World Club Cup finalists

Overall Record: 1976-77 to 1980-81

	Pld	W	D	L	F	A	PTS	GD
League	210	106	62	42	332	160	274	+172
League Cup	32	21	8	3	78	29	50	+49
FA Cup	22	10	7	5	42	27	27	+15
Anglo Scottish Cup	9	6	3	0	20	9	15	+11
County Cup	7	5	1	1	14	6	11	+8
Friendlies	64	40	12	12	162	69	92	+93
Charity Shield	1	1	0	0	5	0	2	+5
European Cup	20	12	4	4	32	14	28	+18
World Club Champ.	1	0	0	1	0	1	0	-1
Super Cup	4	2	1	1	4	3	5	+1
Totals	370	203	98	69	689	318	504	+371

The Legacy

The heights achieved by the players and management of this era will forever set the standards by which all future Forest teams are judged. Its not impossible, but it is unlikely, that these marks will never be reached. Not only were Forest the 'smallest' club to ever win the European Cup, but they also retained it. Something that most of the self-proclaimed giants of British and European football have never managed. This was also achieved when only the champions of each country and holders of the trophy could compete, plus there was no safety-net of multiple group stages to guard against the odd loss here and there. To help put it in perspective, note that Franz Beckenbauer is the only captain to have hoisted the European Cup more times than John McGovern.

The fact that Forest's achievements are more often than not overlooked by the British media still rankles with players and fans alike. A prime example came with a well-known football magazine's poll of the best teams of all time. The blinkered outlook from so-called experts was laughable. While the obvious choices in the Top 20 were all present and correct – Brazil 1970, Holland 1974 and England 1966, Milan 1992 and Celtic 1967 – there were some startling omissions and some strange rankings of teams. These 'experts' put the Manchester United team of 1999 ahead of the Real Madrid team which won five straight European Cups! For course the Forest side of the late 1970s was nowhere to be seen. Even more strange was the fact that he Liverpool side of 1979 was number twelve in the list. That side won the league, but in the very same season Forest won the League Cup, the Charity Shield, the European Cup and came runners-up in the league despite losing less games than the Merseysiders.

It seems that people outside of the East Midlands have very short memories when it comes to Nottingham Forest so here are a few reminders.

The Best Ever English Teams?

It should go without saying that to even be considered, the team in question would have to have at least one European Cup win in the trophy cabinet. The teams that should be compared are Forest (1977-80), Liverpool (1983-86), Liverpool (1980-83), Manchester United (1966-69), Aston Villa (1980-83), Liverpool (1976-79) and Manchester United (1997-2000). The Liverpool teams have three entries because of the turnover of players in the different eras – for example to European Cup winning teams of 1977 and 1981 have only four players in common in the respective starting line-ups.

So in the greatest club competition, the European Cup, which team won most of it's games? Forest did. They won 78% of their matches, while the United team of 1997-2000 won only 68% of theirs – the lowest of this group. The league championship showed that United had the best record over the three seasons, Forest were third out of the six sides; Forest had the best League Cup record and third best FA Cup record despite never winning it.

Over all competitions Forest and United had virtually identical records: United won 71.5% of their games between 1997-2000 and Forest won 70.5% of theirs between 1977-1980 (both of these are above those for the four other sides mentioned). In the three years considered, Forest won seven major trophies to United's five and also set the mark of forty-two league games unbeaten. So why is one side ranked as number two all time and one not even in the Top 20?

As Brian Clough said at the start of the book, 'If anybody else had have done what we'd done in such a short spell of time we wouldn't have only gone down in history, we'd have gone down as the best thing ever. We'd have outdone Penicillin!'

EUROPEAN CHAMPIONS CUP RESULTS 1978 - 1979

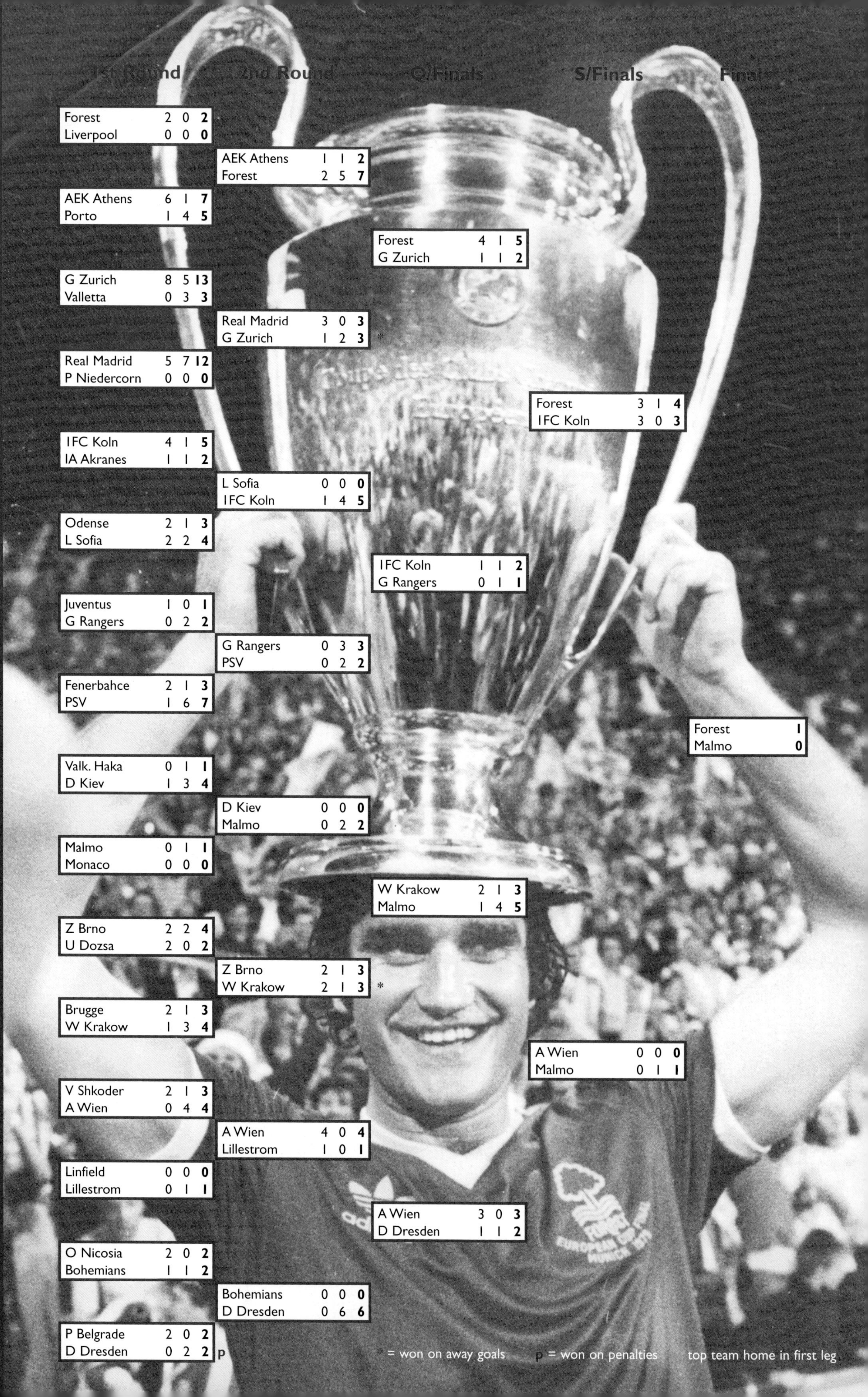

1st Round

Team	1st leg	2nd leg	Agg	
Forest	2	0	**2**	
Liverpool	0	0	**0**	
AEK Athens	6	1	**7**	
Porto	1	4	**5**	
G Zurich	8	5	**13**	
Valletta	0	3	**3**	
Real Madrid	5	7	**12**	
P Niedercorn	0	0	**0**	
1FC Koln	4	1	**5**	
IA Akranes	1	1	**2**	
Odense	2	1	**3**	
L Sofia	2	2	**4**	
Juventus	1	0	**1**	
G Rangers	0	2	**2**	
Fenerbahce	2	1	**3**	
PSV	1	6	**7**	
Valk. Haka	0	1	**1**	
D Kiev	1	3	**4**	
Malmo	0	1	**1**	
Monaco	0	0	**0**	
Z Brno	2	2	**4**	
U Dozsa	2	0	**2**	
Brugge	2	1	**3**	
W Krakow	1	3	**4**	
V Shkoder	2	1	**3**	
A Wien	0	4	**4**	
Linfield	0	0	**0**	
Lillestrom	0	1	**1**	
O Nicosia	2	0	**2**	
Bohemians	1	1	**2**	
P Belgrade	2	0	**2**	
D Dresden	0	2	**2**	p

2nd Round

Team	1st leg	2nd leg	Agg	
AEK Athens	1	1	**2**	
Forest	2	5	**7**	
Real Madrid	3	0	**3**	
G Zurich	1	2	**3**	*
L Sofia	0	0	**0**	
1FC Koln	1	4	**5**	
G Rangers	0	3	**3**	
PSV	0	2	**2**	
D Kiev	0	0	**0**	
Malmo	0	2	**2**	
Z Brno	2	1	**3**	
W Krakow	2	1	**3**	*
A Wien	4	0	**4**	
Lillestrom	1	0	**1**	
Bohemians	0	0	**0**	
D Dresden	0	6	**6**	

Q/Finals

Team	1st leg	2nd leg	Agg
Forest	4	1	**5**
G Zurich	1	1	**2**
1FC Koln	1	1	**2**
G Rangers	0	1	**1**
W Krakow	2	1	**3**
Malmo	1	4	**5**
A Wien	3	0	**3**
D Dresden	1	1	**2**

S/Finals

Team	1st leg	2nd leg	Agg
Forest	3	1	**4**
1FC Koln	3	0	**3**
A Wien	0	0	**0**
Malmo	0	1	**1**

Final

Forest	**1**
Malmo	**0**

* = won on away goals   p = won on penalties   top team home in first leg

EUROPEAN CHAMPIONS CUP RESULTS 1979 - 1980

1st Round

Team	1st leg	2nd leg	Agg
Forest	2	1	**3**
Oesters Vaxjo	0	1	**1**
Arges Pitesti	3	0	**3**
AEK Athens	0	2	**2**
D Berlin	4	0	**4**
D Chorzow	1	0	**1**
Servette	3	1	**4**
SK Beveren	1	1	**2**
U Dozsa	3	0	**3**
Dukla Prague	2	2	**4**
Start	1	0	**1**
Strasbourg	2	4	**6**
HJK Helsinki	1	1	**2**
Ajax	8	8	**16**
Red Boys	2	1	**3**
O Nicosia	1	6	**7**
P Tirana	1	1	**2**
Celtic	0	4	**4**
Dundalk	2	0	**2**
Hibernians P	0	1	**1**
Levski-Spartak	0	0	**0**
Real Madrid	1	2	**3**
Porto	0	1	**1**
AC Milan	0	0	**0**
Valur	0	1	**1**
Hamburg	3	2	**5**
Liverpool	2	0	**2**
D Tiblisi	1	3	**4**
Vejle BK	3	1	**4**
Austria Wien	2	1	**3**
Hajduk Split	1	1	**1**
Trabzonspor	0	0	**0**

2nd Round

Team	1st leg	2nd leg	Agg
Forest	2	2	**4**
Arges Pitesti	0	1	**1**
D Berlin	2	2	**4**
Servette	1	2	**3**
Dukla Prague	1	0	**1**
Strasbourg	0	2	**2**
Ajax	10	0	**10**
O Nicosia	0	4	**4**
Celtic	3	0	**3**
Dundalk	2	0	**2**
Porto	2	0	**2**
Real Madrid	1	1	**2**
Hamburg	3	3	**6**
D Tiblisi	1	2	**3**
Vejle BK	0	2	**2**
Hajduk Split	3	1	**4**

Q/Finals

Team	1st leg	2nd leg	Agg
Forest	0	3	**3**
D Berlin	1	1	**2**
Strasbourg	0	0	**0**
Ajax	0	4	**4**
Celtic	2	0	**2**
Real Madrid	0	3	**3**
Hamburg *	1	2	**3**
Hajduk Split	0	3	**3**

S/Finals

Team	1st leg	2nd leg	Agg
Forest	2	0	**2**
Ajax	0	1	**1**
Real Madrid	2	1	**3**
Hamburg	0	5	**5**

Final

Team	Score
Forest	**1**
Hamburg	**0**

* = won on away goals　　top team home in first leg

Acknowledgements: The authors would like to thank the following -

Brian Clough – for providing the introduction and help in the main text. Thanks to the players for generously giving their time to talk about the events contained in this book: Viv Anderson, Colin Barrett, Garry Birtles, Ian Bowyer, Kenny Burns, Frank Clark, Trevor Francis, Archie Gemmill, Frank Gray, David Needham, John O'Hare, John Robertson, Peter Withe, Tony Woodcock and Chris Woods. All interview quotes are taken from interviews carried out by the authors between spring 2000 and summer 2003. Other quotes are noted within the text or taken from press conferences, TV and newspaper interviews given at the time.

Many thanks to the typing pool of Chris Barlow, Gino Farabella, Carolyn Jovanovic and Susan Wheatley.

The following also gave help, advice and encouragement during the production of this book, so many thanks to: Ann McGovern, Garry Nelson, Kay Wilson, Emily Lewis of Empics, John Sumpter, Keith Gibson, Bob Thomas, Simon Jarvis, Phil Meakin - Elena Hayward - Paul Coffey and Martin Collins at the Nottingham Evening Post, Martin Pittaway of Mirrorpix, James Mather and Nigel Fish of Neartone, Ian Copping, Crispin Morton of The Bridport Red Archive (www.bridportred.com), Zoe Holmes, Daniel Moreira, Paul Ryan, Graham Palmer, Neil Masterton, Dave Brown, Keith Cordon, Mark Arthur, www.u-reds.com, Ailsa Herd of Topps, Becky Lee of Panini, Vicki Harris, Ian Preece and Mike West of the Nottingham Forest Programme Club (Ind) was of great help in sourcing programmes and items of memorabilia. See www.forestprogclub.co.uk or telephone 0115-9811248.

Many thanks also to all those who pre-ordered the book.

1 John McGovern
2 Rob Jovanovic
3 Brian Clough, OBE
4 Mark Arthur
5 Nottingham Forest FC
6 Simon Jarvis
7 Karl Jovanovic
8 Ian Preece
9 Gino Farabella
10 Jack Mason
11 Brian Johnson
12 Malcolm Young
13 Angus Young
14 Cliff Williams
15 Phil Rudd
16 Lee Westwood
17 Martin West
18 Dr Neil Whittemore
19 Stanley Haywood
20 Mike Haywood
21 Jack Walker
22 Crispin Morton
23 Jonathan Morton
24 Peter Morton
25 Nicholas Morton
26 Susan Wheatley
27 John Shaw
28 David Prince
29 Ian Copping
30 Bryn Morgan
31 Dave Brown
32 Steve Walker
33 Jem Bult
34 Dave Bradley
35 Charles Carter
36 Dave Shaw
37 Gary Hall
38 Neil Richardson
39 Troy Eade
40 Peter R. Mitchell
41 Sean Kieron Smith
42 Gary Taylor
43 John Anderson
44 Stevie Wright
45 Paul Terence Weatherbed
46 Steve Ford
47 Mark Dilloway
48 Patrick Gregory
49 Carole Brook
50 Neil Miller
51 Jonathan Bullock
52 Nigel Newbold
53 John Parke
54 Pete Howarth
55 Derek Gascoyne
56 Karen and Michael Gascoyne
57 Richard H. Harrison
58 Henry A. Harrison
59 Mark Sladen
60 Roger A. Cochrane
61 Nathan A. Cochrane
62 Andrew Johnson

63 Frank Eizens
64 Percy Simmons
65 Barry Pearson
66 Graham Baker
67 Graham Smith
68 George Androulakis
69 Adam Lea Wilkins
70 Andy Lyon
71 Tony Walker
72 Anthony Bissett
73 Neal Baxter
74 John Brian Baxter
75 Roger Capp
76 Robert Middleton
77 Andy Rowe
78 Roy Wells
79 Anthony Graham Clipson
80 John Hudson Ward
81 John & Tony Mackness
82 Pete Scott
83 Chris Broughton
84 John Knight
85 Keith Jones
86 Tim Gough
87 John Atkinson
88 Graham Clements
89 Brian Marriott
90 Jon Hurst
91 Alan Hill
92 Tim Hill
93 Graham Hill
94 Stuart Kaye
95 Jeremy Thompson
96 Peter Gibson
97 Carl Baumfield
98 David Skeen
99 Mark Beers
100 Simon Ray
101 Steven Allsopp
102 Stephen Rawlinson
103 Kevin Daybell
104 Brian Franks
105 Patrick Heverin
106 Paul, Abigail & Sam Widdowson
107 Stuart Richardson
108 Paul Gregory
109 Howard Sanders
110 Paul Chambers
111 Roger Peter Towle
112 Mr R. Dosanjh
113 Kevin Cooper
114 Gareth Barker
115 Mr G. Quarton
116 Chris Odell
117 Colin Shields
118 Neil R. Smith
119 Edward A. Smith
120 Kevin Carter
121 Richard Beal
122 Martin Beal
123 Stuart Beal
124 Mark Elliott
125 David Farnsworth
126 Stephen Farnsworth
127 Phil Robinson
128 Lee Darby
129 Mark Hatton
130 Phil Sheldon
131 Richard Whitbread
132 Richard Hanley
133 Michael Hanley
134 Stephen Hanley
135 Ian Whadcoat
136 Gavin Town
137 Ian Clarke
138 Bernard Sullivan
139 Stan Filipowicz
140 John R. Watson
141 Mark Weston
142 Dean Eaton
143 Alan Balchin
144 Anthony Balchin
145 Peter Carey
146 David Mather
147 Martin Edward Walker
148 Clive Hughes
149 Mark Grant Morris
150 Anthony Bowley
151 H.E. Vickery
152 Kevin D. Thompson
153 Nicholas Houldsworth
154 Stephen Houldsworth
155 A.W. Grocock
156 Neil Brown
157 Helen Brown
158 Roy Mullin
159 Michael Lang
160 David F. Johnson
161 Geoff May
162 Paul Hurt
163 David Beaumont
164 Alex Buck
165 James K. Parnham
166 Ian Storer
167 philipwells@hotmail.com
168 Juha Tamminen
169 Peter James Smith
170 Philip Slater
171 Peter Kitt
172 David T. Hack
173 Mark Jackson
174 Peter Thorpe

175 Andrew Lodge
176 Chris Ingle
177 Mat Lamb
178 Carolyn Need
179 Mark Collar
180 Ian Blair
181 Alex Iskandar Liew
182 Peter Lloyd
183 Alun Gadd
184 Mark Allen
185 Allan Draycott
186 Martin Slack
187 Glyn Chamberlain
188 Jeff Hall
189 Mark Jopling
190 Stuart Robinson
191 Don Peterson
192 Andy Cole
193 Mark Fidler
194 David Rowley
195 John Frank Baker
196 Raymond Wilson
197 Edward Redgate
198 Brian Toulson
199 Tony Lamb
200 Nigel Webster
201 Luke Webster
202 John Goodman
203 Paul Bywater
204 Shaun Morley
205 Michael Gascoyne
206 Dawn Odam
207 Robert Richardson
208 Mr S. Purdy
209 Hugh Brennan
210 John Hutchinson
211 Stuart Meehan
212 Carol Kerslake
213 Gary Lambert
214 Philip Colcomb
215 Andy Lowe
216 Christopher McNulty
217 Stephen Groves
218 Steve Plumb
219 Aidan Mulholland
220 Andy Smith
221 Ken Crampton
222 Darren Clare
223 Malcolm Golding
224 Stuart Collins
225 Richard Bignall
226 Mel Egglenton
227 Geoff Walker
228 Paul Walker
229 Grenville Jennings
230 David Wilkins
231 Brett Curtis
232 Mick Curtis
233 Mark Andrew Merriman
234 Raymond Edgar
235 James Raymond Edgar
236 Robin Morris
237 Martin Pullon
238 Lindsey Dickson
239 Dorothy Jessop
240 Rupert Bellamy
241 Ray Ogden
242 Michael Bailey
243 Chris Fagg
244 Wilfred Sharman
245 John Lawson
246 Florence Barlow
247 Alisa Baguley
248 Tony Storey
249 David Cundy
250 Wayne Gallichan
251 Jim Henderson
252 Steve Jamison
253 Steve Williams
254 Russell V. J. Ball
255 Mick Fallon
256 Michele & Martin Cooper
257 Lee Allcock
258 Steve Radmore
259 Richard Parks
260 Leigh
261 V. Buchanan
262 Role Buchanan
263 Philip Clay
264 Richard Binch
265 Simon Jeacock
266 Paul Thomas
267 Stephen Tring
268 Mike Peates
269 Richard Chapman
270 Chris Chapman
271 Dave Fernihough
272 Ivy Trussel
273 Mark Trussel
274 Robert Fox
275 Malcolm Fox
276 Geoffrey Bowyer
277 John Raynor
278 Suzanne Jovanovic
279 Simon Broughton
280 James Hallam
281 Simon Clay
282 Andrew Stubbs
283 Andrew Norris
284 John & Amy Webster
285 Alan Fisher
286 David Sterry

Index

Photographic credits:

Copyright is held by the following agenices for the photographs used as noted below:

Alpha Photography: 42, 44, 46, 47, 50, 51, 52, 55, 57, 70, 72, 73, 75, 76, 78, 79, 81, 82, 88, 89, 115, 116, 124, 131, 133, 135 (top), 141, 162, 101, 211

Empics: 77, 169 (top), 182 (bottom), 200

JMS Photography: back cover, 3, 6, 122-3, 158, 159, 180, 192, 212, 215
These can be ordered by calling 0115-9413184

Mirrorpix: 114 (top right), 195 (bottom), 197 (right) 223

Nottingham Evening Post: front cover, 4-5, 14, 15, 16, 17, 18, 20, 28, 29, 32, 34, 38, 39, 45, 48, 53, 54 (top), 56 (top), 58, 64, 65, 66, 84, 85, 91, 93, 94, 95, 96, 98, 100, 103, 104 ,106, 110, 111, 113, 114 top left and bottom), 117, 119, 120, 121, 125, 126, 127, 128, 129, 130, 135, 137 (bottom), 138, 139, 140, 142-3, 144, 145 (bottom), 146, 147, 150, 151, 152, 153, 154, 161, 163, 164, 165, 166, 167, 169, 170, 171, 173, 174, 176, 177, 179, 181 (middle and bottom), 184, 185, 187, 188, 189 (top), 197 (bottom), 214, 216, 217, 220
These can be ordered from the Evening Post.

Geoff Peabody: 186, 187 (top)

Bob Thomas: 145 (top), 181 (top), 182 (top)

The memorabilia used was taken from the collections of the authors.

Many thanks are given to Topps and Panini for the reporduction of old football cards.

IAN BOWYER
NOTTINGHAM FOREST
M

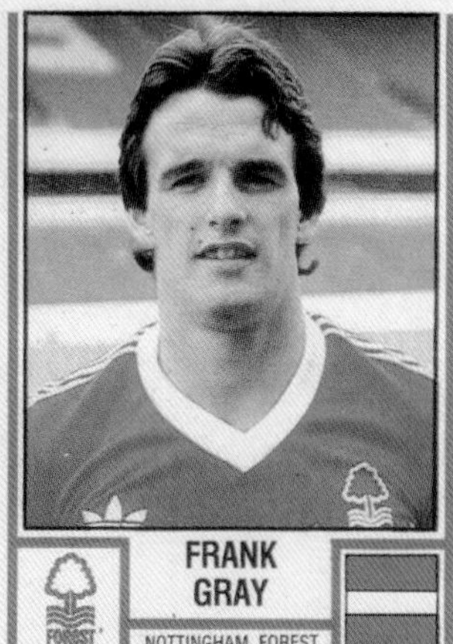
FRANK
GRAY
NOTTINGHAM FOREST

PETER SHILTON
TOPPS ALL-STAR
G
NOTTINGHAM FOREST

TONY WOODCOCK
TTINGHAM FOREST

MARTIN O'NEILL
NOTTINGHAM FOREST
M

RRY LLOY

GARY
BIRTLES
NOTTINGHAM FOREST

JOHN
McGOVERN
NOTTINGHAM FOREST

KENNY
BURNS
NOTTINGHAM FOREST

NOTTINGHAM F.
FRANK GRAY

KENNY BURNS

NOTTINGHAM F.
JOHN ROBERTSON

FRANK CLARK
NOTTINGHAM FOREST

VIV
ANDERSON

JOHN O'HARE
NOTTINGHAM FOREST
M